PLANTING, WATERING, GROWING

PLANTING, WATERING, GROWING

Planting Confessionally Reformed
Churches in the 21st Century

edited by Daniel R. Hyde
and Shane Lems

Reformation Heritage Books
Grand Rapids, Michigan

Reformation Heritage Books
2965 Leonard St. NE
Grand Rapids, MI 49525
616-977-0889 / Fax 616-285-3246
orders@heritagebooks.org
www.heritagebooks.org

Printed in the United States of America
11 12 13 14 15 16/10 9 8 7 6 5 4 3 2 1

Unless otherwise indicated, all quotations of the Belgic Confession, Heidelberg Catechism, and Canons of Dort are from *The Creeds of Christendom*, ed. Philip Schaff, rev. David S. Schaff, 3 vols. (1931; repr., Grand Rapids: Baker, 1996).

Unless otherwise indicated, all quotations of the Westminster Confession, Westminster Shorter Catechism, and Westminster Larger Catechism are from *Westminster Confession of Faith* (Glasgow: Free Presbyterian Publications, 1994).

Library of Congress Cataloging-in-Publication Data

Planting, watering, growing : planting confessionally reformed churches in the twenty-first century / edited by Daniel R. Hyde and Shane Lems.
    p. cm.
Includes bibliographical references and index.
ISBN 978-1-60178-126-0
1. Church development, New. 2. Reformed Church—Doctrines. I. Hyde, Daniel R. II. Lems, Shane.
  BV652.24.P53 2011
  254'.1—dc22
                        2011006918

For additional Reformed literature, both new and used, request a free book list from Reformation Heritage Books at the above regular or e-mail address.

To the councils of the

**Escondido United Reformed Church
and Grace United Reformed Church,**

who heard the Lord's call to
plant the churches we now serve.

Contents

Abbreviations

BC   Belgic Confession

Calvin, *Institutes*—John Calvin, *Institutes of the Christian Religion*, ed. John T. McNeill, trans. Ford Lewis Battles, The Library of Christian Classics, vol. 20 (Philadelphia: The Westminster Press, 1960).

CD   Canons of Dort

HC   Heidelberg Catechism

POPC   *Planting an Orthodox Presbyterian Church* (Willow Grove, Pa.: The Committee on Home Missions and Church Extension of the Orthodox Presbyterian Church, 2002).

WCF   Westminster Confession of Faith

WLC   Westminster Larger Catechism

WSC   Westminster Shorter Catechism

Foreword:
Was the Reformation Missions-Minded?

Michael S. Horton

"Martin Luther was so certain of the imminent return of Christ that he overlooked the necessity of foreign missions.... Calvinists generally used the same line of reasoning, adding the doctrine of election that made missions appear extraneous if God had already chosen those he would save." So writes Dr. Ruth Tucker, professor at Trinity Evangelical Divinity School and author of *From Jerusalem to Irian Jaya: A Biographical History of Christian Missions.*[1]

Well-meaning but ill-informed accounts such as these have been repeated so frequently that they have become clichés in discussions of missions. Tucker repeats the caricature: the Reformers were not terribly interested in evangelism and missions; it was the Anabaptists and Pietists who gave birth to the modern missionary movement.[2] While I am not a missiologist, I do have an interest in this subject, and if the Reformation had negative effects on the advance of the Great Commission, we ought to be the first to point it out. The facts, however, point in quite a different direction.

First is the nature of the Reformation itself. Throughout the late Middle Ages, there was something of a lull in Roman Catholic missions. That is not to say that they did not exist, but it was nothing like the evangelization of the Roman Empire or of the pagan European tribes that preceded it or like the missions of the Jesuits and other Counter-Reformation groups that followed it. It was, in fact, the Reformation itself, combined with other factors (such as exploration and the rise of colonialism), that

Originally appeared in *Modern Reformation* 4, 3 (May/June 1995): 27–29, and is reprinted with permission.

1. Ruth Tucker, *From Jerusalem to Irian Jaya: A Biographical History of Christian Missions* (Grand Rapids: Zondervan, 1983), 67.
2. Ibid., 24.

not only gave birth to Protestant missions but revitalized Roman Catholic missions by reaction.

But what was the Reformation? One's answer to this question will determine one's appraisal of its missiological significance. If the Reformation was simply a period of internecine squabbling that interrupted the more important activity of the church, then it was indeed an appalling distraction. But if it was the greatest recovery of the biblical faith since the first century, the Reformation constitutes the most remarkable missionary movement in post-apostolic church history. If we agree with the Reformers that the doctrine of justification by grace alone through faith alone because of Christ alone is "the article by which the church stands or falls" and that the gospel is "the power of God unto salvation," we can interpret the Reformation as the re-evangelization of Europe. Is this not the point of the Great Commission? The Jews to whom the gospel first came were certainly aware of the prophecies concerning the Messiah, but they did not properly understand them as referring to Christ. The Reformers believed that those who confused the law and the gospel, merit and grace, judgment and justification, were in precisely the same category as the unconverted, even if they were part of Christendom.

This is why, as we read Luther, Calvin, and the other Reformers, we cannot help but come away with a deep sense of admiration for the pastoral, missionary, and evangelistic heart of this movement. Designating themselves the "evangelicals" because they were recovering the gospel (evangel), these Protestants so indefatigably preached the gospel through print, pulpit, and in everyday conversations that the good news spread quickly throughout the Holy Roman Empire. Had the same movement occurred on another continent with the same extensive effects, the Reformation would be considered the most significant missionary enterprise since the apostles. Therefore, the starting point is essential. Those who cannot see the Reformation as anything more than an in-house dispute over less than ultimate issues will not regard this as the re-evangelization of Christendom.

Second, there is the matter of categorization. For instance, in Ruth Tucker's volume, such distinguished Calvinistic missionaries as John Eliot, David Brainerd, Eleazar Wheelock, Isaac McCoy, William Carey, the Judsons and Boardmans, David Livingstone, and many others are treated as products of pietism, when these men and women had their roots in the Reformation-Puritan tradition. In fact, the most prominent names of the modern missionary movement were Calvinists! So much for Tucker's caricature that the "doctrine of election…made missions appear extraneous if God had already chosen those he would save." This is merely an inference of Tucker rather than an effect of this doctrine on the minds and hearts of those great missionary heroes who embraced it. They saw their theology as the engine behind their efforts, not as an embarrassing obstacle.

Besides Carey, Eliot, Brainerd, and Livingstone, there were evangelists such as Whitefield, Edwards, the Tennents, Spurgeon—and on we could go. All of these disciples of the Great Commission credited their theological convictions with their energy and motivation, knowing that it was God alone who saves sinners whenever and wherever He will. While we carry the good news to the poor, only God can grant repentance and faith, and this relieved missionaries and evangelists of either despair on the one hand or proud triumphalism on the other.

At last, however, we return to the Reformers themselves. While their followers may have been great evangelists and missionaries, were men such as Luther, Calvin, Bucer, Knox, and Melanchthon interested in such things?

Interestingly, Tucker makes an observation in the same paragraph as her previously cited remark that appears to be contradictory: "Calvin himself, however, was at least outwardly the most missionary-minded of all the Reformers. He not only sent dozens of evangelists back into his homeland of France, but also commissioned four missionaries, along with a number of French Huguenots, to establish a colony and evangelize the Indians of Brazil."[3]

These missionaries were killed by Jesuits, but another group was sent from Geneva. Not only were the New England Puritans busy building Harvard; they were simultaneously evangelizing the Native Americans (the first Bible published in the New World was in Algonquin by John Eliot in 1663). In fact, the Reformed missionary enterprise was integrating the proclamation of the gospel with the interests of justice and cultural betterment long before it became popular. One thinks of David Livingstone (1813–1873), the Scottish missionary who was also an explorer and, in the words of one historian, "exercised a greater influence on the history of central Africa than any other person, Christian or non-Christian, in the nineteenth century."[4]

---

3. Ibid., 67.
4. *Great Leaders of the Christian Church*, ed. John D. Woodbridge (Chicago: Moody Press, 1988), 329

But history records Livingstone as more than a missionary and explorer; he was an indefatigable opponent of the slave trade. Livingstone knew that the same God who cared for the salvation of the lost also abhorred the bondage of injustice, and sin had not only personal but institutional aspects. He sought to interrupt the slave trade by building East African commercial trade, and he pursued some extraordinarily brilliant ideas, but the British government ended his expedition in 1863. And yet, Brian Stanley concludes, "The Protestant churches of sub-Saharan Africa, many of them born in the aftermath of Livingstone's explorations, are today among the strongest in the world."[5]

American Presbyterian missionary and educator Samuel M. Zwemer (1867–1952) is another example of this integration of preaching grace and doing justice. As a missionary in the Middle East, he earned the title "Apostle to Islam," and he opened up doors to missions throughout the region, especially by building hospitals and schools—a traditional approach to pre-evangelism taken by Reformed and Lutheran missionaries alike. Because these institutions are still among the most important to the locals, these missionaries and their spiritual descendents are among the only trusted Westerners. Zwemer argued that Calvinism could conquer the Muslim world because it was a system, and the Muslims thought very systematically; they would not be won by mere pietistic sentimentality. Various cultural institutions bear his name in Cairo and in other cities in the Middle East.

Far East missions were also led by Reformed Christians. The Scot Robert Morrison, who was the first Protestant missionary to go to China, comes to mind. Confident in God's sovereignty, he prayed for God to place him in a part of the world "where the difficulties are the greatest, and to all human appearance the most insurmountable."[6] Like Zwemer, who saw only a few converts in the entire tenure of his missionary enterprise, Morrison saw fewer than a dozen converts, and, as Tucker informs us, "At the time of his death there were only three known native Christians in the entire Chinese empire."[7] Nevertheless, both missionaries translated the Scriptures for the first time into the native languages and left these few converts to plant the seeds that would eventually produce a harvest of new believers. They did not despair, in spite of few "results,"

5. Ibid., 333.
6. As quoted in Tucker, *From Jerusalem to Irian Jaya*, 167.
7. Ibid.

because all results are God's results, and He will see to the success of His own mission. The story of Korean missions is full of amazing twists and turns, and figuring prominently throughout it all is the Orthodox Presbyterian Church (OPC). By American standards a small but faithful church, the OPC had an inordinately large hand in the evangelization of the region before and after the division of North and South.

The greatest tragedy in modern missions, from this writer's point of view at least, is the sad reality that although Reformation Christians launched modern missions, the "pentecostalization" of the missionary movement has devastated almost overnight the regions where missionaries labored carefully for decades. Huge crusades with spectacular sideshows have replaced the careful exposition of Scripture in large parts of the world. The Two-Thirds World, where the earliest missions produced deep conversions and strong churches, is now dominated by successive waves of Pentecostal phenomena. The results are evident everywhere on the mission field (even more so than in America): hysteria and numerical growth, leading almost as quickly to despair and disillusionment, until the cycle repeats itself.

Just as British missions reflected worldwide missionary activity in the nineteenth century, American leadership in the twenty-first is obvious. "Evangelicalism" around the world is equivalent to American evangelicalism, and with the influence of such institutions as the Fuller School of World Missions, along with the leading trends evident in *Christianity Today,* leading evangelical seminaries and popular movements rather quickly overpower indigenous distinctives, many of the latter derived from the period of earlier missionary activity. Like so many other trappings of American popular commercial culture, when something gets started on the American evangelical scene, it eventually makes its way into the remotest regions.

Speaking for my own tradition, while many Reformed Christians are interested in restoring a sense of vocation and calling, including the vision of transforming culture as salt and light, there does not seem to be a parallel interest in spreading the gospel, either in terms of local evangelism or missions. This is not to say that Reformed churches, whether local or at the denominational level, are not interested in missions: many of them have proportionately large mission budgets. But it is to say that at least this writer is unaware of much thoughtful discussion of what a second Reformation might look like in, for example, Thailand or Tanzania. If we truly believe that many of the crowds turning out for a healing crusade in Uganda or Tulsa are filled with people who have an erroneous understanding of the gospel, we are in precisely the same position as the first Reformers, where "missions" and "evangelism" mean first recovering the biblical gospel. It is not enough for Reformed and Lutheran evangelicals to work side by side with mainstream evangelicals and attempt to influence them. The evangelicals are not simply "off a little" on this or that emphasis; there is quite often these days a fundamentally different message, leading to methods and a general agenda that is at cross-purposes with biblical, historic Christianity. There must be a distinctive Reformational agenda—one that neither attempts to recreate a sixteenth-century European movement in Bombay, nor one that capitulates to American evangelical tendencies on the other.

May God set our hearts and minds to this urgent task, and then may He prepare our feet to bring good news to the captives, whether down the street or around the world.

—Michael S. Horton

Introduction

Daniel R. Hyde and Shane Lems

Who then is Paul, and who is Apollos, but ministers through whom you believed, as the Lord gave to each one? I planted, Apollos watered, but God gave the increase. So then neither he who plants is anything, nor he who waters, but God who gives the increase. —1 Corinthians 3:5–7

Church planting is a hot topic on the American religious landscape. With the mainline denominations in decline, with the fundamentalist sense that America is losing its Christian heritage, and with the constant feeling that our nation is becoming increasingly secular under the influence of "postmodernism," the necessity for church planting is greater than ever. Yet many remedies for this diagnosis fall short. There are websites on which you can get church-plant training in three days or a church-planting degree in six months; you can even find websites where you can choose a place where you want to plant a church and go from there. A person can plant an emergent/emerging church, a cowboy church, a biker church, a typical seeker-sensitive church—and the list goes on. As with much of American Christianity, often church planting is all about the consumer: your way, right away—or your money back.

The experience of the authors of this book will testify, though, that many people are burned out by the church's adaptation of pop culture with bar stools instead of pews, Bluetooth-style microphones that look hip, and "latte-and-a-band" styles of worship. There are many people in America who live in a city in which they cannot find a church that does what the apostle Paul describes in the passage above: plant, water, grow through the "outward and ordinary means whereby Christ communicates to his church the benefits of his mediation...especially the Word, sacraments, and prayer" (WLC, Q&A 154).

Therein lies the true remedy for church planting in our time. Churches are needed that simply spread the seed of the Word through preaching, seek to water those seeds by means of the sacraments of baptism and the Lord's Supper, and humbly pray for the Lord to grant growth. If this is your desire as a Christian, as a potential church planter, or as a congregation, there is some good news for you: Reformed and Presbyterian churches are being planted across the United States that adhere to the "old paths" of the Word of God (Jer. 6:16). Within these churches and denominations there has been some good discussion over the years concerning faithful church planting. The contributors to this book believe the time is ripe for a book that deals exclusively with the many facets of planting Reformed churches that uphold the Word of God and confess the ancient creeds and confessions of the church.

In this book, we have compiled essays on Reformed church planting. We begin with the biblical foundations for church planting and evangelism. Since we recognize the limitations of one book and realize that many other excellent books have been written, we refer you to other books for more details in this area.[1] We have also included a few chapters discussing the theological and Reformational foundation for planting churches. In a word, the great sixteenth- and seventeenth-century documents—the Westminster Standards (Westminster Confession of Faith, Larger Catechism, and Shorter Catechism) and the Three Forms of Unity (Belgic Confession, Heidelberg Catechism, and Canons of Dort)—are "pro-church-planting" confessions.

We also cover the methods for planting churches. The chapters in this section include topics such as methodological examples from the book of Acts, planning a church plant, oversight of church planting, and many others. The final section is a bit more detailed. Here, the authors cover such topics as the church planter, the church plant's core group, the cultural context of planting churches, and preaching in a church plant, among other topics. In summary, the three sections go from biblical/theological foundations, to the outworking of methodology (ways to plant churches), ending with specific application and details of planting churches. All of the chapters must be read in light of the first: church

---

1. E.g., Roger Greenway, *Go and Make Disciples* (Phillipsburg, N.J.: P&R, 1999); Roger Greenway and Timothy Monsma, *Cities: Missions' New Frontier* (Grand Rapids: Baker, 2000); J. I. Packer, *Evangelism and the Sovereignty of God* (Downers Grove, Ill.: InterVarsity, 2009); Will Metzger, *Tell the Truth* (Downers Grove, Ill.: InterVarsity, 2002); John Piper, *Let the Nations Be Glad* (Grand Rapids: Baker, 2003).

planting is the fruit of the preaching of the gospel of God's free and amazing grace.

We would also like to affirm at the outset of this book that we greatly appreciate the Orthodox Presbyterian Church's (OPC) manual for church planting entitled *Planting an Orthodox Presbyterian Church.*[2] We have cross-referenced many chapters of our book to this OPC manual for ease of comparison and study.

We do not suggest that this book will be *the* definitive church-plant guide. We simply could not turn over every church-plant stone out there. However, it is our hope that the readers would use this information as a general guide to help turn over other stones. By giving many general principles as well as specific applications, we hope that other areas we have not covered will be more approachable.

We also highly recommend that the reader, whether a church planter or a church-planting core group member, consult other traditions when undertaking the great task of planting a church. For example, a church plant among the churches in which we minister, the United Reformed Churches in North America (URCNA), can learn much from the OPC and Presbyterian Church in America (PCA) forms of government and methods of church planting. The same can be said of all faithful Reformed and Presbyterian churches with the North America Presbyterian and Reformed Council (NAPARC). Since many of these materials are accessible online, it would be foolish to neglect the wisdom in all of these sources.[3]

In the end, our prayerful goal is that this book might itself be a seed that motivates and assists confessionally Reformed seminary students, ministers, consistories/sessions, seminaries, and churches to continue to plant solid churches in North America and beyond. We pray that as we seek to plant and labor to water these confessionally Reformed churches in the twenty-first century, our Lord Himself, the great Lord of the harvest, will bring tremendous growth, "exceedingly abundantly above all that we ask or think" (Eph. 3:20).

---

2. This volume can be accessed free of charge on www.opc.org, and is well worth studying. The OPC *Book of Church Order,* which includes the Form of Government, can also be found online.

3. OPC: www.opc.org; PCA: www.pcanet.org; and URCNA: www.urcna.org

PART ONE

❧

The Foundations of Planting Churches

CHAPTER ONE

൭

The Fruitful Grain of Wheat

Brian Vos

Pity the nations, O our God,
Constrain the earth to come;
Send Thy victorious Word abroad,
And bring the strangers home.

—Isaac Watts, "How Sweet and
Awesome Is the Place"

As servants of the Lord Jesus Christ living on this side of the cross, we labor with joy in the dawn of the new creation—praying for God's mercy upon the nations, that He would constrain the earth to come, and that He would send forth His Word and bring the strangers home. We pray these things with confidence and boldness, based on the finished work of our Lord and Savior Jesus Christ, for it is His finished work that compels us to plant churches. Many themes, texts, and teachings of Scripture, of which the reader is quite likely aware, demonstrate the need for church plant-ing. For our purposes, however, we will consider this theme in John's gospel, specifically in 12:20–26, where we see the biblical foundation for church planting in Jesus, the fruitful grain of wheat, who died in order to produce much fruit—the salvation of men and women from every nation, tribe, people, and tongue.

When Jesus began His earthly ministry, John the Baptist proclaimed Him as "the Lamb of God who takes away the sin of the world!" (John 1:29). Following Jesus' meeting with the woman at the well, the Samari-tans confessed, "This is indeed the Christ, the Savior of the world" (John 4:42). After Jesus raised Lazarus from the dead, Caiaphas, the high priest, prophesied that Jesus would die not only for the Jewish nation, "but also that He would gather together in one the children of God who were scattered abroad" (John 11:51–52). After Jesus' triumphal entry, the Pharisees—His mortal enemies—were compelled to say, "The world has gone after Him!" (John 12:19). Jesus' ministry and work are for people of all nations, tribes, and tongues. John the Baptist proclaimed it. The Samaritans recognized it. Caiaphas prophesied of it. Even the Pharisees confessed it. Jesus did not make all of these statements, however; others did. It is not until John 12:20–26 that Jesus Himself declares such things. In this pivotal passage, Jesus connects the work He is about to accomplish on the cross with the gathering in of the nations, describing Himself as the fruitful grain of wheat.

The Time of Harvest Has Come

John begins this text in a most arresting fashion, fixing our eyes on the Gentiles: "Now there were certain Greeks among those who came up to worship at the feast" (12:20). The Jews had once complained among themselves: "Does He intend to go to the Dispersion among the Greeks and teach the Greeks?" (John 7:35). Their complaint reveals their blindness, for even now Jesus is beginning to draw all peoples to Himself. The Greeks come to Jesus.

John does not want us to miss the irony here. These "certain Greeks" were "among those who came up to worship at the feast" (12:20). The feast to which John is referring is the great feast of the Jews, the Passover, which celebrated the deliverance of the infant Jewish nation from the land of Egypt, from the house of bondage. Not only did this feast look back on the great redemptive act of the Old Testament, but it also looked forward in hope to the nation's future redemption.[1] It was a thoroughly nationalistic feast that commemorated God's separation of the Jews not only from the Egyptians but also from all the other peoples of the earth. The means by which God separated the Jews from all others was the blood of the lamb. Meredith Kline writes:

> The picture in Exodus 12 is...one of God's...coming to them and abiding with them through the dark night of judgment on Egypt. Like a hovering bird spreading its protective wings over its young, the Lord covered the Israelite houses, keeping watch over them. He was their gatekeeper, their guardian against the entrance of the angel of death.... The Lord shielded his people from his own wrath by himself intercepting the death angel's thrust as he stood guard at the door of their dwellings.... The lamb's blood on these sanctuary

---

1. *The International Standard Bible Encyclopedia*, s.v. "Passover."

tombs presaged their becoming empty tombs in the morning. Their blood-covered doors would be opened and their redeemed occupants would emerge as the children of the resurrection day.[2]

The annual celebration of the Passover should have reminded the Jews of their unique status as those who lived in the freedom of a new day.

Though we do not know what these Greeks were doing at this Jewish feast, we do know they wanted to see Jesus and perhaps begin to enjoy the freedom of a new day themselves: "Then they came to Philip, who was from Bethsaida of Galilee, and asked him, saying, 'Sir, we wish to see Jesus'" (12:21). The Greeks came to Philip, most likely because Philip was one of only two disciples with a Greek name.[3] The point, however, is not that they came to Philip. The point is their request: "Sir, we wish to see Jesus." The implication is that these Greeks were not satisfied with the Jewish feast. The Jewish feast left them empty, unfulfilled, and in the shadows. These Greeks were hungry and longed to be filled; they sought the Light of the World. They wanted to see Jesus.

Here, John gives us a hint of the history of redemption as he takes us from the Old Testament shadows of a Jewish feast to the New Testament reality of Jesus. John is signaling to us that in Jesus the dawn of the new age has arrived—an age in which men and women of every nation, tribe, tongue, and people will be counted among the children of the resurrection day. Though the new age is already intruding in history here in John 12, it has not fully arrived. Notice that the Greeks do not yet come to Jesus; they come to Philip. Nevertheless, they do come to *see* Jesus.[4] Remarkably, the Greeks understand, though only in part, that this Jewish feast is but a shadow. Jesus is the reality. Thus, the Greeks understand—and appear ready to accept—what the Jews do not: Jesus is the Christ, the Son of the living God.

Philip receives the request of the Greeks, proceeds to tell Andrew, and in turn Andrew and Philip tell Jesus (12:22). Thus, John does something remarkable in this text: he fixes our eyes on the Gentiles in order to fix our eyes on Jesus. John's only purpose in introducing other charac-

---

2. Meredith Kline, "The Feast of Cover-Over," *Journal of the Evangelical Theological Society* 37, 4 (December 1994): 497–510.

3. The other disciple with a Greek name was Andrew, the one to whom Philip went in verse 22 (William Hendriksen, *The Gospel of John* [Grand Rapids: Baker, 1954], 194).

4. This is likely a pregnant term in John's gospel, indicating far more than a desire to see Jesus physically. Implied here is a desire to follow Jesus as disciples (cf. John 1:39, 46, 50, 51) (James T. Dennison, "Come and See," *Kerux* 9, 2 [September 1994]: 23–29).

ters in his gospel is to point us to Jesus, that we might behold His glory. Raymond Brown comments, "The coming of the Gentiles is so theologically important that the writer never tells us if they got to see Jesus, and indeed they disappear from the scene."[5] The Greeks disappear from the scene so that we might see Jesus. He is, after all, the Great Harvester who draws all peoples to Himself. Now we see Jesus.

The Great Harvester

Jesus receives the report from Andrew and Philip that the Greeks have come with a request to see Him. Remarkably, Jesus does not address the Greeks. Instead, He simply says, "The hour has come that the Son of Man should be glorified" (12:23). Jesus interprets the coming of the Greeks as the arrival of His hour.

Everything in John's gospel has been pressing toward this hour. At the wedding feast of Cana in Galilee, Jesus says to His mother, "My hour has not yet come" (John 2:4). John tells us later that no one could lay a hand upon Jesus "because His hour had not yet come" (7:30). We find the same thing in 8:20. In the opening half of John's gospel, Jesus' hour has not yet come. But now, with the Gentiles drawing near to Him, Jesus says, "the hour has come."

The hour to which Jesus is referring, of course, is the hour of His death. We learn that from John 13:1, where "His hour" is defined in terms of Jesus' departure from this world. We see it again in John 17:1 as Jesus begins His High Priestly Prayer with those words anticipating His death: "Father, the hour has come. Glorify Your Son, that Your Son also may glorify You." The hour of which Jesus is speaking—the hour that has now come—is the hour of Jesus' death, and it is the drawing near of the Gentiles that signals its arrival. Thus, the inclusion of the Gentiles is brought about through the Jewish rejection of Jesus. The Greeks wish to see Jesus, and the Jews wish to see Jesus no more. Jesus' hour—the hour of His death—has come.

The connection Jesus draws between the coming of the Gentiles and the arrival of the hour of His death on the cross is vital to church planting. Prior to Jesus' work on the cross, the message of the gospel was proclaimed almost exclusively to the Jews. From henceforth, however, it goes forth to

---

5. Raymond E. Brown, *The Gospel According to John I–XII* (New York: Doubleday, 1966), 470.

Jew and Gentile alike—to men and women from every nation, tribe, tongue, and people. The gospel is to be "declared and published to all nations, and to all persons promiscuously and without distinction" (CD, 2.5).

This leads us to one of the most profound ironies of John's gospel: the hour of Jesus' death is the hour of Jesus' glory. In John's gospel, Jesus is not merely glorified after His death on the cross but *in* His death on the cross. John wants us to fix our eyes upon Jesus, hanging on the cross, and to see there His glory![6]

Jesus refers to the hour of His death as the hour "that the Son of Man should be glorified" (12:23). Picture the scene of Jesus' crucifixion. The place itself conjures up the most disturbing images; it is called "the Place of a Skull," in Hebrew, "Golgotha" (John 19:17). Here the soldiers pierced Jesus' hands, nailing them to the horizontal bar. They pierced His feet, fastening them to the vertical bar. They lifted Him up on the cross between two thieves. Above Him they fastened the title "JESUS OF NAZARETH, THE KING OF THE JEWS" (19:19). The soldiers stripped Him of His garments and cast lots for His clothing. Where is the glory in all of this?

How can the hour of Jesus' death be the hour that the Son of Man is glorified? Jesus tells us in John 12:24: "Most assuredly, I say to you, unless a grain of wheat falls into the ground and dies, it remains alone; but if it dies, it produces much grain." The hour of Jesus' death is the hour of His glory, because at the cross, Jesus actually saves His people, securing their redemption for time and eternity.[7] He dies in order to produce much fruit, and the fruit of His death is the salvation of men and women from every nation, tribe, people, and tongue. Jesus explains, "And I, if I am lifted up from the earth, will draw all peoples to Myself" (John 12:32).

In John 12:24, Jesus indicates the absolute necessity of His death if there is to be a church. "*Unless* a grain of wheat falls into the ground and dies, *it remains alone*" (emphasis added). The implication is clear. If Jesus does not die, there will be no church; but He does die, and so He brings forth His church, in which He reveals His glory. In fact, as Raymond Brown has pointed out, "The parable is concerned not with the fate of the grain

---

6. It is noteworthy that in John's record of the crucifixion there is no reference to the three hours of darkness. This is remarkable, for of all the gospel writers, John develops the imagery of light and darkness most fully. Perhaps John doesn't record the three hours of darkness at Golgotha, however, because he wants us to focus only on the glory of Christ, the Light of the World.

7. For a recent, helpful discussion on definite atonement, see Joel Beeke, *Living for God's Glory* (Orlando: Reformation Trust, 2008), 74–100.

but with its productivity."[8] Such is the love and compassion of Christ for His church, that His glory is bound up with His fruit—that is, with the church. Though He is all-glorious in and of Himself, His glory is revealed and demonstrated most powerfully in the salvation of His church.

By His death, Jesus produces much fruit. In His being lifted up, He draws all peoples to Himself. This season of harvest was anticipated from the beginning of the world and will not cease until the world's end. The Belgic Confession states, "This church has existed from the beginning of the world and will last until the end, as appears from the fact that Christ is an eternal King who cannot be without subjects" (BC, art. 27). The Confession goes on to state, "This holy church is not confined, bound, or limited to a certain place or certain persons. But it is spread and dispersed throughout the entire world, though still joined and united in heart and will, in one and the same Spirit, by the power of faith" (BC, art. 27). The Heidelberg Catechism echoes the Confession when it states, "The Son of God through his Spirit and Word, out of the entire human race, from the beginning of the world to its end, gathers, protects, and preserves for himself a community chosen for eternal life and united in true faith" (HC, Q&A 54). The Westminster Standards (WCF 25, WLC, Q&A 61–64) use similar language, stating that the "universal Church" consists "of the whole number of the elect...from all places in the world."

This, then, is the purpose for which Jesus came and died: to produce a great harvest, His church. Francis Turretin observed, "He came into the world and performed the mediatorial office for no other reason than to acquire a church for himself and call it (when acquired) into a participation of grace and glory."[9] The growth of the church from a small band of disciples in Acts 1 to the ends of the earth in Acts 28 is proof, as Johannes VanderKemp puts it, that "the satisfaction of the Son cannot be frustrated."[10] Our Lord Jesus Christ is a most successful harvester. He calls the church into existence by His messianic acts.[11] This is the point Jesus is making when He compares Himself to a grain of wheat that falls to the ground and dies, and by that death produces much fruit. By His suffering and death Jesus produces the church and now calls her to be fruitful.

---

8. Brown, *The Gospel According to John*, 472.

9. Francis Turretin, *Institutes of Elenctic Theology* (Phillipsburg, N.J.: P&R, 1997), 3:1.

10. Johannes VanderKemp, *The Christian Entirely the Property of Christ, in Life and Death: Exhibited in Fifty-three Sermons on the Heidelberg Catechism*, trans. John M. Harlingen (Grand Rapids: Reformation Heritage Books, 1997), 1:427.

11. Geerhardus Vos, *The Kingdom and the Church* (Grand Rapids: Eerdmans, 1958), 78.

The Fruit of His Labor

The fruit that Jesus produces by His death resembles Him. An apple seed produces apples. A pear seed produces pears. A grain of wheat that falls to the ground and dies produces grain. In other words, Jesus' church is conformed to Him. Listen to the words with which Jesus concludes our text: "He who loves his life will lose it, and he who hates his life in this world will keep it for eternal life. If anyone serves Me, let him follow Me; and where I am, there My servant will be also. If anyone serves Me, him My Father will honor" (12:25–26).

Here Jesus speaks of conformity to His image. He produces His image in His people—and His people are made like Him. The true church of Jesus Christ resembles Him. This means that as He died to self in order to produce much fruit, so His church, in conformity to Him, dies to self in order to produce much fruit for His glory. The pattern that we observe in Jesus— dying that others may live—He now reproduces in His church. In Him His church lives and moves and has her being. Sometimes it is said that couples who have been married for a long time come to resemble each other. So also here, the bride resembles her Bridegroom; the church resembles Christ. And the church counts this her joy, delighting to live as "children of the resurrection day." As the Heidelberg Catechism puts it, "By His power we too are already now resurrected to a new life" (HC, Q&A 45).

Thus, the principle of "death to self / life in Christ" articulated by Jesus in John 12:25–26 is the paradigm not only for the life of Christian discipleship but also for the life of the church. Though this pattern is found in every facet of the church's life, perhaps it is most profoundly seen in the work of the church planter and in the corporate life of the church plant.

Not only the church planter, but the church body as a whole, must die to self. Luther once stated, "The Church is misery on earth."[12] He also stated that the church "is like unto her bridegroom, Christ Jesus, torn, spit on, derided, and crucified."[13] Indeed, this is the way it must be so that we do not depend upon ourselves, but always upon Christ—that the glory may never be ours, but that it may always be His. Luther went on to say, "We tell our Lord God plainly, that if He will have His Church, He must maintain and defend it; for we can neither uphold nor protect it. If we could, indeed, we should become the proudest asses under heaven.

---

12. Martin Luther, *Table Talk* (Gainesville, Fla.: Bridge-Logos, 2004), 255.
13. Ibid., 253.

But God says: I say it, I do it."[14] Calvin also recognized the need for the church to be conformed to the image of her Savior: "The Church, so long as she is a pilgrim in this world, is subjected to the cross, that she may be humble, and may be conformed to her Head.... Her highest ornament and luster is modesty."[15] The church's greatest glory is to be found in her conformity to Christ, and that means death to self and life in Him.

How does the church planter die to self? He dies to self each time he gives up another evening of precious time he would otherwise spend with his wife and children to encourage struggling members of the church. He accepts a much smaller salary than he would receive in a larger church. He refuses to build the church upon his personality, choosing instead to decrease that Christ may increase. He gladly spends and is spent for the life of the congregation. He imparts to the congregation not only the gospel but also his life.

How does the church plant die to self? The church plant dies to self by refusing to be discouraged by small numbers. It refuses to give up when the funds are low and instead seeks help from sister churches that are more established. It foregoes its desire for a nice, large building, choosing instead to meet in less-than-ideal quarters, even though each time it gathers the members have to set up chairs for the worship service again. The church plant dies to self as it refuses to promote itself, choosing instead to proclaim Christ to a lost and dying world.

Edmund Clowney reminds us that this is precisely the work to which the servants of Christ Jesus are called: "Jesus came to gather, and to call gatherers, disciples who would gather with him, seeking the poor and helpless from city streets and country roads.... Mission is not an optional activity for Christ's disciples. If they are not gatherers, they are scatterers."[16] Conformity to Christ means the difficult work of missions and evangelism and church planting. Christ came to seek and to save the lost—not the righteous, but the unrighteous—and that work cost Him His life. Even as Christ came to serve sinners, so in Him we are called to serve sinners (John 13:14–17). Clowney goes on to state the great danger for those churches that fail to conform to Christ in terms of seeking the lost: "The congregation that ignores mission will atrophy and soon find itself shattered by internal dissension. It will inevitably begin to lose its

---

14. Ibid.
15. As quoted in Graham Miller, *Calvin's Wisdom* (Edinburgh: Banner of Truth, 1992), 52.
16. Edmund Clowney, *The Church* (Downers Grove, Ill.: InterVarsity, 1995), 159.

own young people, disillusioned by hearing the gospel trumpet sounded every Sunday for those who never march."[17] A church that does not die to self in service to Christ will necessarily turn inward and thereby lose her life. The work of missions, evangelism, and church planting is vital to the life of the church—through it she dies to self and lives to Christ.

As the church dies to self, she begins to experience the transforming power of the gospel, for in dying to self she lives to Christ—better yet, Christ lives in her. She becomes an instrument in the Redeemer's hands as He works in her and through her. [18] In his letter to the Colossians Paul says, "To this end I also labor, striving according to His working which works in me mightily" (1:29). It is no coincidence that Paul, who was the great church planter of the New Testament, writes of these themes of death to self and life to Christ often. In his second letter to the Corinthians, for example, he writes,

> In all things we commend ourselves as ministers of God: in much patience, in tribulations, in needs, in distresses, in stripes, in imprisonments, in tumults, in labors, in sleeplessness, in fastings; by purity, by knowledge, by longsuffering, by kindness, by the Holy Spirit, by sincere love, by the word of truth, by the power of God, by the armor of righteousness on the right hand and on the left, by honor and dishonor, by evil report and good report; as deceivers, and yet true; as unknown, and yet well known, *as dying, and behold, we live*; as chastened, and yet not killed; as sorrowful, yet always rejoicing; as poor, yet making many rich; as having nothing, and yet possessing all things (2 Cor. 6:4–10, emphasis added).

In fact, later in the same letter, Paul defines the marks of a true servant of Christ in these same terms:

> Are they ministers of Christ?—I speak as a fool—I am more: in labors more abundant, in stripes above measure, in prisons more frequently, in deaths often. From the Jews five times I received forty stripes minus one. Three times I was beaten with rods; once I was stoned; three times I was shipwrecked; a night and a day I have been in the deep; in journeys often, in perils of waters, in perils of robbers, in perils of my own countrymen, in perils of the Gentiles, in perils in the city, in perils in the wilderness, in perils in the sea, in perils among false brethren; in weariness and toil, in sleeplessness often, in

---

17. Ibid., 160.
18. Cf. Paul Tripp, *Instruments in the Redeemer's Hand: People in Need of Change Helping People in Need of Change* (Phillipsburg, N. J.: P&R, 2002).

hunger and thirst, in fastings often, in cold and nakedness—besides the other things, what comes upon me daily: my deep concern for all the churches. Who is weak, and I am not weak? Who is made to stumble, and I do not burn with indignation? If I must boast, I will boast in the things which concern my infirmity. The God and Father of our Lord Jesus Christ, who is blessed forever, knows that I am not lying. In Damascus the governor, under Aretas the king, was guarding the city of the Damascenes with a garrison, desiring to arrest me; but I was let down in a basket through a window in the wall, and escaped from his hands (2 Cor. 11:23–33).

The persecutor of the church became persecuted for the church's sake—including churches he had planted. The persecutor of Christ became persecuted for Christ's sake. Yet in this suffering and death, Paul found glory and life. In so doing, he tasted of the power of God, as God's strength was made perfect in weakness. Therefore Paul could most gladly boast in his infirmities, for in these infirmities the power of Christ rested upon him. Therefore he took pleasure in infirmities, in reproaches, in needs, in persecutions, in distresses for Christ's sake. For when he was weak, then he was strong (2 Cor. 12:9–10).

This paradigm of death to self and of life in Christ is not unique to the apostle Paul; it characterizes the life of all true servants of Christ. Indeed, it characterizes the life of the church herself. As the church is conformed to Christ, she proclaims Him in Word and deed, and Christ Himself is then at work producing still more fruit. Thus, as a statement from the Mission to North America points out, "From the beginning of the established church, missionaries have started new congregations from which to share the Gospel to a desperate and hurting world."[19]

But why should mission work take the form of church planting? The answer is simple: Church planting is essential because the risen Christ has bound Himself to the assembly of His people on the Lord's Day. It is in the assembly that He has promised to work through the preaching of the gospel to create faith in our hearts and through the sacraments to strengthen that faith (HC, Q&A 65–68). Michael Horton writes,

> The church is first of all a place where God does certain things.... Christ, both Lord and Savior of his church, appointed an official ministry...so that he could continue to serve his covenant people

---

19. "Frequently Asked Questions," Mission to North America (PCA), accessed July 2008, www.pca-mna.org/churchplanting/faqs.php.

and extend his kingdom of grace to the ends of the earth by his Spirit. Even in the present—every time we gather—it is God who summons us in judgment and grace. It is not our devotion, praise, piety, or service that comes first, but God's service to us. This is why we must assemble at a place where the gospel is truly preached, the sacraments are administered according to Christ's institution, and there is a visible form of Christ's heavenly reign through officers whom he has called and sent.[20]

It is through the "ordinary means" of the church's ministry—namely the foolishness of preaching and the weakness of water, bread, and wine—that Christ has promised to work, bringing sinners to salvation in Christ through repentance and faith in Him.

Geerhardus Vos states, "The church actually has within herself the powers of the world to come. She...forms an intermediate link between the present life and the life of eternity.... The consummation of the kingdom in which all is fulfilled began with [Jesus'] resurrection and ascension."[21] And so, by God's grace, we press on in planting churches, proclaiming Christ, that sinners may be ushered into the life of the world to come. And as they begin to taste the powers of the age to come, they too lay down their lives in service to Christ, knowing that these present sufferings are not worthy to be compared with the glory that shall be revealed in us. As Calvin notes, "The afflictions of the Church are always momentary, when we raise our eyes to its eternal happiness."[22] Thus, in all our labor, we echo the words of Paul: "I press on, that I may lay hold of that for which Christ Jesus has also laid hold of me.... For our citizenship is in heaven, from which we also eagerly wait for the Savior, the Lord Jesus Christ, who will transform our lowly body that it may be conformed to His glorious body, according to the working by which He is able even to subdue all things to Himself" (Phil. 3:12, 20–21).

Conclusion

Jesus Christ is the fruitful grain of wheat who died in order that He might produce much fruit. The church is His fruit, and she exists to bring glory and honor to Him. Thus, the biblical foundation for church planting is the

---

20. Michael Horton, "No Church, No Problem?" *Modern Reformation* 17, 4 (July/August 2008): 17.

21. Vos, *The Kingdom and the Church*, 84–85.

22. As quoted in Miller, *Calvin's Wisdom*, 61.

glory of Christ Jesus our Lord. Therefore, as Vos comments, "The joy of working in the dawn of the world to come quickens the pulse of all New Testament servants of Christ."[23] As we long for the fullness of the day when we behold the Sun of Righteousness in all of His glory, let us go forth and plant churches with the words of Isaac Watts's hymn in our hearts:

> We long to see Thy churches full,
> That all the chosen race
> May, with one voice and heart and soul,
> Sing thy redeeming grace.

---

23. Geerhardus Vos, *Grace and Glory* (Edinburgh: Banner of Truth, 1994), 90.

CHAPTER TWO

ॐ

The Sovereign Spirit of Missions: Thoughts on Acts 16:6–10 and Church Planting

Daniel R. Hyde

The book of Acts is the closest thing we have to a manual for church planting and missions in the New Testament. As we turn to its pages, we see story after story of the Lord's hand in sowing His vineyard as the church grew through missions and church planting. Although the age of the apostles was an extraordinary time in the life of the church, the narrative of the Acts of the Apostles lays out for us many practical principles for church planting that abide in all times and places. One practical point that we as Reformed people must learn from Acts is that we need not only a passion for the work of planting new congregations but also a willingness to respond to the Spirit's leading and engage in the work of planting churches—whether as the overseeing church or as partnering churches. We need to say with eagerness and expectation, "Here am I! Send me" (Isa. 6:8).[1]

In this chapter we will look at Acts 16:6–10 and see how Luke, the author of Acts, speaks about this leading of the blessed Holy Spirit, who is the sovereign creator, source, and leader of church planting. He is the sovereign Spirit of missions. If we are going to be missional and commissional churches, obeying our Lord's command in Matthew 28, we need to be sensitive and obedient to the leading of the Holy Spirit in the twenty-first century.

Adapted from "The Recipe for Church Planting from the Book of Acts" in *Christian Renewal* 25, 12 (March 14, 2007): 24–25 and is reprinted with permission.

1. On the theme of the leading of the Holy Spirit from a Reformed perspective, see the classic work of the Puritan Thomas Jacombe, "The Leading of the Holy Spirit Opened; With Some Practical Inquiries Resolved about It," in *Puritan Sermons 1659–1689* (1682, 1844; repr., Wheaton, Ill.: Richard Owen Roberts, Publishers, 1981), 3:585–610. See also the contemporary works of J. I. Packer: *Keep in Step with the Spirit: Finding Fullness in Our Walk with God*, rev. ed. (Grand Rapids: Baker, 2005) and with Carolyn Nystrom, *Guard Us, Guide Us: Divine Leading in Life's Decisions* (Grand Rapids: Baker, 2008).

The Holy Spirit Sovereignly Leads in Whom He Calls to Plant Churches (Acts 16:6; 13:2)

We begin in verse 6, which says, "When they had gone," and we ask the question, "How did Paul, Silas, and Timothy come to this point in the narrative of going 'through Phrygia and the region of Galatia,' preaching the gospel?" We must look back to chapter 13:1–3 to see how. There we read that while they were engaged in public worship (*leitourgountōn*; the word from which we get "liturgy") and fasting, the prophets and teachers of the church in Antioch were told by the Holy Spirit, "Now separate to Me Barnabas and Saul for the work to which I have called them" (v. 2). Thus, the sending of Paul and Barnabas was of the Holy Spirit's initiation and sovereign choice.

While we read that the Spirit called Paul and Barnabas in this extraordinary manner, we must understand that the Spirit had already been preparing Paul for this calling. The Holy Spirit, then, did not just call Paul "out of the blue." This is important to note, because all across our land today, too many missionaries, church planters, and churches have sprung up because someone claims to feel led by the Spirit. Today many people believe that the only qualification a person needs to be a missionary or church planter is a so-called heart for the lost. And if he has that, he is sent. In fact, one of my former neighbors "felt" that God wanted him to come to San Diego and plant a new church for postmodern people. This group had no oversight, no elders, and no group of supporting churches—nothing. This church no longer exists, yet similar ones do.

What we learn from Paul's experience is that while the internal call must be validated by the outward call, the internal call is tested and strengthened through ordinary means. The Spirit calls missionaries and church planters through the means of the church as it worships and fasts. We see this clearly in Acts 13. However, a church's sending someone is no guarantee of the Spirit's calling. My own secondhand experience validates that even though a person may be sent by a church (whether it is a true church or not), he often comes back as a failure. Why? Because he had not truly been called by the Holy Spirit. Again, the Spirit uses ordinary means, and not only a desire. What I mean by this is that a church planter must be gifted and prepared for the task. We see with Paul that the Holy Spirit had already been preparing him, even before he was internally and then externally called. We see this preparation in three things that made Paul a great church planter.

First, *he was educated in the Word* (cf. Acts 22:3). This applies today, as we need men trained at solid seminaries. We cannot cut corners in education, and we ought not to make any excuses for a person who does. Second, *he was passionate for a specific people group*, the Jews, as Romans 9:2 and 10:1 testify. This means that a church planter cannot be one who is just looking for a job, a salary, or something to do, even if he piously couches this in terms of "just serving the Lord." A church planter must be one who is looking to plant in a particular place, with a particular people. Third, *he was willing to suffer for the sake of Christ*. We see Paul suffering in many ways for the sake of Christ throughout the book of Acts, and he frequently writes of his sufferings in his letters.[2] The Lord prepared Paul for his calling as a missionary who would suffer.

In summary, we see in Acts 16 that the Holy Spirit is sovereign, which means that He can call anyone He desires. But we also learn from Scripture that the Holy Spirit calls those whom He has prepared.

The Holy Spirit Sovereignly Leads in Where to Plant Churches (Acts 16:6, 7, 10)

The second thing that we learn from this text of Scripture is that the sovereign Spirit leads in where to send missionaries to plant congregations. He also leads where not to plant. Again, He can do this because He is sovereign. In his comments on this text, John Calvin asked the difficult question, "Why did the Lord forbid Paul to speak in Asia, and did not allow him to come into Bithynia?" He explained that instead of rooting this in one people group being better than or more worthy than another people group, we should see the answer rooted in God's sovereign wisdom:

Therefore there is nothing better than to leave God the freedom and power to deem those, whom He pleases, worthy of His grace, or deprive them of it. And certainly since His eternal election is of grace, so must the calling, which flows from it, be considered of grace, and it is not founded on men, since it owes nothing to anyone. Accordingly let us realize that the Gospel comes forth to us from the one fountain of pure grace. However God does not lack a legitimate reason why He offers His Gospel to certain ones, but passes others by; but I maintain that the reason is hidden in His secret purpose.

---

2. See chapter 1, "The Fruitful Grain of Wheat" by Brian Vos for a discussion of the many situations in which Paul suffered, "dying to self" for the sake of Christ.

In the meantime let believers know that they have been called gratuitously when others have been neglected, so that they may not ascribe to themselves what belongs to the mercy of God alone. On the other hand as for the rest whom God rejects for no apparent reason, let them learn to wonder at the profound abyss of His judgment, into which it is not permitted to pry.[3]

We most often think of God the Father as the one who is revealed in Scripture as sovereign, and rightly so. For it is He who called everything to be out of nothing (Gen. 1). It is He who elected us by His good pleasure (Eph. 1:3–14). It is He who is the Lord of creation and providentially maintains it (Ps. 104). It is He who raises up kings and casts them down (Prov. 21:1). It is He who appoints nations, their boundaries, and their durations (Acts 17:26).

Yet we also are reminded that the Holy Spirit is revealed in Scripture as sovereign. It was He who re-created the dark, void mass of chaos in the beginning (Gen. 1:2; Ps. 104:30). It is He who powerfully raises dead, lifeless sinners to life (John 3:5–8; 1 Peter 1:3). It was He who called Paul to preach in Acts 13.

So as Paul, Silas, and Timothy were traveling through what is today Turkey, we see the sovereign Spirit in action. Notice where they tried to go and where they were led to go. First, verse 6 says that they were going "through Phrygia and the region of Galatia" because they were "forbidden by the Holy Spirit to preach the word in Asia." They were trying to go north towards the Black Sea but were led through the center of Asia Minor. Second, verse 7 says that when "they had come to Mysia," which is the northwest corner of Asia Minor, "they tried to go into Bithynia, but the Spirit did not permit them." They were still trying to get up into the northern territories, going clockwise around Asia Minor. They were being led in between the region of Asia in the south and Bithynia in the north through a desolate region with no major cities.

We may read this and say, "But I thought the Holy Spirit was the Spirit of missions? Why would He actually forbid the gospel from being preached?" Notice that in verse 9 Paul sees a vision of a man in Macedonia, and in verse 10 they leave for Macedonia. Were the Macedonians more worthy and deserving of the gospel than the Asians or Bithyn-

---

3. John Calvin, *The Acts of the Apostles, Volume II*, trans. John W. Fraser, ed. David W. Torrance and Thomas F. Torrance, Calvin's New Testament Commentaries (1966; repr., Grand Rapids: Eerdmans, 1973), 7:69.

ians? Did God love Macedonia more? God forbid. We must simply say with John Calvin that it was the secret will of God why Paul, Silas, and Timothy were forbidden to preach in Asia and Bithynia, while it was the revealed will of God to preach in Macedonia. By preaching in Macedonia the gospel came to Lydia; the Philippian jailer; Thessalonica, one of Paul's great ministerial joys; the Bereans, the studious believers; Athens, with the great debate on Mars Hill; and Corinth.

This story can be told over and over again by missionaries and church planters. In fact, one of my parishioners told me after we began the Oceanside United Reformed Church that she and her husband had prayed for ten years that a Reformed church would be started on the coast of north San Diego. So why did God wait ten years? I do not know. All I know is that after ten years of praying, several families had come to the knowledge of the Reformed doctrines and all lived in coastal north San Diego County. At the same time I was graduating from seminary, having gone with the purpose of planting a Reformed church in Orange County, to the north, where my wife and I are from and where there are only a few Reformed churches. Yet the mysterious and sovereign plan of the Holy Spirit led us to where we are today—perfectly in His will, not ours.

Therefore, we must learn what Paul, Silas, and Timothy learned—to trust in the timing and direction of the Holy Spirit in the life of a mission work and that He will make that direction and timing clear to us. We must humbly submit to the revealed things of the Word in church planting, and the Spirit will do His work. It is revealed for us to preach, evangelize, make disciples, be outwardly focused, do everything according to the Word, plant seeds, and see what the Lord will do. We know that we are called to be salt and light in the place God has put us, so we must be faithful to that. And when the Spirit's leading is evident as He brings people to us from an area where there is no Reformed church— whether near or far—we need to heartily and joyfully concur with the apostolic mission, "concluding that the Lord had called us to preach the gospel to them" (v. 10).

The Holy Spirit Sovereignly Leads in How to Plant Churches (Acts 16:6, 10)

Finally, Luke's narrative in Acts 16 tells us how the Spirit leads in how Christians are to plant churches. What method and means do we use? Luke tells us: "the word" (v. 6) and "the gospel" (v. 10). We preach Christ and Him crucified. It is the Word—the Word of the gospel—that is the power of God unto salvation (Rom. 1:16). It is by hearing the Word of Christ that faith comes (Rom. 10:17). With all the gimmicks and methods and programs that are out there today masquerading themselves as Christian, we must fix in our hearts and minds that the Spirit uses the Word. As in the days of Isaiah, when the leaders of God's people sought the word of God in mediums and wizards, we need to cry out with the prophet, "To the law and to the testimony!" (Isa. 8:20). The book of Acts focuses our attention upon God's method of preaching:

> Then the word of God spread.... But the word of God grew and multiplied.... And the word of the Lord was being spread throughout all the region.... So the word of the Lord grew mightily and prevailed.... [Paul] dwelt two whole years in his own rented house, and received all who came to him, preaching the kingdom of God and teaching about the things which concern the Lord Jesus Christ with all confidence, no one forbidding him (Acts 6:7; 12:24; 13:49; 19:20; 28:30–31).

Although they were forbidden to speak the Word in Asia, so they spoke it boldly in Phrygia and Galatia; although they were forbidden to preach the gospel in Bithynia, they preached it powerfully in Troas and then Macedonia. When they came to a river where some women were praying, they spoke to them passionately, and "the Lord opened [Lydia's] heart to heed the things spoken by Paul" (16:14).

To plant a biblical church is to send the man the Spirit has chosen, to the place He has chosen, to use the means He has chosen. In saying this, we must be wary of over-spiritualizing this process and task, emphasizing the Holy Spirit's sovereign work to the point that we do not preach to the lost and become hyper-Calvinists as we wait for some sign from heaven to go and preach. We must also be wary of over-emphasizing the method and means of church planting—preaching—lest we become too centered on our hearers' thoughts and feelings and seek to seduce them through the wisdom of man. Instead, we want the sovereign Spirit to do His ineffable work along with the Word, which He has ordained, as both are joined together. It has been said that if we have the Spirit without the Word we blow up; if we have the Word without the Spirit we dry up; but only when we have the Spirit and the Word do we grow up. May God cause His Spirit to lead us by His Word into our world so that mature congregations may spring up all over the globe.

CHAPTER THREE

∾

The Reformed Confessions and Missions

Wes Bredenhof

Most Reformed missionaries and church planters have encountered a familiar derogatory moniker for our churches: the Frozen Chosen. Usually this designation comes from non-Reformed people who believe that the Reformed faith inevitably kills evangelistic outreach, church planting, and missions. Often, those who use the Frozen Chosen moniker place the blame for this alleged neglect specifically at the feet of the Reformed doctrine of election. A sentiment exists in broader Christian circles that confessionally Reformed believers are not, will not, and cannot be enthusiastic about sharing the gospel of Christ with those who are strangers to the promises of God. If such creatures exist, they are like true Christians within the Roman Catholic Church: they simply do not belong in such a place.

What can we expect when church historians and missiologists portray the Reformation as a movement indifferent to the missionary calling of the church? How can any good fruit come from such a tree? For example, one recent mission textbook alleges that the Protestant Reformers believed there was no remaining evangelistic task for the church; therefore they "did not preach the gospel beyond the fence lines of Christendom." Indeed, one supposedly has to look beyond the pale of the magisterial Reformation to find any missionary zeal: "Outside Lutheran and Reformed churches, Anabaptists exhibited considerable enthusiasm for evangelism." However, even the Anabaptists failed "to move outside the walls of Christendom."[1] In the estimation of these authors, like so

A sincere word of appreciation is in order for Ken Wieske, a Canadian Reformed missionary working in Recife, Brazil, for his helpful comments on an earlier draft of this essay.

1. A. Scott Moreau, Gary R. Corwin, Gary B. McGee, *Introducing World Missions: A Biblical, Historical and Practical Survey* (Grand Rapids: Baker Academic, 2004), 120–21.

many others, the Protestant missionary movement really begins with William Carey in the late eighteenth century.

Confessions—An Asset or a Liability?

Unfortunately, we face similar sentiments from some who call themselves Reformed. In our own backyard, the blame for lack of missionary passion is sometimes laid at the foot of the Reformed confessions—products of the allegedly unevangelistic Reformation. For instance, in November 1972, *Calvin Theological Journal* featured a number of articles on the relationship between the Three Forms of Unity and missions. The Heidelberg Catechism and the Canons of Dort came out with passing marks, but the Belgic Confession was singled out as being particularly defective when it comes to stimulating outreach among Reformed believers. Robert Recker concluded that "the Belgic Confession projects an image, in the main, of a church talking with itself rather than a church before the world."[2] He went on: "If I were to construct a missiology today, or if I would hope to be inspired with missionary passion, I would reach for the Bible and not for the Belgic Confession. Reading this Confession with analytical care impressed me with the fact that it is partial. And when I read it to discern the missionary focus of the whole Word of God, then I can only say it is inadequate."[3]

Recker did appear to be *sympathetically* critical. He acknowledged the context, noting that "the document reveals the raw nerves of a particular historical situation and so is limited by the pressures and the insights of the time."[4] But according to Recker, there is no escaping the reality that the Belgic Confession is simply irrelevant to missions and may actually be a liability for a missionary-minded church.

What was implicit in Recker's analysis of the Belgic Confession became explicit in the Christian Reformed Church (CRC) in the process leading up to the adoption of its new confession, Contemporary Testimony: Our World Belongs to God, which addresses contemporary issues unknown to the writers of the historic confessions, such as the Internet and terrorism. During that time (1971–1986), there were many voices in the CRC arguing that not only the Belgic Confession but also the Three Forms of Unity as

---

2. Robert Recker, "An Analysis of the Belgic Confession as to Its Mission Focus," *Calvin Theological Journal* 7, 2 (November 1972): 179.

3. Ibid., 180.

4. Ibid., 179.

a whole insufficiently address the missionary calling of the church.[5] This became part of the rationale for the formulation of this new confessional document. It leaves the rest of us who continue to adhere to the Three Forms of Unity alone wondering whether perhaps we too have an insufficient confessional basis for missions at home and abroad.

It is the goal of this chapter to address that very point. Do the Reformed confessions inhibit or stimulate the task that the Lord Jesus gave His church in the Great Commission? Is our confessional heritage an asset or a liability—a blessing or a curse— when it comes to missions? Do we need to supplement or perhaps even replace these confessions?

Before we proceed, it should be noted that while our focus will be on the Three Forms of Unity (the Belgic Confession, the Canons of Dort, and the Heidelberg Catechism), we will also give some attention to the Westminster Confession and catechisms. Most confessionally Reformed churches in the world accept either or both of these sets of Reformed confessions as faithful summaries of Scripture. These confessions are not above the Scriptures, but they do faithfully represent the crucial doctrines of God's Word. Presbyterian theologians often speak of the confessions as being "subordinate standards"—meaning that they are subordinate to the Bible. This way of speaking also represents the approach of this essay to those documents.

Historical Background

Because the Reformed confessions are rooted in the Reformation, we need to first consider the question of the relationship of the Reformation to Christian missions. When contemporary missiologists and church historians portray the Reformation as a movement lacking in missionary zeal, they invariably judge by the standard of contemporary understandings of the scope and nature of "mission." But what if the Reformed churches of the sixteenth century understood "mission" differently?

To answer that question, consider the Reformed churches in the Lowlands (modern-day Belgium and the Netherlands) in the sixteenth century. The ideals of the Protestant Reformation were propagated in this

---

5. See "Supplement: Report 38," *Acts of Synod 1972*, 403. A survey was distributed to each consistory of the CRC. Of the 135 churches (of 367) who said that it was necessary for the CRC to augment its confessions, ninety said that it was urgent to augment the confessions in the area of the mission of the church while forty-five stated that it was desirable. Only seven said that it was unnecessary.

region mainly by Calvinist preachers and theologians. However, artists, musicians, and actors were also key figures. In the Lowlands, especially in Flanders, we find the Chambers of Rhetoric, which produced numerous dramas reflecting a strongly held anti-Roman Catholic and anticlerical sentiment. The Chambers also organized poetry contests and pageants, and it held annual events at which awards and prizes were given for the best works.[6] During the 1560s, almost every play produced was antagonistic toward the Roman Catholic Church. In at least one play, Roman Catholics were explicitly identified as being the heathen.[7] This sentiment existed in the popular mind as early as 1540. Phyllis Mack Crew cites a Flemish poem from that period:

> [The images] stand in the temple like house beams
> Rusted, dusty, covered with spider webs,
> Dirtied by birds, by cats, by mice.
> And in addition you must also acknowledge
> That they neither smell nor taste
> Nor have any sense of life; that is true.
> Those who love them, must be despised
> And they should not even be regarded as Christians.[8]

This poem alludes to the polemic against idolatry found in Psalm 115 and in doing so, it heightens the sense that the Romanists were truly the pagans in the land.

This sense was also there among the ministers of the Reformed churches in the Lowlands. Herman Moded insinuated that those in the Church of Rome were followers of Baal.[9] It was commonly held by the Reformed that the priests of Rome were sorcerers and magicians who practiced witchcraft.[10] In 1544, a delegation was sent from Tournai to Geneva requesting that a Reformed missionary be sent because of the great paganism in the land.[11]

Among those Reformed ministers we find Guido de Brès, author of the Belgic Confession. Besides the Confession, de Brès also authored polemical works dealing with the Roman Catholic Church and the Anabaptist move-

---

6. Phyllis Mack Crew, *Calvinist Preaching and Iconoclasm in the Netherlands, 1544–1569* (Cambridge: Cambridge University Press, 1978), 52.

7. Ibid., 146.

8. Quoted in ibid., 29.

9. Ibid., 22.

10. Ibid., 23, 25.

11. Ibid., 53.

ment. In his book *Le baston de la foy chrestienne* (The staff of the Christian faith), de Brès made it clear that he regarded Roman Catholicism as another religion. Already in the subtitle of his book, he identifies the Roman church as being an enemy of the gospel.[12] In the preface, he identifies those under the yoke of Rome as pagans and idolaters.[13] When dealing with the marks of the church, de Brès reveals that his vision for the true church of Christ includes what we today call the Great Commission.[14] He saw it as the continuing task of the church to spread the gospel everywhere, and for de Brès and the Reformed churches of the Lowlands, that included the essentially pagan regions of Europe under the Roman yoke.

However, it was not just Roman Catholicism that constituted the darkness in Reformation-era Europe. *La racine, source et fondement des anabaptistes* (The root, source and foundation of the Anabaptists) may be considered the magnum opus of Guido de Brès, and in this work it becomes evident that at least some of the more extreme Anabaptists were also to be regarded as enemies of the gospel of Christ. For instance, de Brès wrote about the infamous history of the Reformation at Münster in Germany. The pure gospel of Christ arrived in 1532, and eventually peace and tranquility came to the city as a result. De Brès goes on to describe what happened in later years: "But Satan, the enemy of peace and of the truth, could not long endure the peace and publication of the Gospel; therefore, just as he had already done in other places, with might he worked to obstruct and overthrow the Gospel. He did this in order to establish in its place these seditious Anabaptists. He did just this at Münster, to the great damage of the faithful and the destruction and infamy of the Gospel."[15] While de Brès recognized the differences among Anabaptist groups (Münster was an extreme), it is clear that he and the Reformed churches saw at least some of them as being essentially sub-Christian or even pagan.

---

12. "...*pour s'armer contre les ennemis de l'Euangile & aussi pour cognoistre l'anciennete de nostre foy & de la vraye Eglise*" (to provide weaponry against the enemies of the gospel and also to recognize the ancient pedigree of our faith and of the true Church).

13. Guy de Brès, *Le baston de la foy chrestienne* (Geneva: Nicolas Barbier & Courtreau, 1558), 3–4.

14. Ibid., 241–45.

15. Guy de Brès, *La racine, source et fondement des anabaptistes ou rebaptisez de nostre temps. Avec tres ample refutations des arguments principaux, par lesquels ils ont accoustumé de troubler l'Eglise de nostre Seigneur Iesus Christ, & seduire les simples* (Rouen: Abel Clemence, 1565), 19 (author's translation).

This prevailing perspective was found not only among the Reformed churches of the Lowlands but also among all Reformed churches in Europe in the sixteenth century. Roman Catholics and many Anabaptists were regarded not as fellow Christians (though erring in certain key respects), but properly as objects of mission—lost people who still needed the true gospel of Jesus Christ. The medieval church had failed in evangelizing Europe, and, hence, it remained a mission field.

It is also worth noting that this broader missionary perspective continued into the seventeenth century among the Reformed churches. Gisbertus Voetius (1589–1676) was one of the most influential delegates to the Synod of Dort (1618–1619). Jan Jongeneel has described him as the first theologian to work out a comprehensive Protestant theology of missions. When he considered the issue of those to whom missionaries are to be sent, Voetius included the Roman Catholics and other heretics and schismatics. They are properly included with self-identifying unbelievers as the object of the missionary enterprise.[16]

Based on this understanding, we can agree with Fred Klooster, who calls the Reformation "one of the greatest home missionary projects of all history."[17] More recently, Scott Hendrix has argued that previous generations of mission historians have "underestimated the extent to which the Reformation as a whole *was* mission."[18] When we survey the views of the Reformers and the Reformed churches of the sixteenth and seventeenth centuries, it becomes clear that there was a much stronger sense of the antithesis between true and false religion than is found today in most of what passes for Christianity, and even among our Reformed churches.

Today, many in the broader Christian context would no longer consider nations or regions dominated by Roman Catholicism to be in need of the gospel. The same can be said for nations or regions where charismatic Pentecostalism (a modern form of extreme Anabaptism) is in ascendancy. However, confessionally Reformed churches cannot allow the broader Christian context to dictate who the objects of mission really are. We need to return to the Scriptures. When we do that we see, for instance, the central significance of the doctrine of justification by faith

---

16. See Jan Jongeneel, "The Missiology of Gisbertus Voetius: The First Comprehensive Protestant Theology of Missions," *Calvin Theological Journal* 26, 1 (April 1991): 60–63.

17. Fred Klooster, "Missions—The Heidelberg Catechism and Calvin," *Calvin Theological Journal* 7, 2 (November 1972): 187.

18. Scott H. Hendrix, *Recultivating the Vineyard: The Reformation Agendas of Christianization* (Louisville, Ky.: Westminster, 2004), 86.

alone through Christ alone—a doctrine that Rome continues to deny. Nothing has changed on that score since the sixteenth century. So, on the one hand, the Reformation saw the home front as a mission field. Europe was the place where the main spiritual battles of the sixteenth century were fought. Yet there was still an eye for the rest of the world. Though it resulted only in much loss of life, the church at Geneva sponsored a pioneering mission to Brazil from 1555 to 1560. Around the same time, a Reformed missionary was also sent out from Budapest to minister among the Muslims.[19] Hebrew translations of Calvin's catechism and the Heidelberg Catechism appeared already in the mid-sixteenth century in efforts to reach Jews in Europe and elsewhere with the gospel.[20]

As the Reformed faith became more established in the Netherlands, attention was soon given to foreign missions there as well. Frans Schalkwijk has detailed the Dutch Reformed missionary efforts in Brazil from 1630–1654. He noted that the Heidelberg Catechism was translated into Tupi, an indigenous South American language—indicating the significance of the Catechism for Reformed missionaries in that area.[21] Others have described the Reformed missionary work done in conjunction with the United East India Company from 1602 to 1799 in such places as South Africa, Formosa (Taiwan), Ceylon (Sri Lanka), and Indonesia.[22] Leen Joosse has extensively documented the Reformed missionary work facilitated by the Dutch West India Company in the United States, the Caribbean, the Guyanas, and elsewhere.[23] Several articles have also been written describing the missionary efforts of Reformed ministers such as Jonas Michaelius and Johannes Megapolensis in New Netherland (present-day New York State) in the early to mid-seventeenth century.[24] Surveying all

---

19. Klooster, "Missions," 183–84.

20. Ibid., 207. Cf. C. van der Spek, "Calvin's Hebrew Catechism," *Lux Mundi* 26, 3 (September 2007): 68–69.

21. F. L. Schalkwijk, *The Reformed Church in Dutch Brazil (1630–1654)* (Zoetermeer, The Netherlands: Boekencentrum, 1986), 181.

22. *Het indisch sion: de gereformeerde kerk onder de verenigde oost-indische compagnie*, ed. G. J. Schutte (Hilversum: Verloren, 2002).

23. Leendert Jan Joosse, *Geloof in de nieuwe wereld: ontmoeting met afrikanen en indianen* (Kampen, The Netherlands: Uitgeverij Kok, 2008).

24. See Charles E. Corwin, "Efforts of the Dutch-American Colonial Pastors for the Conversion of the Indians," *Journal of the Presbyterian Historical Society* 12, 4 (October 1925): 225–46; Charles E. Corwin, "The First Dutch Minister in America," *Journal of the Presbyterian Historical Society* 12, 3 (April 1925): 144–51; Gerald Francis De Jong, "Dominie

these studies and others, it soon becomes apparent that there is no validity to the claim that William Carey represents the true beginning of the Protestant missionary movement. Confessionally Reformed churches were zealously engaged in home and foreign missions long before Carey.

Having established that the Reformed faith has provided a home for the missionary spirit since the sixteenth century, we can now turn to the confessions that express that faith. We will survey those confessions on a number of topics of significance for Christian missions.

The Foundations and Origins of Mission

The first question and answer of the Heidelberg Catechism is well known for its warm, pastoral summary of the gospel. However, these words also speak to the missionary calling of the church of Jesus Christ:
What is thy only comfort in life and in death?

> That I with body and soul, both in life and death, am not my own, but belong unto my faithful Savior Jesus Christ, who with His precious blood, hath fully satisfied for all my sins, and delivered me from all the power of the devil; and so preserves me that without the will of my heavenly Father, not a hair can fall from my head; yea, that all things must be subservient to my salvation, and therefore, by His Holy Spirit, He also assures me of eternal life, and makes me sincerely willing and ready, henceforth, to live unto Him (HC, Q&A 1).

Fritz Krüger has pointed out that question and answer 1 "defines both the foundations and limits of all mission." The Catechism speaks about comfort, highlighting the reality of universal human misery, "of alienation from all comfort." It reminds us that unbelieving man is under the curse. Man is fallen, and he is like an abandoned child with no one to fend for him, no one to defend him. He has "only his own futile efforts which are so easily overwhelmed in this sad world." So the Catechism, right from the beginning, establishes itself as a missionary document. Says Krüger, "It is a pastoral hand reaching out to the lost and the lonely, the suffering and the crying, those lost in despair and hidden in oppression."[25]

Johannes Megapolensis: Minister to New Netherland," *The New-York Historical Society Quarterly* 52, 1 (January 1968): 7–47.

25. J. J. Fritz Krüger, "The Reformed Confessions: Embarrassment or Blessing to a Missionary Church?" *Laden IRTT Site*, accessed 28 Oct. 2010, http://www.irtt.nl/start/start.htm.

The Canons of Dort establish the same foundation: "As all men have sinned in Adam, lie under the curse, and are obnoxious to eternal death, God would have done no injustice by leaving them all to perish, and delivering them over to condemnation on account of sin, according to the words of the Apostle (Rom. 3:19), 'that every mouth may be stopped, and all the world may become guilty before God'; (ver. 23) 'for all have sinned, and come short of the glory of God'; and (6:23), 'for the wages of sin is death'" (CD, 1.1).

Since Adam's fall, all mankind is under the curse of sin and deserves God's wrath and judgment. This is the foundational problem for mankind, and it is the raison d'être for Christian missions. How can a person be delivered from this curse and escape the wrath of God? How can a person be reconciled to God, being restored to fellowship with Him?

In the Belgic Confession, Reformed churches confess, "We believe that our most gracious God, in His admirable wisdom and goodness, seeing that man had thus thrown himself into temporal and spiritual death, and made himself wholly miserable, was pleased to seek and comfort him when he trembling fled from His presence, promising him that He would give His Son, who should be made of a woman to bruise the head of the serpent, and would make him happy" (BC, art. 17).[26] This article teaches us that we can, in some sense, justifiably speak about God as being the first missionary. He is the first missionary, not in the sense that He was sent out on a mission (who could send God?), but in the sense that He set out to seek the lost in Eden. He did so on His own initiative and in an entirely unique way, but it can still be described in missionary terms.

Some missiologists have taken this truth further in unwarranted directions. For instance, in the mission theology of David Bosch, mission is not so much an activity of the church but rather is an attribute of God.[27] Bosch and others use the Latin expression *missio Dei* (mission of God) to refer to this concept, which has come to encompass all sorts of social and political agendas that have nothing to do with the mission of the church as given by Christ. Insofar as God is the one who seeks out that which is lost (also through Christ), there is a kernel of truth in this concept. However, J. DeJong has rightly argued that the concept of *missio Dei* is inadequate, as it "tends to blur the specific mandate given by Christ to

---

26. See also Westminster Confession of Faith, VII.3.

27. David J. Bosch, *Transforming Mission: Paradigm Shifts in Theology of Mission* (Maryknoll, N.Y.: Orbis Books, 1991), 390.

his church."[28] The expansive contemporary missiological notion of *missio Dei* needs to be distinguished from the limited *missio Dei* found in article 17 of the Belgic Confession.

According to the Confession, the missionary task of the church finds its origin with God and His pity for fallen creatures.[29] It is part of God's character to seek the lost and to call them back to Himself. In the garden, He did so without any use of means. Today, He uses the means of men who are sent out by Jesus Christ with the command to preach, teach, and disciple (Matt. 28:18–20). Since God is a missionary God (in the sense that the lost are of concern to Him), His people ought to be a missionary people.

This conclusion from article 17 is supported by passages such as Ephesians 5:1, where believers are called to be imitators of God. Obviously, we cannot imitate God in every respect, but the context of Ephesians 5:1 is that of God's love and forgiveness. We can certainly imitate Him in those ways, and that definitely has a bearing on our missionary calling. Looking to the origins of missions, we ought to be constrained by God's love.

The Need for Mission

One of the most common missiological errors today is the teaching that Jesus Christ will not only save those who hear the gospel and believe but also those who have never heard. The only ones in true danger are the ones who hear the gospel and reject it, and with some missiologists, even these are not beyond hope. Religious pluralism and inclusivism are some of the most deadly errors undermining the Christian missionary enterprise in our day.

Carl Braaten has argued that Jesus Christ is the fulfillment of all non-Christian religions. At the same time that he warns against religious pluralism, he also speaks of Bhakti Hinduism and Mahayana Buddhism as religions of grace and approvingly refers to Paul Althaus and Paul Tillich's recognition of a "real knowledge of God" apart from Christian revelation. Braaten asserts that when it comes to adherents of non-

---

28. J. DeJong, "Even So I Send You—Some Reflections on the Current Missionary Task of the Church–(2)," *Clarion* 45, 21 (October 18, 1996): 473.

29. The Westminster Larger Catechism says the same: "God doth not leave all men to perish in the estate of sin and misery...but of His mere love and mercy delivereth His elect out of it" (WLC, Q&A 30).

Christian religions, "We are free to waffle somewhere between reverent speculation and silent agnosticism."[30]

Braaten's position can be described as a sort of soft inclusivism. It is on the same trajectory as the radical religious pluralism of John Hick. For Hick, "The God-figures of the great theistic religions are different human awarenesses of the Ultimate." Consequently, he asserts that salvation (which he defines as moral transformation) is found in all religions and, by implication, even in non-religion.[31]

The Reformed confessions rebuke both soft inclusivism and radical religious pluralism and establish the dire need for Christian mission. For instance, the Belgic Confession states:

> We know [God] by two means: first, by the creation, preservation, and government of the universe; which is before our eyes as a most elegant book, wherein all creatures, great and small, are as so many characters leading us to contemplate the invisible things of God, namely, His eternal power and Godhead, as the apostle Paul saith (Rom. 1:20). All which things are sufficient to convince men, and leave them without excuse.
>
> Second, He makes Himself more clearly and fully known to us by His holy and divine Word; that is to say, as far as is necessary for us to know in this life, to His glory and our salvation (BC, art. 2).[32]

The book of the universe operates in two ways, depending on the spiritual status of the reader. For the believer, the universe is a most elegant book (*un beau livre*) that leads our thoughts upward in contemplation of God's imperceptible attributes, particularly His eternal power and divinity. In other words, for Christians the universe functions in a doxological manner. However, for unbelievers this revelation works as a curse, convicting them and leaving them without excuse. According to the Confession, building on Paul's treatment of the subject in Romans 1 and 2, nothing else is needed to achieve a conviction of people under sin. For our purposes, the important thing to note is that God is never with-

---

30. Carl E. Braaten, *No Other Gospel! Christianity Among the World's Religions* (Minneapolis: Fortress Press, 1992), 72–81.

31. See John Hick, "A Pluralist View," in John Hick, Clark H. Pinnock, Alister E. McGrath, R. Douglas Geivett, W. Gary Phillips, *Four Views on Salvation in a Pluralistic World* (Grand Rapids: Zondervan, 1995), 29–59.

32. The Westminster Confession of Faith says the same: The "light of nature, and the works of creation and providence do so far manifest the goodness, wisdom, and power of God, as to leave men inexcusable; yet they are not sufficient to give that knowledge of God, and of His will, which is necessary to salvation" (WCF, 1.1).

out a witness in the world, even where the Bible is absent. This witness cannot save, but it does testify that there is a problem in the relationship between God and man and that man is responsible for the problem.

The answer to this problem is found only in the other book, God's holy and divine Word. Through a Scripture-engendered faith, we come to know God better, not only as judge (which we already knew from the first book) but also as our Father through Jesus Christ. The Bible exists to clearly and fully reveal God Himself to us in all His attributes so that we may exalt His worth and be saved. According to the Belgic Confession, the Holy Scriptures are indispensable for salvation. It is the Bible that needs to be proclaimed for the salvation of sinners.

The Westminster Confession reaffirms these truths:

> Others, not elected, although they may be called by the ministry of the Word, and may have some common operations of the Spirit, yet they never truly come unto Christ, and therefore cannot be saved: much less can men, not professing the Christian religion, be saved in any other way whatsoever, be they never so diligent to frame their lives according to the light of nature and the law of that religion they do profess. And, to assert and maintain that they may, is very pernicious, and to be detested (WCF, 10.4).

Likewise, the Westminster Larger Catechism addresses this question:

> Can they who have never heard the gospel, and so know not Jesus Christ, nor believe in Him, be saved by their living according to the light of nature?
>
> They who, having never heard the gospel, know not Jesus Christ, and believe not in Him, cannot be saved, be they never so diligent to frame their lives according to the light of nature, or the laws of that religion which they profess; neither is there salvation in any other, but in Christ alone, who is the Savior only of His body the church (WLC, Q&A 60).

There is only one way to be saved from the wrath to come—by faith in Jesus Christ. That faith comes by hearing the Word. The conclusion can be only that the ministry of the Word, also through missionary preaching, is an absolute necessity in a fallen world.

The same point is readily apparent in the youngest of the Three Forms of Unity, the Canons of Dort, which state that man is totally incapable of any saving good. The Canons state further, "Without the regenerating grace of the Holy Spirit, they are neither able nor willing to return to

God, to reform the depravity of their nature, nor to dispose themselves to reformation" (CD, 3/4.3). Article 4 confesses that unregenerate man possesses the *sensus divinitatis* or light of nature, but it is not used properly and serves to make man inexcusable before God (CD 3/4.4). Article 5 maintains that the law is also inadequate for bringing men to peace with God (CD 3/4.5). Article 6 is the clincher, presenting us with our confession regarding the need for the gospel: "What, therefore, neither the light of nature, nor the law could do, that God performs by the operation of His Holy Spirit through the word or ministry of reconciliation: which is the glad tidings concerning the Messiah, by means whereof it hath pleased God to save such as believe, as well under the Old as under the New Testament" (CD, 3/4.6).

For our purposes in this chapter, we can glean from this the principle that mission work has a necessary place in the scheme of God's kingdom. If men were not sent out with the gospel of salvation, the kingdom would not advance and the Evil One would rejoice. We cannot expect people to be saved from God's judgment apart from the missionary ministry of the church. Salvation is found only in Jesus Christ, so His good news must be universally and indiscriminately proclaimed. The point is reinforced again: "Moreover, the promise of the gospel is, that whosoever believeth in Christ crucified shall not perish, but have everlasting life. This promise, together with the command to repent and believe, ought to be declared and published to all nations, and to all persons promiscuously and without distinction, to whom God out of His good pleasure sends the gospel" (CD, 2.5).

Thus, our Reformed confessions summarize and reinforce the sound biblical doctrine that missions and church planting are not optional—they are an essential part of God's work in this world. If our local churches are not actively engaged in missions at home and abroad, we cannot lay the blame for this at the feet of our confessions. Rather, if that is the case, our own confessions testify against us.

Election and Mission

God works in time to gather those whom He, in His good pleasure, has elected from before the foundation of the world. The doctrine of unconditional election is one of the most important of the Reformed faith, so it is natural that we find it in the Reformed confessions. For instance, it is confessed in the Belgic Confession:

> We believe that all the posterity of Adam, being thus fallen into per-
> dition and ruin by the sin of our first parents, God then did manifest
> Himself such as He is; that is to say, merciful and just: merciful, since
> He delivers and preserves from this perdition all whom He, in His
> eternal and unchangeable council, of mere goodness hath elected
> in Christ Jesus our Lord, without any respect to their works: just, in
> leaving others in the fall and perdition wherein they have involved
> themselves (BC, art. 16).

This article briefly expresses the classical Reformed position that God's election is purely based on divine grace and goodness. Salvation is to be attributed entirely to God. On the other hand, the reprobate are respon-sible for their fallen condition.[33]

Historically speaking, this article has been no stranger to theological controversy. During the late sixteenth and early seventeenth centuries, the Belgic Confession came under fire from James Arminius and those asso-ciated with him. The resulting controversy led to the convocation of the Synod of Dort and the production of its eponymous Canons. Furthermore, at the instigation of the Arminian party, a number of articles of the Con-fession were revised to better establish the Reformed position. However, interestingly, article 16 was not among those articles. Rather than revis-ing the article to strengthen it, the Synod prepared its Canons as a further explanation of the doctrine of election together with its corollaries.[34]

This article, or more properly the doctrine expressed in it, has also faced controversy in the study and practice of missions. As we noted in the introduction, the doctrine of election has been and is regularly maligned as being a death sentence for Christian missions. The infamous words of John Ryland to a young William Carey in 1786 are often mar-shaled as proof: "Young man, sit down; when God pleases to convert the heathen, he will do so without your aid or mine." David Cloud is one modern author who cites Ryland's alleged words as proof that "Calvin-ism tends to cool evangelistic fervor" and that evangelistically minded

---

33. One 1561 version of this article was quite a bit longer, giving further emphasis and explanation to this particular point. See J. N. Bakhuizen van den Brink, *De Neder-landse Belijdenisgeschriften* (Tweede druk) (Amsterdam: Uitgeverij Ton Bolland, 1976), 96.

34. For the entire account of the Belgic Confession at the Synod of Dort, see Nicolaas H. Gootjes, *The Belgic Confession: Its History and Sources* (Grand Rapids: Baker Academic, 2007), 133–59.

Calvinists are the exception rather than the rule.[35] John Piper related hearing a former president of InterVarsity Christian Fellowship state that when he began his missionary career, he was convinced that a belief in predestination was incompatible with Christian missions.[36] Similarly, Terry McGovern, a Baptist missionary in Papua, New Guinea, asserted that Calvinism is one of the biggest dangers to the gospel and missions.[37] Sadly, such sentiments are common. Does the Reformed doctrine of election destroy the missionary impulse? This is a hackneyed question that has been asked and answered repeatedly.[38] Nevertheless, the fact that it is still frequently answered affirmatively indicates that we need to continually attend to it.

Briefly, we may note that the election described in article 16 of the Confession and elsewhere in the Reformed confessions does not come into effect apart from means (BC, art. 16). Context is critical here, because in the following article (BC, art. 17), the Confession states that God sought man and extended the evangelical promise of Genesis 3:15 to him. In article 22, we discover that for believers in every age, the Holy Spirit is the One who kindles true faith in hearts (BC, art. 22). Article 24 states the same thing and adds the "hearing of God's Word" as an instrument of the Holy Spirit to gather in God's elect (BC, art. 24). That preaching is done by human beings, both in established churches and on mission fields around the world. Reformed churches have always recognized that God's decree of election entails a human responsibility, both inside churches and outside.

This is affirmed in the Westminster Confession: "As God hath appointed the elect unto glory, so hath He, by the eternal and most free

---

35. David Cloud, "Calvinism on the March among Evangelicals," *Friday Church News Notes* 7, 38 (September 29, 2006): 1.

36. John Piper, *Let the Nations Be Glad: The Supremacy of God in Missions,* 2nd rev. ed. (Grand Rapids: Baker Academic, 1993), 55.

37. Terry McGovern, "Calvinism," *Missionary Insights,* October 3, 2006, accessed November 3, 2008, http://missionary-insights.blogspot.com/2006/10/calvinism.html.

38. For some efforts, see James Montgomery Boice and Philip Graham Ryken, *The Doctrines of Grace: Recovering the Evangelical Gospel* (Wheaton, Ill.: Crossway, 2002), 111–12; Michael Horton, *Putting Amazing Back into Grace: Embracing the Heart of the Gospel,* 2nd ed. (Grand Rapids: Baker, 2002), 242–43; J. I. Packer, *Evangelism and the Sovereignty of God* (Downers Grove, Ill.: InterVarsity, 1961). For a work that addresses one of election's corollaries (limited or particular atonement) and its connection to evangelistic zeal, see Robert A. Peterson and Michael D. Williams, *Why I Am Not an Arminian* (Downers Grove, Ill.: InterVarsity, 2004), 192–215.

purpose of His will, foreordained all the means thereunto" (WCF, 3.6). In other words, God uses means to bring the elect to glory. The precise nature and identity of those means is expanded upon by the Canons of Dort:

> But when God accomplishes His good pleasure in the elect, or works in them true conversion, He not only causes the gospel to be externally preached to them, and powerfully illuminates their minds by His Holy Spirit, that they may rightly understand and discern the things of the Spirit of God, but by the efficacy of the same regenerating Spirit He pervades the innermost recesses of the man; He opens the closed and softens the hardened heart, and circumcises that which was uncircumcised; infuses new qualities into the will, which, though heretofore dead, He quickens; from being evil, disobedient, and refractory, He renders it good, obedient, and pliable; actuates and strengthens it, that, like a good tree, it may bring forth the fruits of good actions (CD, 3/4.11).

So how does God call the elect? Reformed churches confess that it is through the preaching of the gospel and the efficacious working of the Holy Spirit in the hearts of human beings. This doctrine does not hinder the work of missions, outreach, and church planting but rather boldly animates it. The elect will be gathered in through the preaching of the gospel; therefore, the gospel must be preached! It should be no surprise, then, that it has been vehemently denied that Ryland's words to Carey (quoted earlier) emerge from a Calvinistic perspective; indeed, even the veracity of the legendary account is seriously doubtful.[39] Where the gospel is preached, we can have confidence that the elect will be gathered. The Canons of Dort states this truth beautifully:

> This purpose proceeding from everlasting love towards the elect, has, from the beginning of the world to this day, been powerfully accomplished, and will, henceforward, still continue to be accom-

---

39. "The popular story is repudiated by Ryland's son, John Ryland, Jr., who was Carey's close friend and a fellow member of the Northampton Association, being assistant minister at his father's church at the time when the incident was supposed to have happened. 'I never heard of it till I saw it in print, and cannot give credit to it at all.' Among the reasons he gives for rejecting its authenticity it is interesting to note that he says, 'No man prayed and preached about the *latter-day glory* more than my father'" (Iain Murray, *The Puritan Hope: Revival and the Interpretation of Prophecy* [Edinburgh: Banner of Truth, 1971], 280). Murray cites as source John Ryland, *Life of Andrew Fuller* (1816), 175. For further confirmation, see W. A. Jarrel, *Baptist Church Perpetuity: Or the Continuous Existence of Baptist Churches* (Dallas, 1894), 417. Jarrel quotes Ryland's son as insisting that his father was not even present at the Northampton meeting.

plished, notwithstanding all the ineffectual opposition of the gates of hell; so that the elect in due time may be gathered into one, and that there never may be wanting a Church composed of believers, the foundation of which is laid in the blood of Christ, which may steadfastly love and faithfully serve Him as their Savior, who, as a bridegroom for His bride, laid down His life for them upon the cross; and which may celebrate His praises here and through all eternity (CD, 2.9).

This means that missionaries and church planters can be optimistic as they do their work. Our fundamental orientation is always positive: even if our work does not appear fruitful from a human perspective, God's purposes will not be frustrated. He will gather His elect one way or another. We can submit in hope to God's sovereignty with the sure confidence that the gates of hell will never frustrate His work through us.

We should also briefly give some thought to the place of this doctrine in the preaching and teaching of Reformed missionaries and church planters. Those of us who have been gripped by the wondrous knowledge of God's grace are sometimes faced with a peculiar temptation. Especially when faced with believers who have, perhaps by default, embraced Arminian or semi-Pelagian doctrines of salvation, we may be tempted to fixate on the doctrines of grace, also known as the five points of Calvinism or TULIP. It is *vitally* important that these doctrines be taught and disseminated, but there is a right way and a wrong way to go about it. This was recognized already at the Synod of Dort 1618–1619:

> As the doctrine of divine election by the most wise counsel of God was declared by the Prophets, by Christ Himself, and by the Apostles, and is clearly revealed in the Scriptures both of the Old and New Testament, so it is still to be published in due time and place in the Church of God, for which it was peculiarly designed, provided it be done with reverence, in the spirit of discretion and piety, for the glory of God's most holy name, and for enlivening and comforting His people, without vainly attempting to investigate the secret ways of the Most High (CD, 1.14).

As they put this instruction into practice, Reformed missionaries must take care that their preaching and teaching does not become one-sided. Some missionaries preach virtually nothing but eschatology—the coming of the beast, the mark of the beast, the rapture, and other end times-related topics. Reformed missionaries might face the temptation of preaching virtually nothing but the five points. As mentioned, the doctrines of grace are critically important, but they are not the sum total of God's revelation. We are to preach "the whole counsel of God" (Acts 20:27), and that goes beyond the doctrines of grace toward *all* the riches of God's Word.

The Church and Mission

One of the most neglected doctrines in the study and practice of missions today (especially in the broader context) is that of the church. This is a place where the Reformed confessions provide a much-needed corrective. It seems that in the minds of many, when it comes to missions the church is a footnote. It is a good thing to have, but it is not essential for the work of missions. We often see this, for instance, when the Great Commission is presented as a commission given to individual believers rather than to Christ's church.[40]

Reformed churches have sounded a different note in their confessions. The Westminster Confession states, "Unto this catholic visible Church Christ hath given the ministry, oracles, and ordinances of God, for the gathering and perfecting of the saints, in this life, to the end of the world: and doth by His own presence and Spirit, according to His promise, make them effectual thereunto" (WCF, 25.3).

Therefore, God has given the ministry of the Word to the church. This is not only for the perfecting of those who already believe but also for the gathering of those yet to believe. This can mean nothing other than that mission work belongs to the church as we see it here on earth. It is the responsibility of local, visible churches to send out missionaries and church planters, to support them and to oversee their work. Though parachurch mission organizations are a reality because of the historical lack of mission-mindedness among some churches, we should not accept this situation as normal, nor should we facilitate it. In the present day, such organizations are often usurping the work of the church.

The essential importance of the church for missions is also underlined in the previous article of the Westminster Confession, when it concludes

---

40. See Roger S. Greenway, *Go and Make Disciples: An Introduction to Christian Missions* (Phillipsburg: P&R, 1999), 42–43. Earlier in the book, Greenway states that "the call to missions is not entirely an individual matter. Christ assigns to his church the task of bringing the gospel to the world (Ephesians 3:10). This implies that a personal call to missions needs to be recognized and supported by a congregation of believers." The emphasis, however, falls on the individual believer.

by stating that "there is no ordinary possibility of salvation" outside of the visible church (WCF, 25.2). This is also confessed in the Belgic Confession: "We believe, since this holy congregation is an assemblage of those who are saved, and *out of it there is no salvation*, that no person of whatsoever state or condition he may be, ought to withdraw himself, to live in a separate state from it; but that all men are duty bound to join and unite themselves with it (BC, art. 28, emphasis added).

The italicized words have a long history in the Christian church, dating back to the time of the church father Cyprian.[41] In the *Institutes of the Christian Religion*, John Calvin used similar language to assert that the church is not optional.[42] At the very least, these words mean that salvation and the church *normally* belong together.

We may also reflect on the ecclesiastical dimensions of mission when the Heidelberg Catechism considers the meaning of the ninth article of the Apostles' Creed ("I believe a holy catholic church"): "That out of the whole human race, from the beginning to the end of the world, the Son of God, by His Spirit and Word, gathers, defends and preserves for Himself unto everlasting life, a chosen communion in the unity of the true faith; and that I am, and forever shall remain, a living member of the same (HC, Q&A 54).

As it does elsewhere, the Catechism begins with Christ and His work (HC, Q&A 86). Christ works with His Spirit through the Word as it is proclaimed. This proclamation is to be done only by those who are "duly approved and called to that office" by the church of Christ.[43] Further, we note here the great comfort afforded to missionaries, to sending churches, and to missionary congregations. As Krüger poignantly expresses it,

> Many missionaries will attest that they often find themselves heading for seemingly impenetrable walls, not knowing what to do or how to do it. They sometimes see their work dashed to pieces on the rocks of sin and hardened hearts. They see unfortunate circumstances making months of hard work meaningless in one day. They see people in whom they trusted turn away from Christ and following their old ways. Many are the times they ask in despair: what is the meaning of all of this? Why do we do this? Well, here is the

41. See Daniel R. Hyde, *With Heart and Mouth: An Exposition of the Belgic Confession* (Grandville, Mich.: Reformed Fellowship, 2008), 377–80; G. VanRongen, *The Church: Its Unity in Confession and History* (Neerlandia, Alberta: Inheritance Publications, 1998), 77–90.
42. Calvin, *Institutes*, 4.1.4.
43. See WLC, Q&A 158.

answer: because Christ gathers for himself a community chosen for eternal life! Again, we have to repeat, always in great humility: "I... and yet not I...!"[44]

The fact that it is Christ's church and that He builds it through weak and sinful vessels ought to encourage and motivate us. We also come to realize that we are not indispensable to Christ's work. He may choose to work through us, but then again, He may also choose to work through others. Yet He will accomplish His purpose! According to the Catechism, that purpose is to gather a church, a place where people are "living members," a place where the means of grace (the preaching of the Word and the administration of the sacraments) stand central for the blessing of God's people.

As confessionally Reformed Christians, when we speak about missions and evangelism, the church must have a place of central importance. It is through the church that salvation is designed to be administered. Missionaries are to be sent out by churches, they are to be supported by churches, and they are to be supervised by churches. When the time is right, the missionary institutes a new church, which continues the process. Our confessions teach us to be missional, but they also teach us that our missions must be ecclesio-centric.

However, according to our confessions, there remains an evangelistic calling for all individual members of the church. For instance, Heidelberg Catechism question and answer 86 says that an important part of sanctification is that Christians "by our godly walk may win our neighbors also for Christ." As the church authoritatively proclaims the gospel through the means of grace administered by properly ordained special officers, the members of the church are called to testify and authenticate the message by their transformed walk and talk.[45] This is corroborated by the Heidelberg Catechism:

> But why art thou called a Christian?
>
> Because by faith I am a member of Christ; and thus a partaker of His anointing; in order that I also may confess His name, may present myself a living sacrifice of thankfulness to Him, and may with free

---

44. Krüger, "The Reformed Confessions," 6.

45. For the distinction between the priesthood of all believers and the ordained ministry, see the Second Helvetic Confession, chapter 18 in Schaff, *Creeds of Christendom,* 3:875–84.

conscience fight against sin and the devil in this life, and hereafter, in eternity, reign with Him over all creatures (HC, Q&A 32).

As Krüger points out, each of the offices described here is outward looking. Confessing Christ's name is a prophetic speaking about salvation. It includes convicting others of sin, calling them to repentance, and speaking about Christ in a winsome manner. The priestly office of all believers is drawn out of passages like 1 Peter 2:5 and 9. In these passages, offering spiritual sacrifices to God and declaring His praises are essentially synonymous. The royal office involves warfare against sin and the Devil. Looking to the scriptural proofs for this teaching, we find 1 Peter 2:12, which, Krüger explains, "shows again that there is a missionary intention even in my private struggle against secret sin: I have to live such a good life among unbelievers that they too will end up glorifying God!"[46] Thus the Reformed confessions, while giving priority to the official and authoritative proclamation of the gospel by the church, also make clear that there is a biblical imperative for all believers to always be ready to give an account of the hope within us (1 Peter 3:15) and to live the gospel in such a way that God is glorified.

Praxis

What do the Reformed confessions say about what a missionary ought to be doing? The confessions are clear about his primary task: he is to preach the gospel of salvation in Jesus Christ. The Westminster Confession expounds this biblical teaching: "Repentance unto life is an evangelical grace, the doctrine whereof is to be preached by every minister of the gospel, as well as that of faith in Christ" (WCF, 15.1). Here the Westminster divines succinctly and accurately portray the primary task of a missionary. A missionary must convict of sin and preach God's command for people to repent from their sins. A missionary must preach the gospel and God's command for people to believe in the Lord Jesus. This is not optional.

As previously noted, we may and must preach other doctrines of Scripture as well, but this must always be in the forefront. Jesus Christ must be preached as the one who saves people from their sinful way of life and the wrath of God that justly rests upon it. Jesus Christ must be preached as the one who not only bore the curse on the cross as our substitute but who

---

46. Krüger, "The Reformed Confessions," 4–5.

also lived a perfect life in our place (BC, art. 22). Preaching a Jesus Christ who saves from economic hardship is not mandated, needed, or beneficial. Preaching a Jesus Christ who saves the poor from the rich is not the gospel. Neither is preaching a Jesus Christ who could be confused with Dr. Phil or Dr. Laura. If we were to preach a Jesus whose message is "your best life now" or "become a better you," we should be accursed (Gal. 1:8). Rather, our confessions lead us to see that the gospel is found only in the foolishness of preaching "Christ and Him crucified" (1 Cor. 2:2).

Besides the preaching and teaching of the gospel, our Confessions also lead us to see prayer as an important component of missions, not only for missionaries and church planters but also for the churches that send them. While it does not seem to have been neglected in the practice of missions, prayer is often something forgotten in the systematic study of missions. Thankfully, more recent works have begun to address this neglect.[47] Because our confessions devote much attention to prayer, we Reformed believers have no excuse for neglecting this subject.

Both the Westminster Shorter Catechism and the Heidelberg Catechism include a section on the Lord's Prayer. Both of them offer explanations of the second petition, "Your kingdom come," which offer much help in exploring the place of prayer in mission work. This is what we find in the Westminster Shorter Catechism:

What do we pray for in the second petition?

In the second petition (which is, Thy kingdom come) we pray, That Satan's kingdom may be destroyed; and that the kingdom of grace may be advanced, ourselves and others brought into it, and kept in it; and that the kingdom of glory may be hastened (WSC, Q&A 102).

This means that the church must pray for mission work. Because we pray for it, we must also be involved with it. In fact, we can even say that prayer and mission are inseparable. If we are doing mission, we must be praying. If the church is praying in the manner the Lord Jesus taught us, she must be doing mission.[48]

Teaching about the second petition of the Lord's Prayer is also found in the Heidelberg Catechism:

---

47. See Greenway, *Go and Make Disciples*, especially chapters 11 and 12; J. Andrew Kirk, *What Is Mission? Theological Explorations* (Minneapolis: Fortress Press, 2000), especially chapter 11.

48. Cf. Greenway, *Go and Make Disciples*, 88–89.

What is the second petition?

Thy kingdom come. That is: So govern us by Thy Word and Spirit that we may submit ourselves unto Thee always more and more; preserve and increase Thy church; destroy the works of the devil, every power that exalteth itself against Thee, and all wicked devices formed against Thy holy Word, until the full coming of Thy kingdom, wherein Thou shalt be all in all (HC, Q&A 123).

Just as with the Shorter Catechism, here we find the mention of preserving and *increasing* the church. But what exactly does the Catechism mean when it speaks about "increasing"? The same word is used in the original German as in Martin Luther's translation of Genesis 9:7, "Be fruitful and *multiply*."[49] This would seem to indicate that what is really in mind here is a numerical increase. The Catechism teaches us to pray and look for the numerical increase of God's church. By implication, we are also bound to use the God-given means by which that must happen: the ministry of the Word.

Conclusion

Thoughtful consideration of the Reformed confessions disallows the position that these documents are irrelevant for missions and church planting as well as the sentiment that they are destructive for missions. Those who read them with care cannot help but be amazed and thankful for how much direction we do receive from these documents. At the same time, if they are faithful summaries of Scripture, we ought not to be surprised.

That is not to say that the Reformed confessions will answer every question we may have on missions. These documents are several centuries old, and they bear the marks of their time. For instance, we find little in either the Three Forms of Unity or the Westminster Standards that speaks directly to the challenges world religions present to our missions at home and abroad. The Belgic Confession speaks briefly about Judaism and Islam in article 9 regarding the Trinity, but apart from that there is virtually nothing. Other articles of the Belgic Confession and the other confessions address the reality of false religions, but not directly or specifically. This could be a weakness in certain contexts, and in those particular

---

49. The Heidelberg Catechism: "erhalt und mehre deine kirchen" (Bakhuizen van den Brink, *De Nederlandse Belijdenisgeschriften*, 218). Luther's translation of Genesis 9:7: "Seid fruchtbar und mehret euch und reget euch auf Erden, daß euer viel darauf werden."

contexts we should be open to considering the possibility of supplementing what we have in our confessions. One cannot realistically expect a sixteenth-century Western European confession to directly address all the challenges faced by missionaries and new believers in a variety of global contexts. Recognizing this does not denigrate our confessions in any way, as if there is something inherently wrong with them. Rather, we are simply recognizing that they emerge from an age quite different from our own. Some of the challenges faced by that age are the same (i.e., Roman Catholicism, Anabaptism), while others are quite different.

Our Reformed confessions are a rich repository of scriptural teaching, and this essay demonstrates that we have only begun to mine these riches and their significance for Christian missions. Much more could be said, for instance, on the ways in which these confessions were deliberately contextualized for the most effective communication of scriptural truth in their original setting. We could reflect more deeply on the inherent missionary function of confessions.[50] With the Belgic Confession, we could draw out the context of martyrdom and persecution and explore how that connects to the mission of the church then and now.[51] We might also investigate how the Reformation doctrine of Scripture in Belgic Confession articles 3–7 is related to the explosion of Bible translations into vernacular languages in the sixteenth and seventeenth centuries. What is clear is that we have nothing to be ashamed of in these confessions; rather, we have much for which to be thankful. In these confessions, our churches are taught from the Scriptures to witness to the wonderful work of God in Jesus Christ—for the salvation of men and ultimately for His glory.

---

50. Krüger has some helpful hints on how to begin such a reflection ("The Reformed Confessions," 2).

51. See Wes Bredenhof, "Martyrdom, Mission and the Belgic Confession," *The Confessional Presbyterian* 4 (2008): 109–122.

CHAPTER FOUR

❧

No Church, No Problem?

Michael Horton

How many times have you heard that the church is not a place but a people? Across the board, from more traditional to more experimental approaches to ministry, the dominant perspective seems to be that we gather on the Lord's Day primarily in order to do something for God and each other rather than first of all to receive something from God. Drawing on Darrell Guder, emerging-church leader Dan Kimball has recently argued that in its emphasis on the "marks of the church" (preaching and sacrament), the Reformation inadvertently turned the focus away from the church-as-people who do certain things to the church-as-place where certain things are done.[1]

But there's nothing inadvertent about it. With Scripture itself, the Reformers were very explicit about the fact that we come to church first of all because the Creator of the universe has summoned us to appear before Him in His court. Entering as His covenant people, we invoke the name of Christ for our salvation, God addresses us again in judgment and forgiveness, and we respond with our "Amen!" of faith and thanksgiving for who God is and what He has done for us. The gifts of the Father in the Son by the Spirit come first; our action is a response to God's action.

Why We Need the Church

First, because the church is a place where God does certain things, it becomes a people who do certain things. We cannot take God's action

---

Originally appeared in *Modern Reformation* 17, 4 (July/August 2008): 16–20, and is reprinted with permission.

1. Dan Kimball, *The Emerging Church: Vintage Christianity for New Generations* (Grand Rapids: Zondervan, 2003), 95.

for granted or assume that it has been completed in the past. Christ, both Lord and Savior of His church, appointed an official ministry (including officers) so that He could continue to serve His covenant people and extend His kingdom of grace to the ends of the earth by His Spirit. Every time we gather—even in the present—it is God who summons us in judgment and grace. It is not our devotion, praise, piety, or service that comes first, but God's service to us. This is why we must assemble at a place where the gospel is truly preached, the sacraments are administered according to Christ's institution, and there is a visible form of Christ's heavenly reign through officers whom He has called and sent.

Pastors, teachers, and elders are not life coaches who help us in our personalized goals for spiritual fitness. They are gifts given by the ascended Lord, so that the whole church might become mature and less susceptible to being spiritually duped (Eph. 4:1–16).

From "Every-Member-Ministry" to "Self-Feeders"

The reigning paradigm of churches today, however, seems to be quite different. Two characteristics especially stand out when we think of American Christianity: activism and individualism. Known for our self-confidence, Americans do not like to be on the receiving end. Even when we are receiving something, we prefer to think of it as something we deserve rather than an outright gift.

We're also individualists. We do not like to be told who we are and what we need by someone else—even God—but would much rather decide who we are or will be and determine our own felt needs accordingly. Our emphasis on choice in this culture collides with the biblical emphasis on God's electing, redeeming, and calling grace as well as the covenantal, communal, and corporate nature of our growth in Christ. Even when we come to church, it is often as individual consumers of spiritual experiences, with opportunities for self-expression in worship and "finding our ministry" in the church rather than being beneficiaries of God's gifts to us through servants whom He has called to be our shepherds under Christ (see Eph. 4:1–16).

Not surprisingly, ministers today are regarded more as life coaches who facilitate our self-transformation than as ambassadors of Christ, devoted to the Word of God and prayer, so that they can spread a feast on behalf of the King for His people in this world. If the focus of our message falls on our "willing and running" rather than on God's mercy (Rom. 9:16), it will follow that our methods will concentrate almost exclusively on finding the best techniques for transforming ourselves and others. It is a simultaneously activistic and individualistic approach. Yet this subverts God's whole intention on the Lord's Day. He comes not to help you "become a better you," but to kill you and raise you together with Christ as part of His redeemed body.

God's Service Creates a Redeemed People on Pilgrimage in This Present Age

Churches of the Reformation have always agreed that the true church is found wherever the gospel is truly preached and the sacraments are administered according to Christ's institution. But this means that the public ministry provided on the Lord's Day is primarily God's ministry to us. We are not individuals who come together simply for fresh marching orders for transforming ourselves and our culture; we are sinners who come to die and to be made alive in Christ—no longer defined by our individual choices and preferences (the niche demographics of our passing age)—but by our incorporation into Christ and His body.

Even the purpose of our singing is not self-expression (witnessing to our own piety), but rather it is to teach and admonish one another in all wisdom so that "the word of Christ [may] dwell in you richly" (Col. 3:16), "giving thanks always for all things to God the Father in the name of Jesus Christ" (Eph. 5:20). We come to invoke the name of our Covenant Lord, to hear His law and receive His forgiveness. Only then are we able to receive His gifts with the "Amen!" of faith and repentance, with a heart full of thanksgiving toward God and love toward our neighbors.

But if church is primarily about what individuals do (even if they happen to do it in the same building), then it stands to reason that our services will focus on motivating us for action rather than ministering to us God's action here and now in the Spirit, through Word and sacrament, that which He has already accomplished for us objectively in Jesus Christ. The liturgy will be replaced with various announcements of church programs; the songs will simply be opportunities for self-expression; the preaching will largely consist of tips for transformation; baptism and the Supper will afford opportunities merely for us to commit and recommit ourselves rather than serve as means of grace. Before long, it will be easy for churches to imagine that what happens on the Lord's Day is less important than what happens in small groups or in the private lives of individual Christians. In fact, this is explicitly advocated today.

In a fairly recent study, Willow Creek—a pioneer megachurch—discovered that its most active and mature members are the most likely to be dissatisfied with their own personal growth and the level of teaching and worship that they are receiving. From this, the leadership concluded that as people mature in their faith, they need the church less. After all, the main purpose of the church is to provide a platform for ministry and service opportunities to individuals rather than a means of grace. As people grow, therefore, they need the church less. We need to help believers to become "self-feeders," the study concluded.[2]

The Ultimate in "Self-Feeding"

How far can this trajectory take us? Evangelical marketer George Barna gives us a good indication. Like the Willow Creek study, Barna concludes that what individual believers do on their own is more important than what the church does for them. Barna, however, takes Charles Finney's legacy to the next logical step. A leading marketing consultant to megachurches as well as the Disney Corporation, he has recently gone so far as to suggest that the days of the institutional church are over. Barna celebrates a rising demographic of what he calls "Revolutionaries"—"millions of believers" who "have moved beyond the established church and chosen to be the church instead."[3] Since "being the church" is a matter of individual choice and effort, all people need are resources for their own work of personal and social transformation. "Based on our research," Barna relates, "I have projected that by the year 2010, 10 to 20 percent of Americans will derive all their spiritual input (and output) through the Internet."[4] Who needs the church when you have an iPod? Like any service provider, the church needs to figure out what business it's in, says Barna: "Ours is not the business of organized religion, corporate worship, or Bible teaching. If we dedicate ourselves to such a business we will be left by the wayside as the culture moves forward. Those are fragments

---

2. Greg L. Hawkins and Cally Parkinson, *Reveal: Where Are You?* (South Barrington, Ill.: Willow, 2007).

3. George Barna, *Revolution: Finding Vibrant Faith beyond the Walls of the Sanctuary* (Carol Stream, Ill.: Tyndale House, 2005), back cover copy.

4. Ibid., 180.

of a larger purpose to which we have been called by God's Word. We are in the business of life transformation."[5]

Of course Barna does not believe that Christians should abandon all religious practices, but the only ones he still thinks are essential are those that can be done by individuals in private, or at most in families or informal public gatherings. But by eliminating the public means of grace, Barna (like Willow Creek) directs us away from God's lavish feast to a self-serve buffet.

Addressing his readers in terms similar to the conclusions of the Willow Creek study, Barna writes, "Whether you choose to remain involved in the congregational mold or to venture into the spiritual unknown, to experience the competing dynamics of independence and responsibility, move ahead boldly. God's perspective is that the structures and routines you engage with matter much less than the character and commitments that define you."[6] Believers need not find a good church, but they should "get a good coach." If the gospel is good advice rather than good news, obviously the church is simply "a resource" for our personal development, as Barna suggests.

If the local church is to survive, says Barna, authority must shift from being centralized to decentralized and leadership from "pastor-driven" to "lay-driven," which means that the sheep are primarily servers rather than served by the ministry. Further, ministry must shift from "resistance" to change to "acceptance," from "tradition and order" to "mission and vision," from an "all-purpose" to a "specialized" approach to ministry, "tradition bound" to "relevance bound," from a view of the people's role as receivers to actors, from "knowledge" to "transformation."[7]

"In just a few years," Barna predicts, "we will see that millions of people will never travel physically to a church, but will instead roam the Internet in search of meaningful spiritual experiences."[8] After all, he adds, the heart of Jesus' ministry was "the development of people's character."[9] "If we rise to the challenge," says Barna, America will witness a "moral resurgence," new leadership, and the Christian message "will regain respect" in our culture.[10] Intimate worship, says Barna, does

---

5. George Barna, *The Second Coming of the Church* (Nashville: Word, 1998), 96.
6. Ibid., 68, 138–40.
7. Ibid., 177.
8. Ibid., 65.
9. Barna, *Revolution*, 203.
10. Ibid., 208.

"not require a 'worship service,'" just a personal commitment to the Bible, prayer, and discipleship.[11] His book concludes with the warning of the last judgment: "What report of your commitment to practical, holy, life-transforming service will you be able to give Him?"[12] The Revolutionaries have found that in order to pursue an authentic faith they had to abandon the church.[13]

This is finally where American spirituality leaves us: alone, surfing the Internet, casting about for coaches and teammates, trying to save ourselves from captivity to this present age by finding those "excitements" that will induce a transformed life. Increasingly, the examples I have referred to are what people mean by the adjective "missional."

Like the nineteenth-century revivalist Charles Finney, George Barna asserts that the Bible offers "almost no restrictions on structures and methods" for the church.[14] In fact, as we have seen, he does not even think that the visible church itself is divinely established. Nature abhors a vacuum, and where Barna imagines that the Bible prescribes no particular structures or methods, the invisible hand of the market fills the void. He even recognizes that the shift from the institutional church to "alternative faith communities" is largely due to market forces: "Whether you examine the changes in broadcasting, clothing, music, investing, or automobiles, producers of such consumables realize that Americans want control over their lives. The result has been the 'niching' of America—creating highly refined categories that serve smaller numbers of people, but can command greater loyalty (and profits)." The same thing is happening to the church, Barna notes, as if it were a fate to be embraced rather than an apostasy to be resisted.[15]

However thin, there is a theology behind Barna's interpretation of Jesus as the paradigmatic "Revolutionary," and it is basically that of Finney. "So if you are a Revolutionary," says Barna, "it is because you have sensed and responded to God's calling to be such an imitator of Christ. It is not a church's responsibility to make you into this mold.... The choice to become a Revolutionary—and it is a choice—is a covenant

11. Ibid., 22.
12. Ibid., 210.
13. Ibid., 17.
14. Ibid., 175.
15. Ibid., 62–63.

you make with God alone." In this way, however, the work of the people displaces the work of God.[16]

"Feed My Sheep"

The gospel is good news. The message determines the medium. There is a clear logic to Paul's argument in Romans 10, where he contrasts "the righteousness which is of the law" and "the righteousness of faith" (vv. 5–6). We were redeemed by Christ's actions, not ours; the Spirit applies this redemption to us here and now so that we are justified through faith apart from works; even this faith is given to us through the proclamation of Christ. Since this gospel is a report to be believed rather than a task for us to fulfill, it needs heralds, ambassadors, and witnesses.

The method of delivery is suited to its content. If the central message of Christianity were how to have your best life now or become a better you, then we wouldn't need heralds, but rather life coaches, spiritual directors, and motivational speakers. Good advice requires a person with a plan; good news requires a person with a message. This is not to say that we do not also need good advice or plans but that the source of the church's existence and mission in this world is this announcement of God's victory in Jesus Christ. Coaches can send themselves with their own suggestions, but an ambassador has to be sent with an authorized announcement. If the goal is to get people to go and find Christ, then the methods will be whatever we find pragmatically successful; if it's all about Christ finding sinners, then the methods are already determined. Simply quoting Romans 10:13–15 reveals the logical chain of Paul's argument: "For 'whoever calls on the name of the LORD shall be saved.' How then shall they call on Him in whom they have not believed? And how shall they believe in Him of whom they have not heard? And how shall they hear without a preacher? And how shall they preach unless they are sent?" The evangel defines evangelism; the content determines the methods of delivery; the marks of the church (preaching and sacrament) define its mission (evangelizing, baptizing, teaching, and communing).

The marks of the true church are the proper preaching of the Word, administration of the sacraments, and discipline. The mission of the church is simply to execute these tasks faithfully. Throughout the book of Acts, the growth of the church is attributed to the proclamation of the

16. Ibid., 70.

gospel: "The word of God spread." Waking the dead, this gospel proclamation is not only the content but the method. Those who believed were baptized along with their whole household. They were not simply added to the conversion statistics, but to the church—the visible church, which is no more visible in this world than when it is gathered around the Lord's Table in fellowship with its ascended Head. Furthermore, the apostles and elders—and, by Acts 6 the deacons—served the church as officers representing Christ's threefold office of prophet, king, and priest.

We find no dichotomy between the official ministry of the church as a historical institution and the Spirit-filled mission of reaching the lost. The mission expanded the church; it did not subvert it. Through this ministry, "the Lord added to the church daily those who were being saved" (Acts 2:47). So when evangelists today qualify their invitation to receive Christ by saying, "I'm not talking about joining a church," they are stepping outside of the mission established by Jesus Christ and evidenced in the remarkable spread of the gospel under the ministry of the apostles.

Christ has not only appointed the message but also the methods, and, as we have seen, there is an inseparable connection between them. All around us we see evidence that churches may affirm the gospel of salvation by grace alone in Christ alone through faith alone but then adopt a methodology that suggests otherwise. Christ has appointed preaching, because "faith comes by hearing, and hearing by the word of God" (Rom. 10:17); baptism, because it is the sign and seal of inclusion in Christ; the Supper, because through it we receive Christ and all of His benefits. In other words, these methods are appointed precisely because they are means of grace rather than means of works—means of God's descent to us rather than means of our ascent to God.

In this way, Christ makes Himself not only the gift but the giver, not only the object of faith but the active agent, together with the Spirit, in giving us faith. And He not only gives us this faith in the beginning but deepens, matures, and increases our faith throughout our lives. The gospel is not something that we need to "get saved" so that we can move on to something else; it is "the power of God unto salvation" throughout our pilgrimage. So we need this gospel to be delivered to us regularly, both for our justification and our sanctification.

We also need the law to guide our faith and practice. Christ not only saves, He also rules. In fact, He rules in order to save. His sovereignty liberates us from oppression—not only from the guilt and condemnation of our sins but also from the tyranny of sin. The gospel is not simply enough for our justification; it is the source of our sanctification as we recognize that we are "dead to sin and alive to Christ." The gospel tells us that Christ has toppled the reign of sin; it no longer has any legal authority or determining power over us. It can no longer define us. The old "I"—who was married to sin—has died, and we are now wedded to Christ and righteousness. The gospel is big news indeed. We need it to subdue both our doubts and insecurity and our indwelling sin.

As we submit ourselves to the life-creating gospel and to the life-guiding commands of Scripture, we recognize our need for the spiritual oversight of our pastors and elders and the service of deacons. Like any family, the church needs proper discipline and order so that our personal and corporate life together will imperfectly but truly reflect the fact that the church is an embassy of Christ and the age to come even in this present evil age. God's law, not our spontaneous sincerity, defines what we should do.

The individualistic emphasis of evangelicalism stands in sharp contrast to the covenantal paradigm that we find in Scripture. We are commanded not to become self-feeders who mature beyond the nurture of the church but to submit ourselves to the preaching, teaching, and oversight of those shepherds whom God has placed over us in Christ. We read at the end of John's gospel the account of how Jesus made breakfast for seven of His astonished disciples in His third appearance after His resurrection:

> So when they had eaten breakfast, Jesus said to Simon Peter, "Simon, son of Jonah, do you love Me more than these?"
> He said to Him, "Yes, Lord; You know that I love You."
> He said to him, "Feed My lambs."
> He said to him again a second time, "Simon, son of Jonah, do you love Me?"
> He said to Him, "Yes, Lord; You know that I love You."
> He said to him, "Tend My sheep."
> He said to him the third time, "Simon, son of Jonah, do you love Me?" Peter was grieved because He said to him the third time, "Do you love Me?"
> And he said to Him, "Lord, You know all things; You know that I love You."
> Jesus said to him, "Feed My sheep" (John 21:15–17).

As the passage goes on to relate, Jesus was preparing Peter for a difficult ministry that would culminate in his own crucifixion (vv. 18–19). Unlike the false shepherds who scattered His flock (denounced in Jeremiah 23), the Good Shepherd has laid down His life for them and united them under His gracious rule (John 10). And now, through His undershepherds, Jesus will continue to feed His sheep and lead them to everlasting pastures. The church's ministry is exercised faithfully when the people are fed, not when the sheep are expected to become their own shepherds.

Christ does not deliver us from one tyrant only to leave us weak and isolated, prey to weather, wolves, and our own wanderings. "Obey those who rule over you, and be submissive," Scripture exhorts, "for they watch out for your souls, as those who must give an account. Let them do so with joy and not with grief, for that would be unprofitable for you" (Heb. 13:17).

Yet even this admonition is grounded in the gospel: submitting to the discipline of shepherds is an advantage to us because through it God promises all of His blessings in Christ: "Let us hold fast the confession of our hope without wavering, for He who promised is faithful. And let us consider one another in order to stir up love and good works, not forsaking the assembling of ourselves together, as is the manner of some, but exhorting one another, and so much the more as you see the Day approaching" (Heb. 10:23–25).

PART TWO

The Methods of
Planting Churches

CHAPTER FIVE

∾

Church Planting Principles
from the Book of Acts

Daniel R. Hyde

The Lord is extending His kingdom; nevertheless, the church has much work to do. I work alone in Southern California, a region bordered by Los Angeles to the north and San Diego to the south, San Bernardino to the east and the Pacific Ocean to the west, and there are over thirty million people. And this is just one region in this state, in this country. You can see why I say that there is work to do. My purpose in this chapter is to give a few principles from the book of Acts that I discovered as I preached through this book that are applicable to reaching the vast numbers of non-Christians in our age. Acts is the closest thing we have to a church-planting manual in Scripture. These principles are springboards from which to start new churches. Also included are my suggestions as a church planter on how to reproduce more churches.[1]

Principle 1: Churches Should Be Planted in
Our Own Areas First (Acts 1:8)

We see this first principle in Jesus' instruction to His disciples that they bear witness to the gospel "in Jerusalem, and in all Judea and Samaria, and to the end of the earth" (Acts 1:8). The church followed this outline as it sent missionaries to preach the gospel through the book of Acts:

Adapted from *Christian Renewal* 22, 9 (January 26, 2004): 20–22, and is reprinted with permission.

  1. Chapter 2 of the OPC's manual for church planting lists these sound reasons for beginning a mission work, which are worth noting here: (1) there is a special opportunity to plant this church in this place at this time; (2) this center of population and influence needs the ministry of the new church we will plant; and (3) these fellow believers need our help to carry on what Christ has begun among them (POPC, 15–16). These go hand in hand with the principles found in the book of Acts.

Jerusalem (chaps. 1–7), Judea and Samaria (chaps. 8–12), and the ends of the earth (chaps. 13–28).[2] What this means for us is that churches must shift their missionary focus to home missions first; then only must their attention be towards foreign missions. As Bill Green, a missionary to Costa Rica, comments, "Missions at home will help us understand the complexities of church planting, and will drive us to our knees anew as we seek God's wisdom and strength."[3] Starting in our own areas first will actually get our churches involved in church planting and missions, rather than just sending money to an agency or board. If we set our sights on our neighboring cities, region, and county we will be forced to get involved in the Lord's work.

Principle 2: A Church Should Be Planted in an Area Where Believers Have Gathered and Where Conversions Are Occurring (11:19–26, 18:2, 19:1–7)

This second principle should be an obvious one, yet it has an interesting application for us. It used to be that Reformed churches would start a church plant when families moved from one church or several churches from a denomination to a new area, for example, for work-related reasons. From these members a church would be planted, or better, transplanted. We do not live in such a simple world anymore. For example, in writing on Reformed liturgy, Terry Johnson observes that our age's lack of denominational or "brand" loyalty has affected worship in Presbyterian churches so that no two churches seem to worship alike.[4] The point is that when our people move, we cannot expect that they will be willing to do the hard work that it takes to start another church from scratch when there are existing churches in a given area.

The reality is that we need to start thinking of new ways to gather core group families from which to plant new Reformed churches.[5] Some

---

2. On the structural outline of Acts, see Dennis E. Johnson, *The Message of Acts in the History of Redemption* (Phillipsburg, N.J.: P&R, 1997), 8–12, and Ben Witterington III, *The Acts of the Apostles: A Socio-Rhetorical Commentary* (Grand Rapids: Eerdmans, 1998), 68–77.

3. Bill Green, "Shotgun or Rifle? Thoughts on Missions and the Local Church," *Reformed Missions in Latin America*, accessed October 9, 2008, http://www.reformed-missions.org/shotgun.html.

4. Terry Johnson, ed. *Leading in Worship: A Sourcebook for Presbyterian Students and Ministers Drawing upon the Biblical and Historic Forms of the Reformed Tradition* (Oak Ridge, Tenn.: The Covenant Foundation, 1996), 1–2.

5. The OPC church plant manual discusses this in more detail (*POPC*, 62–65).

very practical and interesting ideas that some of us have tried in our recent church planting efforts include the following:

1. Heavy use of the Internet: making attractive websites that are user-friendly and full of resources. Furthermore, websites need to be capable of soliciting interested people in certain areas to contact us for more information, from which we can gather core groups.

2. Using Christian radio: placing ads about our churches during the time excellent Reformed radio programs such as *Renewing Your Mind* and the *White Horse Inn* are aired, starting call-in programs, and even placing radio ads in areas with no Reformed churches is a way to attract a core group.

3. Conferences: At the Oceanside URC and the nearby Christ URC (Santee), we have hosted our own conferences on Reformed theology, which draw hundreds of potentially interested people.

These are just three basic examples. The point is that we need to be creative and invest in finding ways to be proactive in planting and organizing Reformed churches instead of waiting for our own transplanted people or others to come to us.

Principle 3: Church Planting Should Gather Believers Together and Develop Unity (2:42–47, 4:32–35)

This principle is derived from the example of the early church gathering and unifying around four things: the apostles' doctrine, the prayers, the Supper, and the bond of fellowship. The difficult work of church planting involves the rewarding yet ever-stressful task of unifying a core group. The church planter needs to know what to unify his group around. According to the book of Acts, it is *theology* (the apostles' doctrine), *liturgy* (*the* prayers, the breaking of *the* bread), and *community* (the fellowship).

From the outset, this means that a church plant must be a confessional institution and organism. The Word of God as summarized in the ecumenical creeds and Three Forms of Unity and the Westminster Standards must be central. It is important not only to teach the doctrines as expressed in these documents in the evening service and catechism classes but also to use them in our liturgies, our sermons, and our visitations.[6] We must develop a confessional consciousness.

---

6. On the benefits and practice of catechism preaching, see the following basic resources: Peter Y. De Jong, "Comments on Catechetical Preaching [1]," *Mid-America*

A church plant must also be a liturgical institution and organism. An emphasis on the prayers—that is, the official public worship of the Lord's Day—needs to be a hallmark of a new church, especially in our day and age.[7] The liturgy of the church teaches, reinforces, and baptizes us in our theology. The morning liturgy in the congregation that I pastor incorporates many responses, such as the corporate amen, the great Trinitarian doxologies, the *sursum corda* during the celebration of the Lord's Supper, a corporate prayer of confession, recitation of the creeds, and various Scripture responses throughout the service. We unify our minds and hearts week by week as one people with one voice. Also, Luke mentions in Acts 2:42, that the early church was devoted to "the breaking of *the* bread." He uses the definite article before "bread" to specify which bread he was referring to: the bread of the Lord's Supper (Luke 22:19). One of the reasons for a more frequent communion is that it unites the many members of the church experientially in the one loaf (1 Cor. 10:16–17). An emphasis on the Supper, then, is needed as the means to unite us to Christ and each other.

Finally, a church plant must be a communal, community-focused institution and organism. Some of the practical ways a church plant can begin to develop unity and community is to have monthly picnics, home Bible studies, holiday gatherings, and a prayer chain, but especially by being hospitable with our families and sharing in Lord's Day fellowship together.[8]

Journal of Theology 1:2 (Fall 1985): 155–89; "Comments on Catechetical Preaching [2]," *Mid-America Journal of Theology* 2:2 (Fall 1986): 149–70; "Comments on Catechetical Preaching [3]," *Mid-America Journal of Theology* 3:1 (Spring 1987): 89–134; Daniel R. Hyde, "The Principle and Practice of Preaching in the Heidelberg Catechism," *Puritan Reformed Journal* (2008): 97–117; Nelson D. Kloosterman "Catechism Preaching: Assumptions and Methods in Catechism Preaching," *The Outlook* 38:1 (January 1988): 13–15; R. E. Knodel, Jr., "Catechetical Preaching," *Ordained Servant* 7:1 (Jan. 1998): 16–19; R. Lankheet, "Catechism Preaching: Response to Rev. Kloosterman," *The Outlook* 38:1 (January 1988): 15–16; "Catechism Preaching: Two Ways to Write a Catechism Sermon," *The Outlook* 37:8 (October 1987): 4–5; Donald Sinnema, "The Second Sunday Service in the Early Dutch Tradition," *Calvin Theological Journal* 32 (1997): 298–333; Jan Karel van Baalen, "Why Preach the Heidelberg Catechism?," in *The Heritage of the Fathers: A Commentary on the Heidelberg Catechism* (Grand Rapids: Eerdmans, 1948), 15–26.

7. On the Lord's Day, see R. Scott Clark, "Whatever Happened to the Second Service?" in *Recovering the Reformed Confession: Our Theology, Piety, and Practice* (Phillipsburg: P&R, 2008), 293–342.

8. For more detail on hospitality, see chapter 10, "Being a Welcoming Church Plant," by Kevin Efflandt.

Principle 4: The Sponsoring Congregation Needs to Have a Program of Prayer (4:23–31, 12:5, 13:13)

In the book of Acts we see the church as a praying people. During times of persecution, great need, and at critical junctures we see the church on its knees. Christ's kingdom is a foreign force in the world; therefore, its persecution is inevitable. A regular prayer meeting at both the sponsoring congregation as well as at the church plant is a real way of showing that church planting is a spiritual battle.[9] A church plant needs the prayers of the larger church by means of a note in the bulletin, mention in the pastoral prayer, and on the church's prayer chain. Our Heidelberg Catechism applies here:

> *What is the second petition?*
>
> *Thy kingdom come.* That is: So govern us by Thy Word and Spirit that we may submit ourselves unto Thee always more and more; preserve and increase Thy church; destroy the works of the devil, every power that exalteth itself against Thee, and all wicked devices formed against Thy holy Word, until the full coming of Thy kingdom, wherein Thou shalt be all in all (HC, Q&A 123).

Principle 5: As Church Plants Grow, Qualified Men Need to Take Some of the Responsibility from the Pastor (6:1–7)

The apostles were remarkable men. They planted, preached, pastored, and provided for the early church. Eventually, though, as with Moses (Ex. 18:13–27), the workload was too much, and what would become known as the deaconate was formed. We can apply this to a church plant in the form of delegating a steering committee or some other group from its inception.[10] This is an excellent vehicle for others to take ownership of the growing church by assisting the pastor in the more mundane tasks of church life. This ensures the pastor will have time to preach, teach, evangelize, and care for the spiritual needs of his flock. It is also an excellent way for the pastor to evaluate those on the committee and assess their potential to be office bearers in the church. Simply put, the church planter needs the freedom to pursue his calling of planting a church, which means he is not a fundraiser, a businessman, or a ministry coordinator.

---

9. On this, see Joel R. Beeke, *The Family at Church: Listening to Sermons and Attending Prayer Meetings* (Grand Rapids: Reformation Heritage Books, 2008).

10. On the topic of steering committees, see appendices C and D by Spencer Aalsburg, "The Steering Committee" and "Guidelines for the Steering Committee."

**Principle 6: Other Pastors Should Be Consulted
Before Sending a Church Planter Out (13:1–3)**

In Antioch there were multiple prophets and teachers who were guided by the Holy Spirit to send Paul out to the world. Although this was confined to one local congregation, an application would be that the choosing and sending out of a church planter depends on more than just one man's inward call. The local pastors and elders need to agree and should ask for other church planters to offer an evaluation of a potential church planter as well.

In a setting like the one I am in, here in Southern California, there is a plethora of seminary students who make the rounds to various sister churches to bring the Word of God. This provides an excellent built-in system for evaluating a man's gifts, abilities, and personality that the churches need to make use of. And this can be said elsewhere as well. A local church that knows its own candidate for the ministry would do well to ask other pastors and elders of churches in which he has exhorted these questions: Does this man have the personality for church planting? Is this man gifted as an evangelist? Is he adaptable to constant change? Does he have a vision for a church plant? Would you call him to plant a church for you? Do you have any reservations about his ability and aptitude to be a church planter?

**Principle 7: The Church Planter Needs to Encourage the
Sponsoring Church with Reports on What God Is Doing (15:12)**

Just as Paul returned to Jerusalem and reported about what God was doing among the Gentiles, so too a church planter needs to periodically return in person to report the joys and sorrows of his work. He should report in writing and over the phone, but a personal visit and report of the Lord's work can invigorate a sponsoring congregation to support, pray, and encourage their church planter all the more.

**Principle 8: The Sponsoring Church Must Not Become
Discouraged When Its Plan Seems Unsuccessful (16:6–10)**

As we saw in chapter 2, Paul, Barnabas, and Timothy wanted to evangelize in Asia but were forbidden by the Holy Spirit; they wanted to preach in Bithynia but were not allowed. Instead, the Holy Spirit led them to Macedonia. It seems that they were unsuccessful in their work, doesn't it?

What we learn in Acts 16 is how God measures success. An unsuccessful mission work can be the opportunity for many other opportunities. If we go into an area to plant a church, but it fails, what can we learn? First, we learn that church planting is God's work. Second, we learn how to plant more effectively in the future if we are responsible for the failure. Third, we learn that exposing people to the truth does not always produce results, which most of us already know. Trust the Lord, follow His lead, and let His work go forth.

Principle 9: The Church Planter Must Visit His Flock and Teach Privately (20:20)

Paul was tireless, not only preaching in the synagogues and local church but also catechizing his flock, family by family. This is essentially what Paul was telling Timothy to do when he said, "Do the work of an evangelist" (2 Tim. 4:5). When we seek to plant a church, we must call a man who has this gift. Since church planting is a fragile endeavor, those involved in planting a new church need instruction, encouragement, and the prayers of the church planter. In the first year of our church plant, I visited every family twice and invited them into my home for a meal after the morning service at least once. Preaching is just the beginning. It must be applied in the lives of our hearers in a one-on-one way.

Principle 10: The Church Plant Needs to Be Visited by Those Who Are Planting It (15:36, 18:23, 19:22)

The pastors, elders, deacons, and members need to experience firsthand what the Lord is doing in their church plant. In our congregation, we were privileged to have an elder from our mother church, the Escondido URC, attend every worship service as well as many families who willingly came out on a regular basis—which no doubt helped our singing!

There are many benefits to this practice. First, it encourages both the home church and the church plant; second, it increases attendance at the church plant so that it has the look of viability; third, it aids immensely in the singing, especially if the church plant is made up of "converts" to the Reformed faith and worship (you'd be surprised at the difference just two families can make in a church-planting worship service); fourth, it maintains a level of connection that we believe in as Reformed and Presbyterian churches.

As you can see, we have much work to do in planning, preparing, and supporting Reformed church planting in our areas and beyond. We must begin to think biblically and confessionally about how we are going to do this work. It is a huge task, but the Lord is sufficient to make us capable. After all, it is His work.

CHAPTER SIX

∾

Heart Preparation in Church Planting

Paul T. Murphy

For God so loved the world that He gave His only begotten Son, that whoever believes in Him should not perish but have everlasting life. For God did not send His Son into the world to condemn the world, but that the world through Him might be saved.... So Jesus said to them again, 'Peace to you! As the Father has sent Me, I also send you.' —John 3:16–17, 20:21

I will begin by making a couple of observations about the church growth we sometimes experience in Reformed and Presbyterian churches. Most growth has been biological and transfer growth, and I would like to affirm both. Often these types of growth have pejorative connotations, even in our own circles. Biological growth is consistent with the design of the covenant of grace, that is, that God works in the line of families—God is a God to us and to our children after us (Gen. 17:7). Among American evangelicals, the Dutch Reformed are often envied because our youth stay in church because of catechetical instruction, Christian education, and a strong connection between the church, the school, and the home— the so-called "three legs" of our covenantal understanding. This leaves little time for aggressive programs of evangelism as we would see in many evangelical churches.

Transfer growth is legitimate when people come to Reformed convictions and find a home in our confessional churches. This is not a problem; it is a blessing, and we should view it that way. However, these should not be the exclusive areas of growth among us. Our Lord spoke Matthew 28:18–20, commonly called the Great Commission, to the church, and therefore we should be seeing growth from evangelism as well.

Originally appeared in *Mid-America Journal of Theology* 19 (2008): 223–32, and is reprinted with permission.

A Missionary God

My point of reference in Scripture for this chapter is John 3:16–17 and 20:21. The premise for everything I have to say is that our God is a missionary God. He "so loved the world that He gave His only begotten Son, that whoever believes in Him should not perish but have eternal life" (John 3:16). As a missionary Father, he sent a missionary Son, not to condemn the world but to save the world (John 3:17). How many times do we read the purpose statements for which Jesus came in this gospel? That is, He came not for the righteous but for sinners to repent; He came to seek and to save the lost. These teach us that He is a missionary Son who, together with the Father, has sent a missionary Spirit: "So Jesus said to them again, 'Peace to you! As the Father has sent Me, I also send you.' And when He had said this, He breathed on them, and said to them, 'Receive the Holy Spirit'" (John 20:21–22). This was an indication of what was to occur on the day of Pentecost. After Jesus' ascension, Peter tells us that he received from the Father the promised Holy Spirit, who was now being poured out—what they were now seeing and hearing in Acts 2. The point is that God is a missionary God, who sent a missionary Son, who together sent a missionary Spirit on Pentecost to equip, empower, and enable a new covenant missionary church. This is our identity; this is who we are as the people of God.

Evangelism and missions are not an elective course that we Christians can choose to take or not. Evangelism and missions are not something to be tacked on to the budget after we figure out where we are going to spend our money on everything else. This is our identity. I will add that we were created and redeemed "to glorify God, and to enjoy him forever" (WSC, Q&A 1). Therefore, there is no higher priority in the church than worship; we were created and redeemed to worship God, and we don't want to ever lose that focus. It is the ultimate reason for the church's existence.

The penultimate purpose of the church, then, is most certainly missions—seeking and saving the lost that they might worship with us. This is where we need some serious correction concerning the preparation of our hearts. Let me say a couple of things with respect to missions and evangelism.

Every Church a Missionary Church

Since God is a missionary God who sent a missionary Son, who together sent a missionary Spirit, every church should be a missionary church. What we need to do away with in the hearts and minds of our people is the distinction between a maintenance church and a missionary church. In my former pastorate, I initiated contact with a regional home missionary from another denomination after I found out that denomination was going to begin a church about a mile away from the church where I was pastor. Considering what Paul says in Romans 15:20 about not building on another man's foundation, I thought this was improper, and possibly even unethical. I contacted this man and said, "I hear you're starting a church. You know you're starting it a mile away from where there's been an existing Reformed congregation for some seventy-five years." His response was illuminating, but indicting: "This is going to be a different kind of church; this is going to be a missionary church."

I went on to say to him, "I thought every church was supposed to be a missionary church, responsible for seeking and saving the lost in their community, reaching them with the good news of Jesus Christ, forgiveness of sins, and eternal life through faith in Him."

He replied, "Oh well, you know, you're in a maintenance church, and maintenance churches don't do that. We're going to be different."

Unfortunately, this attitude exists in the hearts and minds of our people. In my former denomination, this was actually institutionalized in a chapel system. There were churches that were considered chapels, where new converts or people who were not "our kind of people" were sent. That seemed to be a kind of ecclesiastical affirmative action, a lowering of the standards to accommodate people that didn't have five hundred years of Dutch Reformed tradition behind them. But this idea exists as a mindset in the hearts of our people, and it's something that needs to change, especially as we consider planting more confessional churches in the twenty-first century.

A couple of statistical points prove this. In his book *A New Look at Church Growth*, Floyd Bartel says 95 percent of all Christians in North America will not win one person to Christ in their entire lifetime.[1] Bob Gilliam surveyed more than five hundred evangelical churches in forty denominations over a ten-year period. While I'm writing this chapter

---

1. Floyd G. Bartel and Richard Showalter, *A New Look at Church Growth* (Newton, Kan.: Faith and Life Press, 1979), 59.

primarily for Reformed or Presbyterian churches, the issue Gilliam's survey reveals is not just an in-house problem; it's a problem nationwide. Including more than 130,000 church members, Gilliam's survey revealed that each year the average evangelical church led 1.7 people to Christ for each one hundred people in attendance.[2] Speaking at Dallas Theological Seminary some ten years ago, Alister McGrath noted that England in the eighteenth century was primarily a Christian nation. However, today, only 10 percent claim to be churched, and this may even be an overestimate. McGrath warned that this was because the church stopped doing evangelism and focused its attention on teaching and the pastoral care of its members.[3]

This is something that we suffer from as well. We are good at taking care of our own people—preaching, teaching, and discipling. We are good at raising children in the covenant of grace, nurturing them in the faith, and, by God's grace, bringing them to know Jesus Christ as Lord and Savior. Yet we have a lack. We do missions by proxy; that is, we pay and pray for somebody else to do it. This needs to change. It should be the goal of every church to reproduce since this is our identity. We are a missionary church; I trust readers of this book essentially agree with me. As we plant churches, we need to be sure that our plants are mission-minded, reaching out to the community with the gospel.

Every Christian a Witness

I also want to emphasize that evangelizing is the responsibility of every Christian. We believe in and affirm the special office of the minister of Word and sacraments—that there is an official proclamation that is conducted by a minister who is authorized by the church to speak for Jesus Christ as he explains and applies his text as the Word of God. As the Second Helvetic Confession (1566) says, the preached Word of God is the Word of God (ch. 1.4). I do not want to diminish the significance of

---

2. Bob Gilliam and Sharon G. Johnson, *A State of the Church Report on Evangelism in the E.F.C.A.: The Results of the 1991 National Evangelism Survey* (Minneapolis: Evangelical Free Church of America, Church Ministries Dept., 1992).

3. See Alister E. McGrath, "Biblical Models for Apologetics: Evangelical Apologetics," *Bibliotheca sacra* 155 (January–March 1998): 3–10; "Biblical Models for Apologetics: Apologetics to the Greeks," *Bibliotheca sacra* 155 (July–September 1998): 259–65; "Biblical Models for Apologetics: Apologetics to the Romans," *Bibliotheca sacra* 155 (October–December 1998): 387–93.

the official nature of that office and proclamation, but in addition to an official proclamation of the gospel in preaching, there is an unofficial spreading of the gospel in evangelism. The minister most certainly evangelizes when he preaches the gospel in the corporate worship assembly of God's people, but the members also have the responsibility to witness.

Members of the church are able to speak about Jesus Christ. This subject ought to be familiar to Reformed people from their catechetical instruction. In its exposition of the Apostles' Creed, the Heidelberg Catechism explains why we call Jesus "Christ": "He is ordained of God the Father, and anointed with the Holy Ghost, to be our chief Prophet and Teacher...our only High Priest...and our eternal King" (HC, Q&A 31). It then asks how this applies to us: "But why art thou called a Christian?" The answer is, "Because by faith I am a member of Christ, and thus a partaker of His anointing." A part of that anointing is that we, too, are not only priests and kings but also prophets "in order that [we] also may confess His name" (HC, Q&A 32). Every member of Christ, by definition, innately and inherently has a prophetic responsibility to speak about Christ to the world.

Sadly, in some Reformed churches this has become somewhat distorted. Some commentaries on the traditional Dutch Reformed Church Order say that this question and answer from the Catechism applies to the public profession of faith of a child who has grown up in the church. This is not what the authors of the Catechism were referring to, though.[4] Rather, every Christian has a prophetic responsibility to speak not for Christ officially, but unofficially. I have met far too many people in our confessional congregations who never talk to anybody else about the faith or Christ. We need to call that what it is: sin.

I would submit to you in light of the Scripture and our Catechism that a silent Christian—somebody who has never told others about Christ or the faith or the claims of Jesus Christ—is a contradiction in terms. It is to be sub-Christian. This is also evident in another question and answer in the Catechism, which speaks about the necessity of good works: "Since, then, we are redeemed from our misery by grace through Christ, with-

---

4. In examining Q&A 32, Zacharias Ursinus wrote that "every one in his place and degree...faithfully, boldly, and constantly" profess the true doctrine of the gospel (*The Commentary of Dr. Zacharias Ursinus on the Heidelberg Catechism*, trans. G. W. Williard [1852; repr., Phillipsburg, N. J.: Presbyterian and Reformed, 1985], 179). Ursinus also quotes Matthew 10:32 in this context, which says, "Therefore whoever confesses Me before men, him I will also confess before My Father who is in heaven."

out any merit of ours, why must we do good works?" At the end of the answer we read, "by our godly walk [we] may win our neighbors also to Christ" (HC, Q&A 86). There is a beautiful balance in the Catechism here. By lips and life, by word and deed we testify to others that it is Jesus Christ who loved me, gave Himself for me, purchased me with His own precious blood, and has called me now to serve Him as a living witness to His grace. This is why it is important to have our members involved in evangelism. The church as church is a Great Commission church, and the Christian as Christian is one who tells others about Jesus. This should be the mindset of all our churches and church plants.

Carl F. H. Henry (1913–2003) wrote of this personal element in evangelism: "A one-to-one approach initiated by every believer still holds the best promise of evangelizing the earth."[5] Writing from a historical perspective, Yale historian Kenneth Scott Latourette says, "The chief agents in the expansion of Christianity appear not to have been those who made it a profession, but men and women who carried on their livelihood in some purely secular manner and spoke of their faith to those they met in this natural fashion."[6] Pieter De Jong, a veteran missionary at home and abroad as well as a confessional pastor, observes, "One of the biggest handicaps to our local evangelism programs is often the indifference of our members to their missionary calling, and their failure to welcome those who do come into our worship from outside. On the other hand, one of the biggest factors in the success of winning these people has often been the interest of a Christian neighbor who tried to reach them, rather than the effects of a busy minister."[7] We would do well to heed the observations of these men and steer away from relegating the task of evangelism simply and solely to professionals in the pulpit or on the mission field. Again, without this emphasis, a church plant may not survive.

Statistics that show the influences that lead people to eventually become Christians and members of churches are revealing. Family and friends usually rank the highest of all. Emphasizing the importance of evangelizing family and friends is a serious omission in many churches. It is one of the main reasons, I believe, that we do not see more converts

---

5. Carl F. H. Henry, "The Purpose of God," in *The New Face of Evangelicalism*, ed. C. Rene Padilla (Downers Grove, Ill.: InterVarsity, 1976), 31.

6. Kenneth S. Latourette, *A History of the Expansion of Christianity* (New York: Harper & Brothers, 1944), 1:230.

7. Pieter De Jong, *A Theology of Evangelistic Concern* (Nashville: Tidings, 1963).

in our congregations. To do evangelism is not just spreading information but sharing the gospel that saves sinners. Evangelism is not just informing sinners but inviting them; it is not just to lecture sinners, but to love them. Such evangelism is not harsh and callous, but concerned and courteous. Evangelism is to be warm-hearted, affectionate, considerate, and adaptable. It is not just to throw truth at people but to get alongside them, to start thinking with them and like them, to speak to them and with them. Evangelism is an enterprise that springs forth from love. As Paul says, "The love of Christ compels us" (2 Cor. 5:14).

Since we know what it is to fear the Lord, we try to persuade men. This personal element is essential. However, evangelism should not be done apart from seeing people come to church. Evangelism should be done in the covenant context of the church, not with "lone rangers" doing their own thing, developing their own individualistic ministries. Evangelism is like the family. Family members go out every day to do different things, each one advancing the family's interests. This is the "grass roots" type of work in a church plant.

Application

We need to get this perspective into the hearts of those in our church and those who desire to become core families of a church plant. Here are a few applications of the principles that I've been explaining.

Programs

Often when I give evangelism seminars, people get excited and want to program their church for evangelism. I would discourage you from doing that. Do not program your church plant. Rather, program the hearts of the people in the church plant. People's hearts need to be inclined towards other people, and they should be sensitive to their needs. Also, start inculcating this in the minds and hearts of the next generation. We often have groups from other churches come to New York City to the church plant I pastor to do evangelism, and we train them in that. We take them out and go door to door. We throw them in at the deep end right away. I tell people when they arrive, "Tomorrow morning we're going door to door, and you're going to be forced to talk to people about your faith. You're going to have to talk to people about Jesus Christ." There are a lot of all-night prayer sessions. As they go out to share their faith with others, they experience a variety of reactions—everything from antagonism to reception. When the groups return to their churches, excited about talking to people about their faith, it has a tremendous effect—it lights fires. It is amazing, because excitement like this is better caught than taught. It may be short lived, but those who come begin to form evangelism habits of the heart—sharing the gospel with others.

Use Old and Young in the Church Plant
In my experience, we put an unfair burden on people in the church who are thirty to fifty years old. We have few expectations for young people until they make profession of faith, which usually extends until they get married and have children. Then we start having expectations. We should use young people because they have the energy to do this work, which is very tiring. Get young people out there, and get older people out there as well. We constantly have problems getting elders and deacons established in the church because older people often go to Florida or Arizona—a warmer climate—in the winter months. They seem to be saying, "I put in my time. I did my part." The aged are the people who have acquired wisdom, knowledge, and experience in the church. When they leave for months at a time, we are losing an enormous asset. If thirty- to fifty-year-olds are doing all the work of the church, of course they will be burned out and not want to do anything when they get older. We need to spread responsibilities out more when it comes to evangelism and church planting. Make sure to enlist the different age groups in the church-plant core group.

Prayer
Furthermore, ministers need to pray from the pulpit. Pray for the lost. Pray for opportunities for the congregants to witness and testify. Pray for the people to have eyes of faith so that when God brings open doors, they see them for what they are. Pray for God to give courage to the people and boldness to speak up. If you are a church planter, be unashamedly evangelistic in your prayers; if you are a member of a steering committee, a core group, or a group of elders, pray hard for the lost.

Instruction
Include teaching on evangelism in your profession of faith classes and new members' classes. At the church I pastor in New York City, when I go through the rights and responsibilities of church membership in our classes, I always include evangelism as a responsibility of those who profess

faith in Christ. I ask questions such as, "If being a Christian was a crime, would there be enough evidence to convict you?" "Do people know you're a Christian?" "Are you a silent Christian, just keeping it to yourself?"

Again, missions and evangelism are activities of Jesus Christ, things that need to be in the hearts and minds of all our people. We see this in the very beginning of the book of Acts, where Luke writes, "The former account I made, O Theophilus, of all that Jesus *began* both to do and teach" (Acts 1:1, emphasis added). The clear implication is that Luke is going to write about what Jesus *continues* to do and teach. How does Jesus do this? He continues to work in and through His church. The risen and reigning Lord Jesus Christ is working in and through His church to take the gospel from Jerusalem, to Judea, to Samaria, and to the uttermost parts of the earth—to church plants in North America today and beyond. Jesus promised Peter—and us, "I will build My church, and the gates of Hades shall not prevail against it" (Matt. 16:18). Jesus spoke the words of the Great Commission: "All authority has been given to Me in heaven and on earth. Go therefore and make disciples of all the nations, baptizing them in the name of the Father and of the Son and of the Holy Spirit, teaching them to observe all things that I have commanded you; and lo, I am with you always, even to the end of the age" (Matt. 28:18–20). The power and presence of Jesus Christ is what is important in missions and evangelism. We are merely His instruments.

There are many times when you just want to give up and go home, though. I have to remind myself as I remind other people often: this is the Lord's work. We plant, another man waters, but God has to give the growth—as the title of this book reflects. An emphasis on the sovereign grace of God is the most encouraging thing I can think of. The risen Lord Jesus Christ is building His church, and He will add to it as He pleases and when He pleases. That's a great comfort and encouragement, and it is a great motivation. We just have to be faithful to what the Lord has called us to do. He has His sheep out there, and they must come also, Jesus says (John 10:16).

Context

There is a difference that needs to be accounted for between the first and the twenty-first centuries. During the time the church was being built in Acts, people were living in a pre-Christian era. They had never heard the gospel. God had been largely confined to the borders of Israel, with the occasional exception in the Old Testament. Now Jesus universalizes the gospel, "Go therefore and make disciples of all the nations" (Matt. 28:19). That situation is not ours. We live in what Chuck Colson has designated the new dark ages. We live in a post-Christian era. We live, by and large, in America among people who have heard the gospel and rejected it. When I approach people even in New York City, which is an immigrant city with masses of immigrant population from non-Christian countries, most still have some sort of Christian or church background. These are people who have heard the gospel, and they know about Jesus. When I talk about Matthew, Mark, Luke, and John, they know about the New Testament, but they have rejected it. These are not people who have never heard. This is a huge difference from what we find in the book of Acts. Today, people have become resistant to the gospel that they have already heard, just like a disease becomes resistant to medicine.

We need to be looking not only at the book of Acts but the Old Testament prophets. They went to a people who knew the God of Abraham, Isaac, and Jacob—who knew the Scriptures. They knew the temple sacrifices. But by and large these people were disobedient and unbelieving. The prophets called them on the basis of what they knew: to repent and believe, to come back to the claims and demands of the covenant. The Old Testament prophets ought to be our model in America today along with the book of Acts.

Pragmatism

Beware of pragmatism when it comes to missions, evangelism, and church planting. The question unfortunately for far too many is no longer, "Is it true?" but "Does it work?" Evangelistic methods in the church are often secular, pragmatic, and pluralistic. Many are looking for tricks, tips, gimmicks, and books that will tell them what unbelievers think. The reason many people want to read books about what unbelievers think is so that they can become like them. But that becomes their undoing. In our congregation in New York, our theme from the outset has been "making a difference by being different." And we need to take seriously and recapture the doctrine of the antithesis in our missions and evangelism programs. Make a difference by being different. Do not succumb to pragmatism, although it is very tempting to do that.

On a related note, we must understand that strictness of faith does not equal failure in mission. There are far too many people among Reformed and Presbyterian churches who think that if you do missions and evangelism you have to dismiss or downplay your Reformed distinctives. On the other hand, there are people who are not very winsome and want to hammer away on their Reformed distinctives. I am not advocating that. Yet we do not want to dismiss or downplay our Reformed distinctives. When people come to our church they see it in our name: Messiah's *Reformed* Fellowship. People may not know what "Reformed" is. This is the most frequent question we get: "What's Reformed?" We invite them to sit down, meaning that they should come among us and learn. Our faith cannot be explained on a bumper sticker, and it does not make for a good sound bite. To explain what it means to be Reformed needs at least a few cups of coffee!

Conclusion

I would encourage you not to lose confidence in the power of the gospel. Churches that grow are based on preaching the gospel. Make the gospel the driving force of your church plant. I have talked to enough ministers in my twenty years of ministry to know there are many faithful ministers who do not always understand that. But it was Paul who said, "I am not ashamed of the gospel of Christ, for it is the power of God to salvation for everyone who believes" (Rom. 1:16). Paul says elsewhere: "The weapons of our warfare are not carnal" (2 Cor. 10:4). We do not need tricks, gimmicks, and manipulation.

The weapons we fight with are not the weapons of the world. On the contrary, they have divine power to demolish strongholds. We demolish arguments and every pretension that sets itself up against the knowledge of God, and we take captive every thought to make it obedient to Christ (2 Cor. 10:5).

CHAPTER SEVEN

∾

Church Planting:
A Covenantal and Organic Approach

Paul T. Murphy

In this chapter, I will discuss two points concerning church planting: the *practice* of church planting and the *posture* of church planting. Though I will be talking about the things we at Messiah's Reformed Fellowship have done as a church plant, you must understand that there is not a "cookie-cutter" approach to church planting. What one church planter experiences and the practices described in other chapters of this book will not apply exactly in every situation. What works in San Diego will not necessarily work in New York City, and what works in Seattle will not necessarily work in Atlanta.

The Practice of Planting a Confessional Church

In the practice of church planting, I would encourage you to pursue an organic, covenantal approach. What do I mean by that? I see two ways of doing outreach evangelism in the local church. One is what I would call an "imposition" on the community. This is the door-to-door, on-the-street work of going out and giving Bibles, tracts, and other literature to people on the streets. We have also set up book tables in various places where we give out literature and Bibles to people who will fill out a survey and tell us a little about themselves. Occasionally we do street preaching. These examples are really an imposition on the community. They tend to be somewhat impersonal, detached, and dispassionate. These are fine things to do, but I don't think they are optimum or ideal.[1]

Originally appeared in *Mid-America Journal of Theology* 19 (2008): 233–41, and is reprinted with permission.

1. This type of outreach is quite inexpensive. It costs very little to print out some pamphlets, purchase some Bibles (between three and five dollars each), and take a few hours a week going door to door.

What I do think is optimum and ideal is, by contrast, taking a more organic approach to the community. Specifically, the mission strategy would be this: find out where the needs are in your community and meet them with the gospel. It is earthy, human, and organic. What we have done in New York City is have three main ministries with respect to outreach. First, we have a Wall Street Bible study in the financial district. New York City's financial district in the Wall Street area is the economic engine for the country and the world. We also teach English as a second language at a local public high school. I am also a volunteer chaplain at the local hospital, and we have a number of people in our church plant who have been trained to be spiritual providers or caregivers at the hospital as well. The following is an explanation of these specific approaches.

Bible Study
The Wall Street Bible study is interesting because it is unique. Rather than studying a book of the Bible, it is a topical, targeted study in order to educate the people in the Wall Street area. That is, it is a Bible study on work and what the Bible has to say about work, finances, and other related topics. We do a study of about three dozen different subjects having to do with these broad topics. Things are changing for the better to some extent, but when I was first converted years ago, Christians had a reputation for being the worst workers in New York City. I worked in construction as a job superintendent for a contractor in New York City doing interior renovations. I knew other business owners in New York City, and they refused to hire Christians. If someone applied for a job and the employer found out he was a Christian, it was an automatic reason not to consider him.

In our Bible study, then, we address this situation and show people what the Bible has to say about work—that really the main way that people can serve the Lord is in their work. And the best way to witness for the Lord in the workplace is not to get out your Bible and start talking about Jesus Christ to your colleagues, but to be the best employee. You have to realize that not everyone works hard. Here again is an illustration of the consequences of doctrine. We believe that Christ alone saves sinners' bodies and souls. When people begin to see that the Bible has something to say about where they spend much of their day, they are amazed. Jesus Christ is the Lord of every area of life. We are to take captive every thought to make it obedient to Christ (2 Cor. 10:5). People understand this.

We literally meet people where they are: at Wall Street and Broadway every Tuesday at lunchtime, 12:30–1:15. How do we get people to come to a Bible study? We hand out leaflets on the street. We've had remarkable results. The leaflet is very simple: "Feed Your Heart at Lunchtime." As we hand them out, to avoid waste, we say, "Christian Bible study" and give it only to the people who are interested.

We have handed out thousands of pieces of literature over the time that we have been in New York. In one spring alone we had eighteen people come to this Bible study as a result of just handing out flyers on the street. This was an encouraging response to literature distribution. Once a few people come, we encourage them to invite friends as well.

Teaching within the Community
Second, we teach English as a second language at a local school for business careers, although the public school environment in New York City is hostile to the Christian faith. I'm on the business advisory council at a school where people are preparing to enter into business careers after graduation. The reason I am there is because, ironically, as pastor of a local church I am considered to be a business owner. One day when I was at a council meeting, the parent association president was talking to the principal about all the difficulty that they have with the parents of students because they do not speak English. There are 3,500 students in this school; 1,100 are non-English speaking. One-third of the student population is immigrants who speak no English. I overheard this conversation, and I said, "I think I might be able to help you. I have a program to teach English as a second language."

After that, the dean of the school wanted to see the curriculum, which is published by the Southern Baptist Convention of the American Mission Board. It uses the gospel of Mark as the English text; then it teaches grammar and vocabulary based on Mark. I was certain they would reject it, but instead they said it looked great.

So I and others from the church plant began teaching. We had classes on Saturday mornings and Tuesday afternoons. The first sentence that students read is, "This is the good news of Jesus Christ, according to Mark." This provides marvelous opportunities to talk to people about the faith, the Lord, and the gospel. We have even discussed the grammar of a direct article rather than an indirect article (so Jesus is *the* Way, *the* Truth, and *the* Life as opposed to *a* way, *a* truth, and *a* life) to an unbeliever, which was an opportunity to explain the uniqueness of Christ and His gospel. Things like this happened often as we went through the English text of Mark's gospel.

One day I went in with a box of John Piper's book *Fifty Reasons Why Jesus Came to Die.* After I entered, I had to go past the police check-gate. So I put down the box to get out my ID. Of course the police officer was interested: "What's in the box?"

I said, "Oh! This is a great book: *Fifty Reasons Why Jesus Came to Die.*" He went on to ask, "Can I have one?"

I responded, "You can have one if you promise to read it. Now you know I'm here every week, and I'm going to follow up with you. You have to read this book."

His answer? "All right, I promise I'll read it."

I gave him a copy and later, during class, a different policeman came in. I was thinking to myself, "I'm caught! I'm evangelizing in a public school!"

He asked, "Are you the guy who was handing out books in the lobby?"

I said, "Yes, that was me."

He said, "Can I talk to you over here?" We went to the corner of the room and he whispered, "Do you think I can get one of those books?"

Chaplaincy

Our third organic approach to the community is serving as a volunteer chaplain and spiritual providers in the hospital. There was no chaplain in our local hospital for a long time, so they gladly welcomed us. We ended up having six people in our congregation undergo training to be spiritual providers to the hospital. There have been more opportunities at this hospital to talk about the gospel than almost anything else we have done. It is meeting people in the community at a time of need.

Some of these people are bored sitting in the hospital with nothing to do. I just walk into the room and say, "My name is Paul Murphy. I'm the chaplain. Is there anything I can do for you?" I could spend considerable time discussing all of the interesting and wonderful discussions I have had with people—drug addicts, FBI agents, and all sorts who have never heard the gospel.

These are only a few examples of how to approach outreach and church planting in an organic way. Find out where there are needs in your community, and meet them with the gospel. This is not just a matter of doing good deeds; it is meeting a need with the gospel. This is the mission strategy. Examine your community with eyes of faith and prayer. Do some research; ask librarians, policemen, high school counselors, and others involved in the community where the needs are.

Other Organic Approaches
Some church planters have devoted a certain time each week to studying in a coffee shop or library—to study, but primarily to be available to anyone and to position themselves in a way to share the gospel and invite people to church. Other church planters have had pizza lunches at college campuses, over which theological discussions take place. Still other planters have a pub night, where, in good Reformation fashion, they simply chat about things of the faith in a place where people are relaxed. Other church plants have seminars, lecture series, or other types of Bible studies addressing certain topics that seekers or unbelievers would be interested in. All these things can be advertised on the church plant's website, in its bulletin, with flyers, or in the local newspaper.

The Posture of Planting a Confessional Church
The posture of planting a confessional church is to be covenantal as well. A covenantal approach has to do with families. In outreach and evangelism we aim not just for individuals but also for families. We know, as Reformed Christians, that God's grace runs in the line of families—that God is God to us and to our children. It is the same on the mission field.

Families: Not Just Individuals
A number of families have come to church because when I met with one individual initially, I expressed an interest in the other members of the family. I do that every time I meet with somebody. Often when we discuss family life, we find out that we are dealing with a lot of broken homes, fragmented individuals, and shattered, sinful lives. I suggest talking to church plant visitors about their families, showing genuine love and concern for them.

Christian Day Schools
Something that goes along with a covenantal approach to missions is Christian schools. In our tradition, whenever a church was started, a Christian school was started along with it. That custom would serve us well on the mission field. If you want to do church planting, I would

encourage you to consider starting a school as well. It is consistent with the demands of the covenant of grace and with our understanding of Scripture—that God is God to us and to our children. It is also consistent with taking a long-term approach to mission in any community. If you want to have a long-term impact in terms of a kingdom perspective, then you have to plan to stick with the community and teach them, their children, and their children's children.

A young Dutch couple was attending our congregation. I asked them to give their testimony because they were the unusual ones: they had been raised in a Christian home. We have only two families now in our church that were raised in Christian homes; the rest are first generation. This is a common experience in a church plant. We asked the husband, "How long has the faith been in your family?"

He said, "Four to five hundred years."

I said to everybody, "That's what we want." Whenever I go and preach in other churches, I always encourage people to come with me, because I want them to see what a congregation of Christian families is like. For them it is amazing to see what goes on in these churches: Christian families. What we need to have is families just like in Acts. We must approach church planting in a way that is consistent with the covenant of grace.

Children in Worship

We have a lot of children in our church plant. The one thing that visitors comment on most when they come to worship with us is the number of kids. The children can sit through a service that is more than an hour long, and this is a miracle in the eyes of the world. It is a powerful witness to a watching world—and it is fully covenantal. This is teaching our children like the Bible emphasizes—in the presence of God. God is speaking to us. We come to give God the worship and glory due His name because His promise is to you and to your children.

In both the practice and posture of planting confessional churches, meeting the needs of the community as a vehicle for evangelism and stressing the life-long, familial, and covenantal aspects of the Christian faith are essential for the planting, watering, and future growth of the church plant.

CHAPTER EIGHT

❦

Planning the Plant: Some Thoughts on Preparing to Plant a New Church

Kim Riddlebarger

Church planting is not a science in which fixed laws can be applied with predictable results. Although church planting may be closer to an art—in which intuition and the subjective experiences of the participants might indeed predominate—the fact of the matter is church planting is a matter of faith. Make no mistake about it: a successful church plant depends upon the sovereign will of God. And yet there can be little doubt that it is God's revealed will to provide for His people a church where they can hear the Word rightly preached, receive the sacraments properly administered, enjoy the fellowship of the saints, and use their spiritual gifts for the common good. This essay is written for congregations, prospective church planters, and those who desire to see such a church planted in their community.[1]

One of the great joys of being a participant in the national radio broadcast *White Horse Inn* is the continuing feedback I get from those who, after embracing the doctrines of grace and Reformed doctrines, desire to see a Reformed church planted in their community. Many times people will write or contact me, expressing the same basic dilemma: "We live in a city where there is no Reformed church. What do we do?" I have heard the same basic story line many times. Not counting the Kingdom Hall and the local Mormon stake, many new converts live in a town where there might be a mainline Protestant church (or two), a Church of Christ, an independent fundamentalist church, one or two Pentecostal churches constantly in the midst of revival, and, of course, a large Roman Catholic church. For good reason, Reformed Christians don't feel comfortable attending any of these places. The nearest confessional Reformed or Presbyterian church is too far away to attend on Sundays. What are such people to do?

---

1. For more information, see *POPC*, 17–26.

My first piece of advice to people facing this dilemma is to seriously consider moving (if at all possible) to an area where a solid Reformed church already exists. Membership in a confessional Reformed or Presbyterian church is such an important part of the Christian life that living near such a church should be very high on the list of a Reformed Christian's priorities. Listen to how the Belgic Confession (1561) expresses the necessity and vitality of the church for the believer:

> We believe, since this holy congregation is an assembly of those who are saved, and outside of it there is no salvation, that no person of whatsoever state or condition he may be, ought to withdraw from it, content to be by himself; but that all men are in duty bound to join and unite themselves with it; maintain the unity of the Church; submitting themselves to the doctrine and discipline thereof; bowing their necks under the yoke of Jesus Christ; and as mutual members of the same body, serving to the edification of the brethren, according to the talents God has given them. And that this may be more effectively observed, it is the duty of all believers, according to the Word of God, to separate themselves from all those who do not belong to the Church, and to join themselves to this congregation, wheresoever God has established it, even though the magistrates and edicts of princes were against it, yea, though they should suffer death or any other corporal punishment. Therefore all those who separate themselves from the same or do not join themselves to it act contrary to the ordinance of God (art. 28).

If relocating or commuting is not possible, then planting a Reformed church becomes a real option. While it is a real option (in the sense of being a desirable option), it is not an easy option. The reality is that planting a new Reformed/Presbyterian church is an expensive, all-consuming process that will test your faith, your patience, and your sanctification. It is not as though there are thousands of people eager to flock to this new church with their checkbooks open, wildly enthusiastic about Reformed doctrine and just dying to join the new work.

In fact, anyone who desires to plant a confessional Reformed church must consider the fact that membership in NAPARC churches (the North American Presbyterian and Reformed Council, www.naparc.org) is about 750,000 in North America. This is a good indicator that confessional Reformed and Presbyterian Christians make up a small minority of those who profess faith in Christ. Those desiring to plant a Reformed church need to realize that the vast majority of professing Christians in their area will have little, if any, interest in attending. While this is sad, it is reality, and those who want to plant a church need to keep such things in mind from the beginning.

The reason for my gloomy assessment is simple. To plant a Reformed church you need to know what to expect, you need to plan accordingly, and, most importantly, you must realize that the success of this endeavor depends upon the will and grace of God in providing what He has promised for His people. So while it is essential to be realistic about what goes into planting a church, at the same time, those desiring such a church must not lose sight of the fact that God has promised to provide for His people and has unlimited resources to do so. One of God's greatest blessings is to see that dream of a new church go from the dream to reality.

Some Background

Before I turn to some specifics about planning the church plant, a few qualifications are in order. Although some of the church-planting gurus imply that church planting will inevitably succeed if one simply follows the prescribed recipe, remember that in real life, one size does not fit everyone. If you desire to see a new Reformed church open in your community, you face a unique set of circumstances. Every core group who seeks to plant a church will have a particular vision for the new church, and that core group will be composed of people with unique personalities and expectations. This is why not everything I suggest in the following will apply in every circumstance and why every attempt to plant a new church will face a unique set of circumstances.

In addition to the queries I often receive about what to do when there is no Reformed church where the inquirer lives, my interest in church planting also stems from the fact that over the course of twelve years, Michael Horton and I have planted two Reformed churches in Orange County, California. Both church plants taught me a great deal and serve as the context and background for the suggestions that follow.

Our first church plant was St. Luke's Reformed Episcopal Church (a congregation of the Reformed Episcopal Church [REC]). St. Luke's still exists—though with greatly different doctrinal emphases and membership. Other than a retired minister, the REC had virtually no presence in Southern California when St. Luke's was formed in the early 1980s. When Horton and I got involved with this effort, it was clear that the REC wasn't in much of a position to help. They did secure a facility—the beautiful Church of Our Fathers at the Cypress Forest Lawn. They gave us two offering plates, a communion set, a cordless microphone, a few prayer books, and that was it. Given Horton's presence as a student at a local Christian university, Biola, the church was composed almost entirely of university students in their twenties. There was very little oversight from the REC. We gladly worked for free. At the time, I had a full-time job running our family business. But we loved it. At least, we loved it at first.

Aside from the theological issues with our bishop amid the growing indications that the REC was moving away from its Reformed roots, as the fledgling church grew, we soon found ourselves struggling to find permanent facilities. We quickly discovered that many of the college students who made up our membership were zealous for the Reformed faith but could not support the church financially. The REC was not able to support the work and even expected us to begin to contribute to their board for church extension. Although the work was very rewarding, I was working full time elsewhere while trying to be a pastor in my spare time, and the workload gradually brought me to the point of mental and physical exhaustion. Church planting is difficult work, and I have a hearty respect for those called to devote themselves to it.

When the theological issues with the REC became too great, Horton and I both departed. We were a bit bruised and burned out, but certainly much wiser. On the one hand, it was clear that a church plant could never succeed without great enthusiasm and effort from the church's initial core group. It was also clear that a church plant could never succeed based solely upon the enthusiasm of its initial core group. There is much more to church planting than enthusiasm. St. Luke's never had the funds it needed. Survival was a constant struggle, and this slowly ate away at the soul of the church. While the REC's hands-off approach had certain benefits—there was no meddling or red tape—we never really did know what we were doing, and we never did get any help. Eventually, we burned out and became embittered. This is the sad fate of many church planters, and those who desire to plant a church need to realize from the beginning that this will likely happen if they jump in and plant a church without sufficient planning and preparation.

Twelve years later (after the *White Horse Inn* went on the air), the church-planting issue resurfaced. I had transferred my membership and ordination to the Christian Reformed Church (CRC). My family and I were attending a local CRC, and a number of people eventually joined that church through the influence of the *White Horse Inn*. But the longtime members of that church had great trouble identifying with the needs of all of these ex-evangelicals converting to Reformed theology. These new converts were extremely zealous for the same doctrines with which these CRC old-timers had become increasingly uncomfortable. The sad fact is the members of this church were not interested in adding these Reformed "zealots" to their church. Over time, it became painfully clear that we needed to find another church that could accommodate all of these recent converts and help meet their specific pastoral and catechetical needs.

The defining moment came on Easter evening of 1996. Dr. Robert Strimple of Westminster Seminary California was our guest on the *White Horse Inn*. Before the broadcast, when Horton and I explained the difficulty we were having in accommodating all these new families and recent converts to Reformed theology, Dr. Strimple looked at us and, without missing a beat, exhorted us, "These are Christ's lambs. You men must feed them." With that, both Horton and I made eye contact, and, without saying a word, we instantly knew that we would be planting another church. But this time, the new church would not be St. Luke's revisited. Neither of us was willing to do that again.

To make a long story short, we approached the Christian Reformed Church about planting a new church in the North Orange County area. Our vision for the new church was based squarely upon the distinctives that we had long since identified as things we would want to see in a new church—redemptive-historical preaching, utilization of the historic Reformed liturgy, weekly communion, and stress upon adult education and catechism. Initially, our plea fell upon deaf ears since at the time the CRC was heavily invested in the church-planting methods of Rick Warren and Bill Hybels. But we persisted, and the local CRC officials responsible for church planting graciously gave us an audience.

After a long and rather tense meeting over principled differences about church-planting methods, the CRC decided to support the new work. They issued us a sizeable check, assigned an overseeing church to the effort, and gave us their blessings. Christ Reformed Church opened in a rented Lutheran church building on Reformation Sunday, 1996. For two years we were the fastest-growing church plant in the CRC, and we were able to organize (particularize) in just eight months. Despite the growth and quick organization, the CRC wasn't quite sure what to do with us, and in 1998 Christ Reformed Church left with a number of like-minded churches and joined the fledgling United Reformed Churches in North America (URCNA).

The reason this bit of history is important is because people often (and mistakenly) assume that the opening of Christ Reformed Church came about because of the sheer power of radio and the fact that Horton was gaining something of a local following. It is true that these things contributed greatly to the initial success of Christ Reformed Church. But this was not merely a matter of picking a start-up date, renting a facility, opening the doors, and—presto, a bunch of people were ready to join. There were two difficult years of preparation and planning that laid the groundwork for that first service and sustained the initial growth once Christ Reformed opened and began conducting services.

There is one more qualification to keep in mind. The URCNA goes about church planting differently than other Reformed/Presbyterian denominations such as the Orthodox Presbyterian Church (OPC) or the Presbyterian Church in America (PCA).[2] I write as a minister in the URCNA, with all the prejudices and blind spots that entails. What follows are not *the* principles of church planting, but instead suggestions that, if duly considered, may help you to plant a Reformed or Presbyterian church in your community.

The moral to the story is simple: *you need to plan the plant*. First, you must crawl. Then you walk. And only then do you attempt to run. Opening the doors and conducting services without such a plan is often fatal to a new church. I've seen it happen many times. In the initial phases, planning a new church has little to do with things people most often associate with opening a new church, such as renting a facility and scheduling services. These things come at the end of the process, not the beginning. There is much to do first, which, if done properly, will help secure success further down the road.

What follows are some of my thoughts for those interested in planting a Reformed church. I would hope that you would carefully and prayerfully consider them and tweak them as needed. The suggested phases are guidelines, and the timeframe will be different for each prospective church plant.

---

2. The OPC *Book of Church Order*, which can be found in PDF format at http://www.opc.org/BCO/BCO_2005.pdf, discusses mission works in chapter XXIX. The PCA *Book of Church Order*, which can be found at http://www.pcaac.org/BCO.htm, discusses the same in chapter 5.

Phase One: Establishing a Core Group

The first question those who desire to plant a Reformed church must face is the most difficult: "Where do we begin?" The answer is beginning right where you are. If the time has come to seriously consider planting a confessional Reformed church, the first step should be to establish a core group of several individuals and families who would be interested in such a church.

The core group should be small at first and arise out of the common interest and passion of people of like mind in seeing a Reformed church take root. The core group should be self-conscious about this effort (no "bait and switch tactics") and fully aware of the time, energy, and personal sacrifices that will be involved. Be intentional about the purpose of this group from the beginning, as it is meeting because you desire to plant a new church.

The core group should begin meeting informally in someone's home and spend time brainstorming and discussing what kind of church they would like to see planted. This brainstorming should include things like possible denominational affiliation and confessional identity (will the group adopt the Three Forms of Unity and/or the Westminster Standards), the kind of distinctives the church should have, and an honest assessment about whether the core group members are willing to do what it takes to go any further.

Throughout this initial formation period, the core group should seek to identify and then invite people who might be interested and who share similar concerns to join the core group. Network! Identify people who might be interested and contact them. Carefully evaluate the amount of interest there is in a new church. If a new church isn't viable, then you have an answer to prayer.

From the first meeting, the core group must begin to seek God's will through prayer and through establishing some initial benchmarks that will indicate whether the dream will become a reality. These include a timeframe ("we'll give this six months"), concrete ways to judge progress ("we hope to have a dozen or so people in the core group"), and so on. Meeting these goals will encourage the members and give the church plant momentum. Failing to meet these goals gives you a way to suspend, or even cease, the process while that is still easy to do.

As the core group continues to meet and dream about what it would like to see in a new church, a clear vision should begin to develop. What will the new church be like? Will it be Presbyterian and adhere to the Westminster Standards? Will it be Reformed and embrace the Three Forms of Unity? What will the particular theological emphases of the new church be? What kind of a liturgy will be used? What about things like frequency of the Lord's Supper and the role that catechism and Christian education will play in the life of the church? What about missions and outreach to the community? All of these things ought to be on the agenda and candidly discussed. Don't just assume that everyone in attendance is on the same page. They might not be.

One of the most pressing questions the core group will face early on is who will lead. Will it be someone within the group who naturally rises to fill that role? Is there a pastor or someone with theological training willing to help out? In any case, someone will need to take charge, schedule meetings, handle inquiries, and keep everyone on the same page and moving forward. It is likely that those who lead (and who are involved in the core group) during the initial phases will go on to become some of the new church's first deacons and elders.

Throughout this initial phase, it is vital that all of these matters be discussed thoroughly until the core group reaches a consensus and comes to a clearly defined vision and set of expectations. You can't plant a church if you don't know what kind of church you want. This is vital, and these steps are too often overlooked or assumed. Don't overlook them, and don't assume anything!

Phase Two: Ramping Up

Throughout these initial phases, the core group should be carefully identifying potential new members of the core group as well as those who might be interested in the new church should worship services actually begin. This determination will usually be based upon how involved these people wish to be and how committed they are to the core group's vision. As new faces begin attending core group meetings, there is a sense of excitement and anticipation that also serves as a good benchmark and sign of God's blessing. If, after a period of time, the core group stagnates and shows no growth, then the group ought to consider suspending meetings for a time and trying again later, or even disbanding altogether. It is also vital that the core group not engage in "sheep stealing"—inviting people who are already members of neighboring confessional Reformed or Presbyterian churches.

One way to facilitate the necessary networking is to use social media such as an e-mail group, a blog, or a Facebook page in which information can be disseminated and announcements and updates distributed. It is also helpful for the core group to schedule social activities such as picnics and shared meals. Not only do these activities give the core group opportunities to get further acquainted and build community, but they also serve as great occasions for inviting those who are just checking things out but are not sure about whether they wish to get involved.

A helpful activity for the core group to arrange is field trips to Reformed churches that may be serving as models for the new church plant. Talking about what you want in a church is one thing; seeing it practiced and actually participating in a worship service similar to what you desire is another. We found that spending Saturday night as a group in a hotel and then worshiping together the next morning in a Reformed church like the one we wanted to start got everyone excited about what could actually come to pass. This was a great source of encouragement and served to solidify our group and our resolve to press ahead.

When the core group has shown some growth and established a clear vision, it is time to approach the various NAPARC church bodies with whom the group may wish to affiliate. This can be done by contacting the closest congregation of the particular denomination or federation under consideration or by gleaning information from that denomination's website. This is also a good time in the process to begin arranging for meetings between the core group and representatives of the preferred denominations. These initial contacts and discussions ought to focus on the willingness of those church bodies to plant a church in your area and to provide a church-planting pastor and gives the overseeing denominational church the opportunity to list the resources it can make available to the core group.

But the core group should be very careful about its expectations. The group should not expect that any of these denominations will immediately provide unlimited funding and send a pastor, so that within two months its hoped-for church will be up and running. The core group should expect help from the denomination with which it affiliates, but from the beginning, the core group should set a goal to be as self-sufficient as possible. The reality is that a successful church plant (no matter how much help it receives from the denomination with which it affiliates) will become self-supporting within several years of its opening. A church that does not become financially stable quickly struggles and eventually fails. This is why being self-sufficient should be a goal of the core group from the beginning.

Regarding being self-sufficient, early in the process the core group should openly discuss the finances of church planting. This includes information gathering about the cost of facility rental and of supporting a pastor-church planter, as well as pre-plant expenses like advertising and arranging for travel and lodging for any ongoing denominational contacts. One thing that worked well for us during the planning phase was that we established an escrow account and asked each of the members of the core group to contribute a sizeable amount of money. When we needed funds to advertise, arrange for travel, and other operating expenses, we were able to do so. We also agreed that should the church plant not come to pass, the remaining money would be returned to those who contributed. Again, the grim reality is that planting churches costs money, and establishing and continually enlarging some sort of start-up fund is an absolute necessity. If it is clear that people are unwilling to fund the new church, then viability becomes a real issue and should clearly factor in any decision to proceed to additional steps.

Phase Three: Getting Serious
Once the core group has established a clear vision, sees demonstrable signs of growth and interest in the new work, and is sufficiently organized to manage taking the next steps, it is time to firm up the two most critical decisions the core group will make: denominational affiliation and choosing a church-planting pastor. Assuming that the core group has identified and is already in contact with its preferred denomination, this matter might have already taken care of itself. If it has not established a denominational affiliation, now is the time to solidify such a relationship and make a final decision.

As for a church planter, the core group needs to remember that those ministers most interested in church planting are often recent seminary graduates with little or no pastoral experience. This can be both good and bad for a church plant. Someone new to the ministry is more often willing to make the financial sacrifices that go with church planting, and while he is worthy of his hire (and needs to be supported sufficiently to devote himself to the difficult work of church planting), he will not command a high salary. But since such a man is untried, you face uncertainty about his abilities and how thoroughly he shares the core group's convictions. You may have to rely largely upon the advice and recommendations of the sponsoring denomination about who is available and whom to select.

It is vital that both the core group and the church planter be on the same page and mutually enthusiastic about what might come to pass. The core group should choose someone who is genuinely interested in actualizing the group's vision and who has the gifts and skills to add to its vision and build upon it. How quickly this relationship will develop will largely depend upon the zeal, skills, and availability of the church planter, the support of the sponsoring denomination, and the willingness and ability of the members of the core group to support the new church with their time and, more importantly, their money.

One thing that also needs to be considered at this point is some sort of an advertising campaign that focuses on informing people of like mind in the community that a church plant is being considered and they are invited to be part of the process. This can be done through the local Christian radio station, a local newspaper, and website. Getting the word out to a broader group (beyond the core group and the initial contacts) is very important. Run your group's distinctives and vision up the flagpole for all to see. Invite all those interested to join you. Be clear about your vision (dare I say "sell it"?), and be crystal clear about the kind of church that will be planted. Be careful to attract people of like mind—because they are interested in the core group's vision.

Be intentional in prayer. Ask God to bless the planting efforts and to bring about the things that will allow the new church to open its doors. At this point, you should be getting excited about the possibilities. Such excitement is contagious and will attract others to the new church that may at this point be a bit hesitant. Talk and dream about what can be! This gets people excited.

It is also critical to stay unified in terms of the initial vision. With a small core group this is relatively easy. But as more people join the group or show interest in attending a new church when services actually begin, there will be those who want to change or tweak the original vision. Sinful human nature being what it is, some people will be all too eager to try to impose their vision on the rest of the group. One of the toughest things to do during this phase of planning the plant is to realize that there are some people who would be better off not getting involved. If someone is opposed to infant baptism or wants a style of worship that conflicts with the core group's vision, it is much better (and pastoral) to talk them out of participating. This is hard to do, but it will save everyone much grief over time.

Phase Four: Getting Up and Rolling—Finally!
At last you've come to the point where it is time to investigate potential facilities in which to conduct official services, and even when to think about an opening date. But it will take you a while to get here, and let me remind you again of the importance of the prayer, personal sacrifices, hours of planning, networking, and brainstorming that are required to get you to this point. This is a process that takes months and years, not days and weeks.

Oversight of the church plant will now shift to those whom the denomination has assigned to oversee the work, most often the closest church in that denomination. These contacts will be able to answer questions and help with the many details. From this point forward, various members of the core group will begin to make the transition from core group member to officers in the new church.

With the denomination's approval and oversight, this is the time to begin a weekly in-home meeting in which the focus shifts from planning and preparation to Bible study or to a study of the Reformed confessions and catechisms of the denomination in which the new church will be a member. Visitors and inquirers should be heartily welcomed to these initial Bible studies, especially those people who have expressed interest in the new church but who didn't want to be part of the core group. All those attending should be encouraged to bring their friends and others who might be interested in the new church. It is important that growth and momentum be maintained.

Also, this is the time for the core group to be on the lookout for people with the particular skills needed to plant a church. Be looking for musicians with the requisite skills who will be comfortable with the new church's style of worship. You may want to find a trustworthy realtor who knows the area and who understands the kind of facility your group will need and begin the process of investigating any zoning or administrative restrictions your community places on public assembly. It would also be wise to become acquainted with a lawyer who is familiar with church-related matters to ensure the proper nonprofit state and federal laws and other such regulations are obeyed (including certain details of church bylaws or covenants). Also, keep in mind insurance policies— property, injury, and sexual misconduct as well as any others that may apply in your situation. While these matters are often overlooked, they are quite important and are the concrete signs that the dream is about to become a reality!

Some Final Thoughts

Planting a new church is an extremely difficult but rewarding task. If, in the providence of God, you are privileged to witness your dream become a reality, then God be praised! If, in the providence of God, a new church never forms despite your best efforts and there is simply not enough interest in such a new church, then let God be praised as well. Christ is the Lord of His church, and He has promised to provide for His people. If now is not the time, then maybe that time will come later. Don't give up hope, but do be realistic.

Throughout the years I have had many people approach me about planting a new church, precisely because no confessionally Reformed church exists where they currently live. This is certainly a difficult situation. But I have long since gotten over my reticence to give people an honest assessment about their circumstances. If there is not a confessional church near them, my first question is, "Is it an option for you to move to a city where there is a good church?" I ask this question not as a test of someone's commitment to Reformed Christianity but because, in many cases, this is the best (if not the only) and most realistic option. People think nothing about moving to a locale because of employment concerns or the quality of life or schools. But isn't church attendance and membership at least as important as any of these other concerns? A confessional Reformed Christian will live an impoverished Christian life if he or she is unable to attend a confessional church where the Word is properly preached and the sacraments are properly administered. This should be a priority, and if relocation is possible, it is a good option. But if moving is not an option and church planting is something you desire to do, then it is hoped that this list of suggestions will give you some guidance and direction.

Planting two churches has consumed much of my adult life, but I wouldn't have it any other way. But know what you are getting into and be fully prepared for the difficult but blessed struggle that lies ahead. By all means, get started planning the plant. And trust that God, in His grace, will see your dream through to fruition. That first Sunday the church opens will be one of the most joyous occasions of your life.

PART THREE

The Work of
Planting Churches

CHAPTER NINE

❧

On Being a Church Planter

Daniel R. Hyde

What does it mean to be a church planter of a confessionally Reformed church? How can a seminary student or experienced pastor who is interested in the work of church planting prepare himself to be a church planter? As one who is a church planter and has been since before I graduated from seminary in 2000, I can say that there is not much literature from a confessionally Reformed persuasion offering guidance for church planters. Instead, Reformed church planters like me have too often been left to sift through the haystacks for the needle of applicable truth in the modern church growth movement's literature,[1] in Pentecostal church-planting material,[2] or in information from the emerging-church movement, such as the Acts 29 Network.[3]

Originally appeared in *Mid-America Journal of Theology* 20 (2009): 159–75, and is reprinted with permission.

1. For examples see G. A. Pritchard, *Willow Creek Seeker Services: Evaluating a New Way of Doing Church* (Grand Rapids: Baker, 1996); Nelson Searcy and Kerrick Thomas, *Launch: Starting a New Church from Scratch* (Ventura, Calif.: Regal, 2006); and Rick Warren, *The Purpose-Driven Church: Growth without Compromising Your Message and Mission* (Grand Rapids: Zondervan, 1995).

2. For examples see C. Peter Wagner, *Strategies for Church Growth: Tools for Effective Mission and Evangelism* (Ventura, Calif.: Regal, 1987); Elmer L. Towns, C. Peter Wagner, and Thom S. Rainer, *The Everychurch Guide to Growth: How Any Plateaued Church Can Grow* (Nashville: Broadman, 1998), and C. Peter Wagner, *Church Growth and the Whole Gospel: A Biblical Mandate* (Eugene, Ore.: Wipf & Stock, 1998).

3. For examples see Ed Stetzer, *Planting Missional Churches: Planting a Church That's Biblically Sound and Reaching People in Culture* (Nashville: Broadman, 2006); Ed Stetzer and David Putman, *Breaking the Missional Code: Your Church Can Become a Missionary in Your Community* (Nashville: Broadman, 2006); or the Acts 29 Network website, which is "a network of pastors from around the nation and world whose dream is to help qualified leaders called by God to plant new churches and replant declining churches" (http://www.acts29network.org/).

During my time as a church planter, I have benefited most from read-ing and applying the Word of God in my context and using the Reformed confessions and classic Reformed theological principles—all in concert with other experienced Reformed ministers and church planters in brainstorming sessions. In the past several years, though, several helpful materials have been published. In 1999 Westminster Seminary Califor-nia held its second biennial missions conference on the theme of church planting at home and abroad.[4] In 2002 the Orthodox Presbyterian Church (OPC) published a manual entitled *Planting an Orthodox Presbyterian Church*.[5] Finally, four lectures from Mid-America Reformed Seminary's 2008 church-planting workshop were published in that year's issue of *Mid-America Journal of Theology*.[6] These resources have made a small beginning of remedying this situation for the confessionally Reformed church planter.

We are living in an exciting time when even the American media rec-ognizes the interest in and spread of what it calls the "New Calvinism,"[7] so as seminaries and churches, we need to equip our potential church planters to minister. We must "[redeem] the time" (Eph. 5:16). My pur-pose in this article, then, is to give those who seek to minister as church planters in confessionally Reformed churches as well as the churches that will call these men to that ministry some practical material that will encourage a passion for spreading the Reformed faith in our generation. As a result, what I say will not be merely a discussion of the principles of

---

4. The eighteen audio lectures are available from Westminster Seminary California: http://wscal.edu/.

5. The Committee on Home Missions and Church Extension of the Orthodox Pres-byterian Church, "Planting an Orthodox Presbyterian Church," Orthodox Presbyterian Church, accessed April 3, 2009, http://www.opc.org/chm/chplant/planting.pdf. Cf. *Manual for Presbytery/CHMCE Partnership*, 2nd ed. (Willow Grove, Pa.: The Committee on Home Missions and Church Extension of the Orthodox Presbyterian Church, 1997), accessed April 3, 2009, http://www.opc.org/chm/HM_Manual_97.pdf.

6. The two lectures given by Paul Murphy have been reprinted in this book as chap-ters 6 and 7, "Heart Preparation in Church Planting" and "Church Planting: A Covenantal and Organic Approach." See also Phil Grotenhuis, "Session Two: The Romance and the Reality," *Mid-America Journal of Theology* 19 (2008): 233–41; Phil Grotenhuis, "Session Three: Extreme Makeover—A Kingdom Approach to Mission," *Mid-America Journal of Theology* 19 (2008): 243–50.

7. David Van Biema, "10 Ideas Changing the World Right Now: The New Calvinism," *Time* 173:11 (March 23, 2009): 50; cf. Collin Hansen, *Young, Restless, Reformed: A Journalist's Journey with the New Calvinists* (Wheaton, Ill.: Crossway, 2008).

church planting but how those principles should be applied to the practices of the person and character of the confessionally Reformed church planter. The necessity of such an approach is found in the fact that our theology is practical, as William Ames (1576–1633) observed: "Theology is the doctrine or teaching of living to God."[8] It is also necessary because church planting is extremely difficult and trying work physically, emotionally, mentally, and spiritually.[9]

Foundational Principles

To begin, I will first address what the necessary foundational principles for a church planter are. These principles are foundational in that they are the beginning ideas, presuppositions, and commitments that a church planter must be committed to in doing the work of church planting and that lay the groundwork for everything else a church planter does in his ministry.

These foundational principles are found in texts such as Acts 2:42: "And they continued steadfastly in the apostles' doctrine and fellowship, in the breaking of bread, and in prayers." Frances Turretin (1623–1687) emphasized the importance of Acts 2:42 as a programmatic text for the life of the new covenant church, explaining that this text gives us three particular things for the foundation of the church.[10] In his commentary on this text, John Calvin (1509–1564) also spoke of the foundational principles it establishes: "Luke is recording those things which constitute the form of the church visible to the public eye. Indeed, he defines four marks by which the true and genuine appearance of the Church may be distinguished. Do we seek the true Church of Christ? The picture of it is here lively painted to the life."[11]

---

8. William Ames, *The Marrow of Theology,* trans. John Dykstra Eusen (1968; repr., Grand Rapids: Baker, 1997), 77.

9. For a practical article on this topic see Grotenhuis, "Session Two: The Romance and the Reality," 233–41.

10. Francesco Turrettino, *Institutio Theologiae Elencticae* (Genevae: Samuelem de Tournes, 1690), 3:100. For the English text see Francis Turretin, *Institutes of Elenctic Theology,* trans. George Musgrave Giger, ed. James T. Dennison, Jr. (Phillipsburg, N.J.: P&R, 1997), 3:89.

11. *Calvin's New Testament Commentaries,* eds. David W. Torrance and Thomas F. Torrance, trans. John W. Fraser and W. J. G. McDonald, *The Acts of the Apostles, Vol. 1* (1965; repr., Grand Rapids: Eerdmans, 1982), 6:85; cf. *Institutes of the Christian Religion,* ed. John T. McNeill, trans. Ford Lewis Battles (Philadelphia: The Westminster Press, 1960), 4.17.44.

We see that the church is firmly based upon three principles: it is a theological, liturgical, and communal institution and organism. Luke's words are not only a historical description of what the earliest New Covenant community was like, but they also apply to many areas of what we do as church-planting pastors. For example, our corporate worship is based on these principles, as it is to be doctrinal, liturgical, and communal. Our Christian life is found in these principles as well as we devote ourselves to theology, liturgy, and community. Finally, our purpose in membership classes is to initiate new believers and new members in these three principles.[12] As those who may be sent out as church planters in areas with no confessionally Reformed churches, we must keep these three principles always before us as the first things, the foundational principles of our life and ministry.

The Church Planter Must Be Devoted to Theology
As Luke records in Acts 2:42, the church planter must be devoted to "the apostles' teaching," that is, their doctrine or theology. As such, he confesses all that is taught in the Word of God: "We believe that these Holy Scriptures fully contain the will of God, and that whatsoever man ought to believe unto salvation, is sufficiently taught therein" (BC, art. 7).[13] The Reformed church planter does not confess the teaching of the Word of God as if he were on an island, according to his "private interpretation" (2 Peter 1:20). He confesses the Word of God according to the Spirit of the ascended Christ's leading of the church into all truth (John 14:26; 15:26). While the church planter is starting something new in a church plant, what he starts is not new. This is why he needs a deep-rooted appreciation for the catholicity of "the faith which was once for all delivered to the saints" (Jude 3), as expressed in the ancient church's ecumenical creeds. This is why church planters must be absolutely convinced and confident in the Reformed confessions and catechisms—because they agree with the Word of God.[14] The Reformed church planter promises in the Form

---

12. For example, see how I relate this text to catechizing new members in "Teaching Membership Classes," *Ordained Servant* 14:1 (March 2005): 11–14. For a full new members' course, see Daniel R. Hyde, *The Good Confession: An Exploration of the Christian Faith* (Eugene, Ore.: Wipf & Stock, 2006).

13. *The Creeds of Christendom*, 3:387–88.

14. For a standard discussion of confessional subscription see *The Practice of Confessional Subscription*, ed. David W. Hall (Oak Ridge, Tenn.: The Covenant Foundation, 1997), especially W. Robert Godfrey, "Subscription in the Dutch Reformed Tradition," 67–75.

of Subscription from the Synod of Dort: "We, the undersigned, Ministers of the Gospel...do hereby, sincerely and in good conscience before the Lord, declare by this our subscription that we heartily believe and are persuaded that all the articles and points of doctrine contained in the Belgic Confession and Heidelberg Catechism of the Reformed Churches, together with the explanation of some points of the aforesaid doctrine made by the National Synod of Dordrecht, 1618–19, do fully agree with the Word of God."[15]

One of the things a young church planter will learn and experience is that everything is theological, and theology gives stability to everything. An example of this truth occurred on a Lord's Day evening early in my ministry. The evening service was finished, and I had returned home only to be greeted by four phone calls within five minutes telling me that four of my parishioners had gone into the hospital. Needless to say, this news was overwhelming, causing mental as well as physical stress.

The only thing that gave me confidence—and sanity—was that I was rooted in the Reformed doctrine of God's fatherly providence. The Heidelberg Catechism beautifully expresses this doctrine in its exposition of the first article of the Apostles' Creed: "I believe in God the Father Almighty, Maker of Heaven and Earth." The answer is that "the eternal Father of our Lord Jesus Christ" not only created everything "of nothing" but also "upholds and governs the same by His eternal counsel and providence." Because of this, "I so trust as to have no doubt that...whatever evil He sends upon me in this vale of tears, He will turn to my good; for He is able to do it, being Almighty God, and willing also, being a faithful Father" (HC, Q&A 26). The Catechism goes on to teach about the providence of God, which is His "almighty and every where present power..., whereby, as it were by His hand, He still upholds heaven and earth, with all creatures" and that therefore "all things, come not by chance, but by His fatherly hand" (HC, Q&A 27). The benefits of knowing this are three: "That we may be patient in adversity, thankful in prosperity, and for what is future have good confidence in our faithful God and Father that no creature shall separate us from His love, since all creatures are so in His hand that without His will they can not so much as move"

---

15. This is the Form of Subscription used in the United Reformed Churches in North America, which may be found at www.urcna.org. Cf. *Psalter Hymnal* (Grand Rapids: Board of Publications of the Christian Reformed Church, 1976), 117; and *The Practice of Confessional Subscription*, 69.

(HC, Q&A 28).[16] God used these questions and answers to impress upon me that even in my anxiety as a young church planter I was coram Deo, before the face of my almighty God and Father, and I was so not only in theory but in reality as well.

The church planter's devotion to the theology of the apostles is also applied in preaching. A church planter must view himself as God views him as a minister. He should meditate on the prevalence of the metaphor of the prophetic herald in Scripture (e.g., Isa. 40; 2 Tim. 4) and what that means for him as a pastor. The prophetic pastor is to stand as a voice in the wilderness and a herald on the mountaintop and earnestly speak this gospel, this good news, to the worst of sinners.[17] Church planters need to recapture that consciousness as they go out to minister in a post-everything world. We are prophets who proclaim a message of law and gospel to the world around us—a law that no one can obey (Rom. 8:7–8) and a gospel that no one is willing to believe (Ps. 2:1–3; Rom. 8:5–8; 1 Cor. 2:14). The church planter is to minister the *message* of Christ according to the *method* of Christ.

This means that the message must be conveyed in the way God has instituted. What we must realize is that God has not called us ministers for nothing. We are ministers of the Word, *His* Word. The ministry is no place for ingenuity. We are not to create new measures—relevant, visual, and experiential methods of "translating" the gospel to a modern culture. Many churches in America believe the gospel can be communicated well through drama and skateboard exhibitions or by having a large playground for children on the church's "campus." Yet the New Testament is clear that this is contrary to the way of the Word. We are called to speak what Christ says in the way Christ says to speak it! The message and method are inseparably intertwined.[18] The method of Scripture is oral, verbal proclamation, for "faith comes by hearing, and hearing by the word of God" (Rom. 10:17). This proclamation of the glorious gospel has a multi-faceted vocabulary in 1 Timothy: "charge" (1:3); "instruct" (4:6); "command" (4:11; 6:17); "teach" (4:11, 6:2); "reading" (4:13); "exhortation" (4:13); "doctrine" (4:13, 5:17, 6:1); "word" (ESV) or "preaching" (5:17);

---

16. Schaff, *Creeds*, 3:316–17.

17. See John Angell James, *An Earnest Ministry* (1847; repr., Edinburgh: Banner of Truth, 1993).

18. See Michael Horton, "Is Style Neutral?" *Modern Reformation* 5, 1 (Jan/Feb 1996): 5–10.

"exhort" (6:2). We are called to use our God-given abilities to bring the Word of the gospel to a world that needs to *hear*.[19]

Church planters especially must have a sense of urgency in preaching for many reasons, including the possibility that no one may show up next week! A church planter is, as Paul called Timothy, an "evangelist" (2 Tim. 4:5), one who spreads the evangel, the gospel. As a church planter I have preached to a congregation of ten people, and it was depressing to see so few in attendance. But I was still called to preach the gospel to those ten as if they were the last ten souls on earth. Richard Baxter (1615–1691) said, "I preached, as never sure to preach again, and as a dying man to dying men." A church planter will be an evangelist, announcing the news of the King and His kingdom. A church planter will be a missionary, going someplace near or far with the mission and purpose of speaking the Word. A church planter will be a pioneer, trailblazing a path for the coming of Christ's kingdom of grace among the kingdom of Satan, who is "the god of this age" (2 Cor. 4:4). A church planter does not start a social club or try merely to draw a crowd; instead, what he does is theological, confronting "this present evil age" (Gal. 1:4). This last point is important to remember, given how a-theological the church in our culture has become. The temptation is to tone it down to attract people, and you will be tempted and you will give in, at least in your thoughts if not in your actions. While this strategy may attract tourists, it will not attract those "the Father is seeking…to worship Him" (John 4:23).[20]

If a Reformed church planter is not committed to a Reformed view of preaching, he will be tempted to capitulate on all sides. On one side he will be tempted to make the church look like the culture. On another side he will be tempted to replace preaching with high church liturgy. On yet another side he will be tempted to give in to the sinful desires of himself and his people.

---

19. See Daniel R. Hyde, "The Principle and Practice of Preaching in the Heidelberg Catechism," *Puritan Reformed Journal* 1, 1 (January 2009): 97–117; "Portrait of a Pastor," *Covenanter Review* 16, 2 (Fall 2007): 5–12.

20. This language of "tourists" and "seekers" comes from Michael S. Horton, "Seekers or Tourists? Or the Difference between Pilgrimage and Vacation," *Modern Reformation* 10, 4 (July/August 2001): 12–18; cf. "How the Kingdom Comes," *Christianity Today* 50, 1 (January 2006): 42.

The Church Planter Must Be Devoted to Liturgy
The church planter must also be devoted to liturgy, that is, the public services of the people of God. This is what Luke called "the breaking of [the] bread and the prayers" in Acts 2:42.[21] A church planter must be devoted to the public worship of the triune God and pass that devotion on to his young parish. As one who is presumably beginning a Reformed congregation in an area where there is not another, this devotion must be palpable. What does a devotion to liturgy look like?

First, from the outset of a church plant, make it a non-negotiable principle to emphasize Lord's Day worship. This is who we are as Christians, and this is what we do. We are called to ascend the heavenly mountain of God so that we can fall before His throne in confession and be welcomed around the table of the Lord in thanksgiving as we receive His grace (Ps. 24; Heb. 12:18–25). This "rest one day" and "work six days" pattern needs to be a pattern of a church planter's life as well as the life of his congregation. Just as they downplay theology, the surrounding churches and culture will downplay Sunday as the Lord's Day, and many churches near the confessionally Reformed church plant will have services on Saturday night as an alternative. The sabbatical pattern will certainly not be attractive to the culture. Once the church planter is committed to this, though, and the congregation follows his lead, then he ought to add a midweek Bible study or activity for members and their children.[22]

Second, let me give a strong exhortation to the presumptive Reformed church planter to be confident in Reformed worship. Not only is Reformed theology different to most people who come to our churches, but our worship is strikingly different as well. The reason it is different is our theology. Our worship is a result of our theology, not in spite of our theology.[23] The content of our theology drives both the content and form of worship, and these cannot be divorced.[24] We worship the way we wor-

---

21. For some practical advice on liturgy in the church plant, see *POPC*, 42.

22. On the Lord's Day see John Owen, "Concerning a Sacred Day of Rest," *An Exposition of the Epistle to the Hebrews*, ed. W. H. Goold (1855; repr., Grand Rapids: Baker, 1980), 2:265–546; R. Scott Clark, "Whatever Happened to the Second Service?" in *Recovering the Reformed Confession: Our Theology, Piety, and Practice* (Phillipsburg, N.J.: P&R, 2008), 293–342.

23. Cf. Daniel R. Hyde, "Liturgy as Catechism," *The Journal of the Church Music National Conference* (2005): 17–20. For a principled and practical explanation of Reformed worship for those new to it, see Daniel R. Hyde, *What to Expect in Reformed Worship: A Visitors' Guide* (Eugene, Ore.: Wipf & Stock, 2007).

24. See Michael Horton, "Is Style Neutral?," 5–10.

ship because we believe the way we believe—not vice versa. Pastorally speaking, this means that the church planter needs to be patient with non-Reformed evangelical Christians who are not used to our worship. Work with them. Meet with them. Talk to them. Train your congregation through a catechism or midweek class or through writing to know what they do and why they do it in worship and to be patient with those who do not understand.[25]

Third, the study of the history of Christian worship and the forms of historic worship needs to be a favorite subject for church planters today. I would encourage those interested in church planting to study worship by devoting themselves to the writings of contemporary scholars such as Hughes Oliphant Old as well as the Reformers. My studies have revealed that we as a Reformed people have always been a self-consciously liturgical people, in the past more than we are today.[26] The churches of the Reformation had common worship, meaning they used set liturgies, forms, and prayers. When I have used these historic forms of worship in my setting, I have been amazed to see that we have drawn the same people that the emerging church movement is seeking to draw. Those young twenty-somethings who yearn for community, transcendence, and stability are drawn—not repelled—by liturgical worship. A recent article in *The Christian Science Monitor* that describes why European women are converting to Islam serves as an illustration of the power of history, transcendence, and structure on our postmodern culture. These women are leaving behind their nominal "Christianity" for Islam's transcendent worship, structured prayers, and rigorous life of morality. As one convert said, "Islam demands a closeness to God. Islam is simpler, more rigorous, and it's easier because it is explicit. I was looking for a framework;

---

25. For an example of short, basic articles on key aspects of Reformed worship that I wrote for my congregation, see Daniel R. Hyde, "What Is Reformed Worship? (I): It Is Biblical," *The Outlook* 57, 5 (May 2007): 5–9; "What Is Reformed Worship? (II): It Is Historical," *The Outlook* 57, 6 (June 2007): 6–9; "What Is Reformed Worship? (III): It Is Covenantal," *The Outlook* 57, 7 (July/August 2007): 5–9; "What Is Reformed Worship? (IV): It Is Evangelical," *The Outlook* 57, 8 (September 2007): 4–7; "What Is Reformed Worship? (V): It Is Reverential," *The Outlook* 57, 9 (October 2007): 5–8; "What Is Reformed Worship? (VI): It Is Joyful," *The Outlook* 57, 10 (November 2007): 5–8; "What Is Reformed Worship? (VII): It Is Liturgical," *The Outlook* 57, 11 (December 2007): 6–9.

26. For a discussion of one aspect of historic Reformed worship in the area of the evangelical feast days (i.e., church calendar), see Daniel R. Hyde, "Lutheran Puritanism? *Adiaphora* in Lutheran Orthodoxy and Possible Commonalities in Reformed Orthodoxy," *American Theological Inquiry* 2, 1 (January 2009): 61–83.

man needs rules and behavior to follow. Christianity did not give me the same reference points." A Muslim scholar reflected on why women are converting: "A lot of women are reacting to the moral uncertainties of Western society.... They like the sense of belonging and caring and sharing that Islam offers."[27]

The Church Planter Must Be Devoted to Community

The third principle is that the church planter must be devoted to the community of the church-plant parish. Luke tells us in Acts 2:42 that the early church was "devoted" and steadfast in their love of "the fellowship"; likewise, the church planter must be committed to his church community. This means that church planters must be tireless in visiting their parishioners and getting to know them, counseling and catechizing them to turn from the world's ways to the Word's ways, and living among them in their highs and lows. As Reformed people, we are intimately acquainted with the idea of family or home visitation as the elders' annual duty, and church planters must make that practice their own.[28] As shepherds, church planters must know their sheep by name intimately, just as our Chief Shepherd does (John 10:3). The OPC's church-planting manual points out, "You must know who they are and where they are both physically and spiritually. Know what they do for a living and the location of their workplaces. Know the condition of their marriages and their family relationships. Know what provokes them and what encourages them. Know the needs of the little ones and the elderly ones in the church."[29] As teachers, church planters must be tireless in going "house to house" (*kat'oikous*; Acts 20:20). There are no elders to assist; the church

---

27. Peter Ford, "Why European Women are Turning to Islam," *The Christian Science Monitor*, December 27, 2005, accessed April 2, 2009, http://www.csmonitor.com/2005/1227/p01s04-woeu.html.

28. The Church Order of the Synod of Dort says, "The office of elder is...to conduct family visiting for the edification of the congregation insofar as this can be done before and after the Lord's Supper, especially to comfort the members of the congregation, to teach, and also to exhort others to profess the Christian religion" (art. 23) (P. Biesterveld and H. H. Kuyper, *Ecclesiastical Manual Including Decisions of the Netherlands Synods and Other Significant Matters Relating to the Government of the Churches*, trans. Richard R. De Ridder [Grand Rapids: Richard R. De Ridder, 1982], 165). Cf. Idzerd Van Dellen and Martin Monsma, *The Church Order Commentary* (1941; repr., Wyoming, Mich.: Credo Books, 2003), 108–111; Peter Y. De Jong, *Taking Heed to the Flock: A Study of the Principles and Practice of Family Visitation* (Grand Rapids: Baker, 1948).

29. *POPC*, 37; cf. 38.

planter is preacher, teacher, spiritual counselor, and functioning elder. Visiting the members of a church plant regularly—several times a year—is a means of instruction and an opportunity for prayer for particular and congregational needs. It builds the trust and openness needed in a shepherd-sheep relationship.

Another way we see the community of the saints illustrated in the New Testament is through the hospitality of the saints. Paul exhorts the brethren to be "given to hospitality" (Rom. 12:13). Among the apostle's many exhortations in Romans 12, none may be more powerful for the life of the Christian and the Christian's local church. It is one thing for Paul to say "be kindly affectionate to one another with brotherly love" (Rom. 12:10) but quite another to say "[be] given to hospitality." The former is an attitude while the latter is an action; the first is a creed, and the second is a deed. Hospitality is love in action. It is Paul's way of saying what James says: "I will show you my faith by my works" (James 2:18). Hospitality shows love, breaking down walls and opening the way of fellowship. It says to its recipient, "You are welcome here; I am privileged to have *you* in my home, at my table." It does this because the New Testament word translated "hospitality" is *philoxenia*—the love of strangers. Church planters need to set the example of hospitality by being hospitable to their parish as well as to their neighbors. Regarding those who are saved, Peter exhorted the body of Christ, "Be hospitable to one another *without grumbling*" (1 Peter 4:9, emphasis added). Regarding those who are strangers, Hebrews exhorts us: "Do not forget to entertain strangers, for by so doing some have unwittingly entertained angels" (13:2). By extending hospitality, church planters will live transparent lives in community with their parishioners and will build community, trust, and a godly atmosphere in which to labor and pray.[30] When you invite members, visitors, and neighbors to your home, you will be surprised to learn how few people have ever been invited to a pastor's home. This is a powerful way of showing that you are not untouchable in your ivory tower, but rather you care for souls and desire to be open to them.

These three points are an extended way of saying that the confessionally Reformed church planter must be the most convicted and principled

---

30. For two excellent books on this and similar themes, see Mary Beeke with Joel Beeke, *The Law of Kindness: Serving with Heart and Hands* (Grand Rapids: Reformation Heritage, 2007) and Marva J. Dawn, *Truly the Community: Romans 12 and How to Be the Church* (Grand Rapids: Eerdmans, 1992).

man among our churches. He must be as one out there virtually on his own with temptations at every corner. He must be devoted to his biblical and confessional theology, to his biblical and historic liturgy, and to his church and broader community. He is not a man who will represent his Lord and King if, time after time, he gives in to religious and social pressure, let alone the persecution of those with whom he speaks such serious words.

Aptitude Principles

Along with the three foundational principles that shape who the church planter must be, the church planter must have certain aptitudes—that is, certain skills, gifts, and personality traits. Recall that Paul exhorted young Pastor Timothy to lay before the congregation those men who not only desired to be overseers but also who were "able to teach" (*didaktikon*; 1 Tim. 3:2). He said this in his second epistle to Timothy as well: "And a servant of the Lord must not quarrel but be gentle to all, able to teach" (*didaktikon*; 2 Tim. 2:24). The overseer-minister must not only have the desire to teach the Word, but he must also have the ability to apply that Word to his hearers. The distinction is between knowledge and wisdom. Whereas knowledge is mastery of content, wisdom is the skillful application of that content. We might say that wisdom in the area of teaching is mastery of content. What follows are several aptitudes that a church planter must have.

Passion for Planting (Rom. 10:1)

A church planter must have a passion to be in the church-planting ministry. This means that he must be passionate about spreading the gospel of Jesus Christ to areas where it is not prominent. The church planter must understand that he is a prophet, bringing a foreign, yet needed, message to the world. The OPC church-planting manual explains that he must be "so intensely gripped with the significance of the doctrine of the church that, at the bidding of his presbytery, he is willing to move to a place where he is needed."[31] From the vantage point of Reformation history, the church planter must have the evangelistic and church-planting fervor of our Reformed forefathers, including John Calvin.[32] It was the example

---

31. *POPC*, 35.
32. On the mission emphasis of John Calvin see G. Baez-Camargo, "The Earliest Protestant Missionary Venture in Latin America," *Church History* 21, 2 (1952): 135–45; R. Pierce

of Geneva that led to the modern missions movement, under the leadership of pioneers like David Brainerd (1718–1747) among the American Indians; William Carey (1761–1834) in India; Henry Martyn (1781–1812) in India and Persia; Adonirum Judson (1788–1850) in Burma; John Patton (1824–1907) in the New Hebrides; and Jonathan Goforth (1859–1936) in China.[33] After chronicling the state of the nations in his day, William Carey asserted, "All these things are loud calls to Christians, and especially to ministers, to exert themselves to the utmost in their several spheres of action, and to try to enlarge them as much as possible."[34]

The church planter's passion must be evidenced in fervent prayer that non-believers would come into contact with his church members as well as visit church services and be converted by the Holy Spirit. He must pray passionately that evangelicals who wallow in works-righteousness

---

Beaver, "The Genevan Mission to Brazil" in *The Heritage of John Calvin*, ed. John Bratt (Grand Rapids: Eerdmans, 1973), 55–73; Joel R. Beeke, "Calvin's Evangelism," in *Living for God's Glory: An Introduction to Calvinism* (Orlando, Fla.: Reformation Trust, 2008), 275–88; Keith Coleman, "Calvin and Missions," *Western Reformed Seminary Journal* 16, 1 (February 2009): 28–33, accessed April 2, 2009, http://www.wrs.edu/Materials_for_Web_Site/Journals/16-1_Feb-2009/Coleman—Calvin_Missions.pdf; Amy Glassner Gordon, "The First Protestant Missionary Effort: Why Did It Fail?" International Bulletin of Missionary Research 8, 1 (1984): 12–18; Frank A. James III, "Calvin the Evangelist," *Reformed Quarterly* 19, 2 (Fall 2001), accessed April 2, 2009, http://rq.rts.edu/fall01/james.html; W. Stanford Reid, "Calvin's Geneva: A Missionary Centre," *Reformed Theological Review* 42, 3 (1983): 65–73; Kenneth J. Stewart, "Calvinism and Missions: The Contested Relationship Revisited," *Themelios* 34, 1 (April 2009), accessed April 27, 2009, http://www.thegospelcoalition.org/publications/34-1/calvinism-and-missions-the-contested-relationship-revisited/; James Tanis, "Reformed Pietism and Protestant Missions," *Harvard Theological Review* 67 (1974): 65–73; Samuel M. Zwemer, "Calvinism and the Missionary Enterprise," *Theology Today* 7, 2 (1950): 206–221.

33. John Thornbury, *David Brainerd: Pioneer Missionary to the American Indians* (Darlington, England: Evangelical Press, 1996); Vishal and Ruth Mangalwadi, *The Legacy of William Carey: A Model for the Transformation of a Culture* (Wheaton, Ill.: Crossway Books, 1999); David Bentley-Taylor, *My Love Must Wait: The Story of Henry Martyn* (Downers Grove, Ill.: InterVarsity, 1975); Courtney Anderson, *To the Golden Shore: The Life of Adoniram Judson* (Valley Forge, Pa.: Judson Press, 1987); John G. Paton, *Missionary to the New Hebrides, An Autobiography Edited by His Brother* (1889; repr., Edinburgh: Banner of Truth, 1965); Rosalind Goforth, *Goforth of China* (Grand Rapids: Zondervan, 1937); William Carey, *An Enquiry into the Obligations of Christians to Use Means for the Conversion of the Heathens* (Leicester, England: Ann Ireland, 1792), accessed April 2, 2009, http://www.gutenberg.org/catalog/world/readfile?fk_files=51264&pageno=21.

34. William Carey, *An Enquiry into the Obligations of Christians to Use Means for the Conversion of the Heathens* (Leicester, England: Ann Ireland, 1792), accessed April 2, 2009, http://www.gutenberg.org/catalog/world/readfile?fk_files=51264&pageno=21.

churches would find "the liberty wherewith Christ hath made us free" in his parish (Gal. 5:1 KJV).

This passion must be evidenced in the church planter training and motivating his parishioners to do the work of witnessing as well.[35] Hyper-Calvinists and preachers who are concerned merely with "maintenance ministry," that is, keeping those they already have, must not apply. The OPC's church-planting book gives some excellent advice in this vein:

> Reaching out to the unsaved is not just the responsibility of a pastor or a Christian leader. It is the responsibility of every believer to bear witness to the grace of Jesus Christ. So let your example serve to encourage others to do the same. Make clear to your people that not everyone in the church is called or gifted to be an evangelist, but that is not what this is about. Show them through your example the significance of being salt and light, and stress the importance of faithfulness rather than success.[36]

In light of this necessary passion for evangelism, if you are a candidate for the ministry in a Reformed church, you must not take a call to church planting merely because it is your only option. Further, if you are a seminary graduate and a candidate for the ministry and your desire is to be a pastor in a large, more established congregation or even to be an associate pastor who does a lot of counseling, for example, you must not take a call to be a church planter. In situations where a candidate accepts a church-planting call when he would rather do something else, not only does he end up unhappy but his church—at least what is left of it—is unhappy as well. Being a church planter is not just another job; it is a calling and passion. I say this not as one who is always on fire for church planting. Feelings come and go, but my God-given passion remains the same. We see this in the example of Paul, who told the Romans that his "heart's desire and prayer to God" was for unbelieving Israel to be saved (Rom. 10:1). He reveals his passion for establishing new churches when

---

35. Cf. chapter 6, "Heart Preparation in Church Planting," by Paul Murphy.

36. *POPC*, 41. For some helpful books on witnessing and evangelism from a Reformed perspective, see *Reformed Evangelism: A Manual on Principles and Methods of Evangelization* (Grand Rapids: Baker, 1948); Calvin Knox Cummings and John Murray, *Biblical Evangelism Today: A Symposium* (Philadelphia: The Committee on Christian Education of the Orthodox Presbyterian Church, 1954); R. B. Kuiper, *God Centered Evangelism* (Edinburgh: Banner of Truth, 1966); Will Metzger, *Tell the Truth: The Whole Gospel to the Whole Person by Whole People* (rev. ed., Downers Grove, Ill.: InterVarsity, 2002); Joel R. Beeke, *Puritan Evangelism: A Biblical Approach* (2nd ed., Grand Rapids: Reformation Heritage, 2007).

he says, "I have made it my aim to preach the gospel, not where Christ was named" (Rom. 15:20). His final goal was to pass through Rome and go to Spain, the outmost edge of the Roman Empire and the known Western world (Rom. 15:24). You should not be ashamed if this is not your passion. There are many congregations in which God can use you.

Ability to Be Personable

It is also important for a church planter to be personable. The church planter needs to be able to communicate to all sorts and conditions of people, interacting with unbelievers, visitors to church, and potential new members; getting involved with and recognized in the community; and conducting meetings with church-plant members. The OPC's book on church planting says, "If you do not care deeply for people, if you do not get along well with them generally, and if you find yourself not liking them nearly so much as you like your books and your study, then the work of church planting will not go well for you. Nothing else in Reformed ministry works very well, including preaching, if you do not care deeply for people."[37]

To reach those outside the church, the church planter needs to get out into the community. The community in which a Reformed church plant is begun needs a man who is comfortable spending a lot of social time with people, not one who spends all his time in isolation in his study. The church planter must leave the house and the study. He should study at coffeehouses and small community restaurants. He could join the neighborhood watch—the list of places to go to begin building relationships is extensive. As the story goes, Dr. Cornelius Van Til went to a pub every week in Philadelphia as a means of getting to know people, to answer their questions, and to evangelize them.

In his dealings with those in the church, the church planter should remember the example of the apostle Paul: "I kept back nothing that was helpful, but proclaimed it to you, and taught you publicly and from house to house" (Acts 20:20). We see Paul preaching in traditional settings like the synagogues (Acts 13:5) as well as in untraditional situations such as at Mars Hill, where he preached to philosophers (Acts 17:16–34). He also testified while he was imprisoned (Acts 16:25–34).

This does not mean that church planting is personality driven. Church planters must be known as personable, not as personalities. In his classic

---

37. *POPC*, 37.

work on Reformed liturgy, *Our Worship,* Abraham Kuyper (1837–1920) critiqued what he saw in American Christianity: "Only in America and in some of our own small independent churches is there such a free-reigning spirit. It is quite common in America, especially in the larger cities, for a minister to start his own church, attract whoever will come, and maintain his church from the contributions that come in. Such a church is thus literally an independent business run by the minister, without any confessional forms and without connections to other churches. It is nothing other than a circle gathering around a talented speaker."[38]

This situation exists today, even among those subscribing to New Calvinism. For the confessionally Reformed church planter, though, it is not about personality. As John the Baptist said, "[Jesus Christ] must increase, but I must decrease" (John 3:30).

Ability to Handle Disappointment
Because the church planter will be "starting from scratch," he must not only be passionate about what he is doing but also be able to handle the many disappointments that will come his way.[39] For example, church planters must be able to handle the disappointment of members falling into gross public sin. In the first couple years of my ministry, just as my congregation was being planted and watered and was seeing some stable growth, I came back from vacation twice to learn about serious sin within the church that had come to the surface while I was gone. And those involved were core members who helped to start our church. Was this disappointing? Absolutely. Was this impossible to deal with? Absolutely not in the strength of Christ, although practically it was as difficult as anything I had dealt with to that point in my life.

Another disappointment that the Reformed church planter must handle is the many visitors and seemingly serious inquirers who will never return. Whether they call Reformed services "Catholic"; whether they cannot stand the message of guilt, grace, and gratitude that is preached from the pulpit; or whether they complain that the church is too small for their families' needs, you will be disappointed. In their excellent and encouraging book, *Preaching and Worship in the Small Church,* William

---

38. Abraham Kuyper, *Our Worship,* ed. Harry Boonstra, trans. Harry Boonstra, Henry Baron, Gerrit Sheeres, and Leonard Sweetman (Grand Rapids: Eerdmans, 2009), 6–7.
39. *POPC,* 37.

Willimon and Robert Wilson contrast the mentality of the megachurch Christian world with that of the small church. Some people

> have a gnawing feeling that the small church is somehow second-rate and does not quite measure up to what it ought to be in today's world. Other persons...view the small church as an anachronism, kept alive by stubborn people who are holding on to an institution that should be allowed or even encouraged to die. They see such churches as impediments to the development of the kind of congregation needed today. In the meantime the small congregation continues to exist, doing what it and the Christian Church have always done, albeit imperfectly: winning adherents, nurturing them in the Christian way of life, gathering them each week for worship and preaching, and in many rural communities, finally burying them in the adjacent cemetery, confident that they have successfully run the race and received the reward of the faithful.[40]

If you are called to church planting, you are called to small-church ministry initially, if not for your entire career. In light of this reality, there are two practical ways to deal with disappointment. The first is one of the most important pieces of wisdom I learned from a colleague and friend in the infancy of my ministry. He related to me that when he was church planting he had to learn that he was not the Holy Spirit. I needed to learn that also. This is part of what Paul said to the Corinthians in 1 Corinthians 3:5–7: "Who then is Paul, and who is Apollos, but ministers through whom you believed, as the Lord gave to each one? I planted, Apollos watered, but God gave the increase. So then neither he who plants is anything, nor he who waters, but God who gives the increase."

Church planting is God's work. The church planter is only a servant who sows and waters seeds. As such, he must have a long-term mindset. Week by week people will come and go, but if his eyes are on the goal of planting, watering, and establishing a solid, confessionally Reformed church, he will be able to handle the ups and downs of the work. It is not about the church planter anyway; it is about Christ: "For we do not preach ourselves, but Christ Jesus the Lord" (2 Cor. 4:5).

The second practical means of dealing with the struggles and sadness of disappointment is to develop close relationships with seminary classmates who go out into the ministry with you as well as to find an

---

40. William H. Willimon and Robert L. Wilson, *Preaching and Worship in the Small Church* (Nashville: Abingdon, 1980), 14.

experienced ministerial colleague who is either nearby or is willing to encourage you over the phone. Do not discount human contact and conversation as means the Holy Spirit uses to lift you up "out of a horrible pit" (Ps. 40:2). The church planter must rely on his fathers and brothers in the Lord for counsel: "As iron sharpens iron, so a man sharpens the countenance of his friend" (Prov. 27:17). The church planter must use these brothers as sounding boards when he is feeling down and desperate. Practically, the church planter should make it a habit to call other pastors with whom he is close so that they can hold him accountable, since some church plants do not have mature saints who can help him in this way. These weekly phone calls or meetings should also be for the purpose of encouragement, prayer, and help.

Ability to Be a Self-Motivator
Church planters are pioneers—those who go out to begin a work that no one else has done so that others may follow. One aspect of having a pioneering spirit is to be self-motivating. If you are not a hard worker in your ordinary life as an employee, husband, and father, then do not think you are called to be a church planter—let alone a pastor! If you skidded by in college and seminary, finishing with average work at the last minute, or if you do not work well with a set routine that is often interrupted, you will not be able to handle planting a church. Starting a church plant is not the way to learn self-discipline, and it is not the place for on-the-job training. If you do not have self-motivation and self-discipline, for the church's sake, do not become a church planter! Few will heed the call and be able to meet the challenge of church planting. Others will be needed in the important task of pastoring larger, established congregations that will serve as overseeing and supporting churches of Reformed church planting.

Church planters have to be able to wake up on Monday morning and get back to work, even though Monday is the usual day off for the pastor, his Sabbath rest. He needs to re-energize on Monday morning after preaching two sermons on Sunday so that he can work in his church that may be financially struggling. He must work despite life's challenges, which may include sick children, a throbbing headache, and coping with the death of a dedicated church member. With two sermons to preach, Bible studies to teach, phone calls to make, visitors to follow up with, counseling to do, fellowship to facilitate, meetings to chair, and all the regular responsibilities that most people face, the church planter has no time to spare. In many respects, a church planter is on an island. He has no pastoral staff and does not have the luxury of working in an office where he can take breaks and chat with co-workers. Often, it is just the church planter in his study or on the road doing what needs to be done.[41] Church planters need to have the attitude of the apostle Paul and apply it to church planting: "Forgetting those things which are behind and reaching forward to those things which are ahead, I press toward the goal for the prize of the upward call of God in Christ Jesus" (Phil. 3:13–14).

Ability to Lead by Delegation
Along with being a self-motivator is the ability to lead a church plant by delegation.[42] Yes, the church planter has a lot of regular pastoral work to do, but he also must pay the church's facility rental, call the A/C repairman because it is too hot on Sundays, and take meals to a family that just had their first baby. There is no one else to do these things initially. This is why he must learn to delegate things that are nonessential to his calling to other responsible people in the congregation according to the pattern of the apostles in Acts 6:1–7. As soon as possible, he should organize a steering committee under the oversight of the local consistory that will serve as an advisory council and will take mundane tasks off of his hands. Also, he must find and develop helpful parishioners who may have abilities he does not have to assist with everyday tasks, such as producing bulletins and other printed materials.[43]

Church planters are a "one-man show" in many respects, but they cannot get comfortable being the one man. They are not micromanagers or tyrants, but pastors. Others can do things like change the font of the bulletin, organize snacks and nursery workers, and deal with church

---

41. "The rigors of pastoral ministry are doubled for the organizing pastor.... It will be imperative for you to keep a calendar and operate with a schedule. But being a wise manager of your time also means allowing for interruptions to alter that schedule, since it is not actually your time that you are managing, but the conduct of your ministry. Furthermore, it will be important for you to keep some form of a list of tasks and responsibilities and to incorporate them into the scheduling of your time. And finally, it will be vital for you to learn to distinguish between the things that are urgent and those that are really important as you budget the 168 hours in your ministry week" (*POPC*, 49).

42. Two helpful books on leadership that may be adapted for pastoral use are by John C. Maxwell, *The 21 Indispensable Qualities of a Leader: Becoming a Person Others Will Want to Follow* (Nashville: Thomas Nelson, 1999) and *The 21 Irrefutable Laws of Leadership: Follow Them and People Will Follow You* (1998; rev. ed., Nashville: Thomas Nelson, 2007).

43. *POPC*, 42–43.

banking. Although the church planter may have to do many of these tasks initially, making a commitment to turn things over little by little as God brings people to the congregation is essential for his growth as a pastor and the congregation's growth as servants.

Ability to Handle Stress

Finally, the confessionally Reformed church planter in the twenty-first century *must* be able to handle all the stress of being a pastor, husband, and father, but especially being a church planter. He must learn to be even-keeled, patient, and calm. This is not easy. If he does not have any hobbies, he needs to get one. Listening to classical music—learning about its genres, composers, and history—is a wonderful hobby that relieves stress. Gardening, learning about the mental and psychological development of your children, and even raising a dog can be effective stress relievers as well. With all that the church planter does, he needs to learn to get away from time to time so that he does not lose his mind or lead his church into the ground. Especially, the church planter must pray in times of stress as the Lord has called him to: "casting all your care upon Him, for He cares for you" (1 Peter 5:7).

Conclusion

The confessionally Reformed church planter must have foundational principles concerning theology, liturgy, and community as well as aptitudes such as a passion for church planting, a personality that relates well to others, and an ability to handle disappointment. He must be a self-motivator who leads by delegation and deals well with stress. A prospective church planter either has these qualities, or he does not. Church planting is not a stepping-stone to the bigger church in your denomination.[44] It is a calling. Willimon and Wilson's conclusion to their book on ministry in the small church is applicable to church planting:

> If you measure the success of your ministry by the size of the crowd, the prestige of the church you serve, or the praise of denominational

---

44. Willimon and Wilson address the capitalistic influence in the church that emphasizes that "bigger is better," so that pastors of small churches are viewed as less important than pastors of big churches as well as the notion that a pastor has not "arrived" until he's the senior pastor of a large church. They observe, "If the figures are going up, the congregation and its pastor are presumed to be succeeding. If they are remaining the same or decreasing, something is obviously wrong" (*Preaching and Worship in the Small Church*, 30).

authorities, you are in deep trouble in the small church.... But if you sense that you are called of God—if you know that your ultimate authority and final validation of your ministry come from the faithful service and celebration of the Word and its confrontation by God's people, your servanthood will continue to be blessed. You will have the joy of knowing that you are faithfully proclaiming the Word, and that you are an instrument of God's grace for the people who worship in a church of small membership.[45]

It ought to be a source of great encouragement to us as Reformed church planters that our forefathers pastored small churches. For example, the church John Owen (1616–1683) pastored from 1673 to the end of his life in 1683 began with about forty members. During the last ten years of his ministry, the church received 111 new members.[46] That means John Owen, the Prince of Puritans,[47] the Calvin of England,[48] whose epitaph describes him as "worthy to be enrolled among the first Divines of the age,"[49] pastored a church that grew by eleven souls a year. That is the kind of slow, steady growth that the small church-planting ministry should pray for.

What I have outlined here are only some of the things that we as Reformed churches must begin to consider and discuss if we are going to train and send church planters into our culture. May this outline cause us all to examine ourselves—our principles, our gifts, our abilities, and our personalities—so that our great missionary God may raise up a generation of zealous confessionally Reformed church planters as well as established pastors to go into church planting so that the kingdom of our Lord Jesus Christ may come and that it may be "from shore to shore, till moons shall wax and wane no more!"[50]

---

45. Ibid., 123.

46. Peter Toon, *God's Statesman: The Life and Work of John Owen* (Grand Rapids: Zondervan, 1971), 151, 154–55.

47. Andrew Thomson, *John Owen: Prince of Puritans* (1850; repr., Ross-shire, Great Britain: Christian Focus Publications, 2004).

48. Toon, *God's Statesman*, 173.

49. Ibid., 182.

50. Isaac Watts, "Jesus Shall Reign Where'er the Sun," in *Psalter Hymnal* (Grand Rapids: Board of Publications of the Christian Reformed Church), no. 399.

CHAPTER TEN

∾

Being a Welcoming Church Plant

Kevin Efflandt

There was once a man in his mid-thirties, with a wife and two young children, who were looking for a church where the gospel was faithfully preached and where the Reformed faith was taught. However, he did not want to go to church in a particular town because that town was viewed as closed to and quite suspicious of outsiders, particularly of those who were not of a certain ethnicity. This man, you see, was not only an outsider ethnically but also in the sense that he had not grown up in the Reformed church.

Finally, though, after months and months of trying to find a church and hearing that there was a faithful Reformed church in the town that this man was hoping to avoid, he and his family attended the Reformed church one Sunday morning. As they went, this family—especially the husband and father—was sure that they would not be welcomed. He knew that because his last name was not a certain ethnicity, his family would be viewed as outsiders and ignored.

Much to the family's surprise, however, they soon found out that the things they were so sure of were all misconceptions. The first Sunday they attended the church, one of the elders and his wife invited them over for lunch after the service. The next week, they received a call from one of the members of the church, inviting them over for lunch the following Sunday. And on their third Sunday, they went to the pastor's home for lunch. Even though they weren't from this particular town, and even though they didn't have a last name that was "typical" for this town and this church, the family was welcomed with open arms from the beginning and made to feel right at home.

That's an easy story for me to tell because I was that husband and father. I was converted and spent most of the first thirty-five years of my life in Baptist churches. But when we went to this particular church, in spite of our misgivings and misconceptions, we found a warm, welcoming group of believers and a church for which we had been searching for a long time.

Warm, Welcoming, and Friendly

When we think of the work of church planting, we often ask questions like "What are we going to do to get people in the door?" "What methods of advertising should we use to attract visitors?" But one of the questions that we seldom ask but should is, "What are they going to find when they come here?" Our advertising may get people to check us out, but what good does that do us if we're not prepared to welcome them when they come?

The purpose of this chapter is to orient our thinking toward being a welcoming church. That certainly does not mean that a church should condone or tolerate sin or water down the truth of Scripture. Instead, it means self-consciously being the kind of church that visitors find to be warm and welcoming. Hand in hand with outreach, mission, and evangelism is being prepared to warmly receive people when they visit. Unfortunately, Reformed churches have earned a reputation—deserved or not—of being cold, unwelcoming, and unfriendly. It should be our prayer and hope that what visitors would find at our churches are people who are just the opposite—warm, welcoming, and friendly.

Much of what I will share with you in this chapter comes from my own experience as a church planter and pastor in Bellingham, Washington. The Bellingham congregation has a commitment to be a body of believers that is welcoming to outsiders and to those who are visiting. They are certainly not a perfect church—there are none of those in this life—but they are striving to keep a mission mindset at the forefront of all they do. They also strive to have a mindset that always considers what they could do to make visitors and newcomers feel welcome and at home.

The danger in not doing this is becoming a church that is incredibly inwardly focused. We think of nothing outside of our own group of people and really give no consideration to what visitors might think. And when people do visit, we gather in our cliques after the sermon, never really giving much thought or attention to those who are new.

Again, what needs to be made clear from the outset is this: being a welcoming church does not mean that we cater our worship services to the seeker or unbeliever. Sadly, in our day, we find this in many churches. This is the idea that in order to get new people through the doors, we need to focus on what they want—whether it is the kind of music that they like to hear or the kind of topics that they want teaching on. And not only that, but we also don't ask people for money, and we certainly don't ask them for a commitment. Instead, we want them to feel at home, so our music and our preaching and everything that we do caters to the felt needs that they have.

This approach, however, is contrary to Scripture. The focus of our Lord's Day worship is not the visitor, or "audience." Instead, it is God condescending to meet with His people and spiritually nourish them. Our focus is on the glory of God and the gospel of Jesus Christ. However, that doesn't mean that we should ignore visitors or not make them feel welcome and cared about when they visit our church. But if being a welcoming church doesn't mean catering to every felt need of visitors or gearing our worship and our preaching toward them, then what does it mean? There are six things that we can focus on as church plants that will help our churches to be welcoming to those who are new.

Love One Another

In John 13:35, Jesus said these well-known words, "By this all will know that you are My disciples, if you have love for one another." One of the most powerful ways that we testify to the Lord's work of grace in our lives is by loving our brothers and sisters in Christ. What a wonderful thing it is when visitors come to our churches to see that we actually care for one another, that we rejoice with those who rejoice and weep with those who weep.[1] This kind of love is not something that we can program but must arise out of a heart of gratitude for God's grace. But it begins with the church leadership—with the church planter/pastor, the core group, the leaders of the church plant, and the overseeing elders to tangibly show love to their fellow believers.

Church planters and church-plant leaders must encourage the people of the church plant to love one another authentically. We must encourage them to see the church plant as the family of God—to see the plant as their family. We must care for one another, just like we would care for

---

1. One great teaching of the Westminster Larger Catechism is that of "improving upon" our baptism (Q&A 167). Of the many ways to do so, "walking in brotherly love" is included, which is what hospitality is about.

a member of our family who is hurting in some way. And when visitors come to our church plants and see that kind of love displayed, when they see that the people genuinely love and care for one another, it will have a huge impact on them.

Have Greeters

A church that wants to be a welcoming church must be intentional in having people serve as greeters. Typically, visitors will not walk up to one of the members and ask, "Where can I get a bulletin?" or "Where can I find a Bible?" Instead, they will walk into your building, and, unless they are with a member of your church, they will be somewhat lost. They won't know where the restrooms are or where the nursery is. They won't know where to get a Bible or a bulletin. Some may have no idea what a liturgy is—they may look at the church planter with confusion as he raises his hands and blesses God's assembled people. This requires that you help them, which is not watering down the gospel; it is simply being courteous. If you invited someone to your house for the first time, you would want him to feel welcome and to know where everything is. The same thing should go for those who visit our churches.

Church plants can do several things to make visitors feel welcome. They can have families, couples, or individuals assigned, on a rotating basis, to serve as greeters at worship services. Greeters stand at the door, and, as people come in, they welcome them and shake their hands. Another idea is to have a rotating group of people who serve as "floating greeters." These floating greeters stand in the area where there are Bibles and bulletins, and their sole responsibility is to look for visitors.

Floating greeters approach visitors, introducing themselves and welcoming guests. They might hand newcomers a brief visitor pamphlet that tells them a little about the church. They point visitors to the Bibles and bulletins, as well as the nursery, restrooms, and anything else that they might need. Also, inside the visitor pamphlet, include a little card that the floating greeter can encourage the visitor to fill out and place in the offering bag. The deacons can then give those cards to the pastor so that he can follow up with a note, an email, or phone call later in the week, provided that he was not able to introduce himself personally to the visitor after the service. The Bellingham congregation finds this to be a very helpful way to make visitors feel genuinely welcomed and cared for.

One thing is vital for selecting floating greeters: they must not be grumpy people. You want greeters who exhibit the joy of the Lord and are genuinely warm and welcoming. Rather than asking for people to sign up to be floating greeters, have your council or your steering committee pinpoint four or five key individuals they think would be particularly good at this, and ask those members to serve one Sunday a month.

There is also another aspect to assisting visitors. This spills over into the worship service. It is important to remind the church-plant members that if they see someone who is struggling to find their place in the Bible or who doesn't even have a Bible, they should help him. If he doesn't have a hymnbook, they should get one for him. It's awkward to be a visitor and not know what you're supposed to be doing or where to find the book of Habakkuk. Remember, many visitors to our churches will not know Habakkuk from Hebrews. When my family and I started attending a Reformed church for the first time, there were no hymnbooks where we were sitting. The pastor announced the first song, and at that point, I'm sure we looked like deer in the headlights—completely lost and confused. Thankfully, however, a lady sitting near us must have noticed how lost we looked. She got up, grabbed two hymnbooks from the rack, and handed them to us.

Encourage your congregation to keep their eyes out for those who may need help. For example, I know of a small church that witnessed a young lady sneak in through the back door of the church a few minutes late one Sunday morning. She was clearly not an "insider"; she was wearing black leather and had tattoos and strangely colored hair. A dear old godly man sitting near the back walked over to her, gave her a bulletin and a hymnal, and invited her to sit with him, which she did. That's the courteous welcome we need to offer to all those who worship with us.

Practice Hospitality[2]

In Romans 12:13, the apostle Paul writes that we are to be "given to hospitality." In Hebrews 13:2 we read, "Do not forget to entertain strangers, for by so doing some have unwittingly entertained angels." Perhaps we do not fully know what the word *hospitality* means. It is not referring to the cookies, fruit punch, and coffee that we share in the church plant's fellowship hall or rented gymnasium after the worship service is over.

---

2. See *POPC*, 66.

Hospitality literally means "a love for strangers." One of the things that must characterize the child of God is a love for strangers, for those who are outsiders. And this has a direct correlation to being a welcoming church. As I mentioned in the introduction, one of the things that drew my family to the first Reformed church we joined was the incredible hospitality that was shown to us. Our first three Sundays there, we were in three different homes for lunch. From the beginning, we felt welcome.

We have to recognize the fact that people who visit our churches are not going to know many people. In fact, one of the most awkward things about going to a new church is standing alone after the service, holding a cup of coffee, with no one to talk to. What better way is there to make visitors feel welcome and seek to incorporate them into the life of the church than to have them over for a meal? After all, everyone needs to eat. Most of our morning services end around lunchtime, when our stomachs are starting to growl, so a very nonthreatening way to get to know visitors and to allow them to get to know you is to invite them for a meal.

This can be done in a couple of different ways. One way is to divide everyone in the church into about four or five different groups, each group led by an elder and his wife. These groups then take turns having a potluck meal together after the morning service. An announcement is placed in the bulletin and is also made from the pulpit that after the service a number of people will be staying and sharing a meal together, and visitors (or anyone without a place to go for lunch) are welcome to stay and enjoy a meal with the designated group. This has been effective in encouraging everyone in the church to practice hospitality. However, the sizes of these groups (20–30 people) can be somewhat intimidating to visitors and hard on the hosts.

Another way that we have sought to practice hospitality is to ask for several families to volunteer to host a meal in their home on Sundays after the morning service. Try to get enough volunteers so that each host needs to take a turn only once every other month. Hosts can even partner with another family in the church to ease the workload. We have found this to be the ideal method because it's much easier to get to know people in the nicer environment of a home. Each week the bulletin will list who is hosting that particular Sunday so that the floating greeter can direct visitors to the host family or vice versa.

Another way to practice hospitality, of course, is to invite visitors to your home for a meal on a weeknight. This allows them to see you outside of Sunday at a time when you are not wearing your "Sunday best." It helps newcomers see that you are real people, just like they are.

Whatever method you use, it requires that you be self-consciously looking for visitors. Typically, visitors will not just show up for a meal unless they are invited. And so it's very important that you and your church members are always keeping your eyes out for those who are new to the church.

One other thing in this area: the leadership in the church sets the tone in practicing hospitality. Very seldom does the congregation rise above its level of leadership. If the church planter, core group, or overseeing consistory/session of the church doesn't practice hospitality, if the office bearers are not proactive in looking for and reaching out to visitors, probably the members of the church won't either. The practice of loving hospitality may also help the church planter and overseeing consistory recognize men for the offices of elder and deacon. The heart of a deacon is mercy shown in Christ's name, which is inseparable from mercifully reaching out to visitors.

Have a Book Table

One thing that church plants should be encouraged to have is a well-stocked book table filled with free, readable, theologically solid books. Often, visitors who come to church plants are just beginning to learn about the Reformed faith through their personal reading and have a limited understanding of the doctrines of grace. These types of visitors enjoy reading, so it is imperative to have a good book table. This table should be set up in a location that is easily seen and accessible. Don't put the book table in some dark recess of the church building where no visitor could possibly find it. Place it somewhere near the entrance so that it will be easily seen.

In addition, include books on the book table that will appeal to those who do not have an in-depth interest in theology. In other words, John Calvin's *Institutes of the Christian Religion* or Herman Bavinck's *Reformed Dogmatics* or Francis Turretin's *Institutes of Elenctic Theology* are books the pastor and possibly elders or informed parishioners have, but not material that visitors should start out with. Don't let these books make up the primary source of reading material on your book table.

Instead, I would encourage you to place books on the book table that are easy to understand and allow visitors to learn who you are as a church. These should not be superficial or trivial, but they should communicate in basic terminology what you believe and practice. Also, make sure you put a sticker or stamp somewhere in or on the book with the church plant's website, phone number, and email. Here are a few recommendations that are not only appropriate for visitors but also for those of us who want to be prepared to speak to others in an intelligent way about what we believe and why we believe it.

The Three Forms of Unity or Westminster Standards

I can think of no better book to give to a person who is interested in the Christian faith in general or the Reformed faith in particular than the Westminster Standards or Three Forms of Unity. In addition to the Presbyterian or Reformed standards, have the creeds available as well (the Apostles' Creed, Nicene Creed, and Athanasian Creed). Many of these can be downloaded free of charge from websites such as www.urcna.org and then inexpensively made into booklets.[3]

Banner of Truth Booklets

Banner of Truth has produced a number of helpful booklets that are inexpensive ($1.50–$3.00) and easy to read while not being superficial. They deal with subjects such as "What is true faith?" "What is the significance of the cross?" "What is the church?" "What are the five points of Calvinism?" and "How do I grow as a Christian?"

Putting Amazing Back into Grace

Written by Michael Horton, this book was used greatly by God in my life to turn me from broad evangelicalism to embrace the Reformed faith. Horton deals with doctrines such as the sovereignty of God, total depravity, unconditional election, justification, and the sacraments, and he does so in a very clear and easy-to-understand way.

Chosen by God

This book by R. C. Sproul has impacted many. Sproul deals with the difficult subject of election in a biblical and gracious way.

---

3. Churches that belong to NAPARC might print a brief note in their bulletins explaining that they are members of NAPARC (www.naparc.org), which helps visitors understand who they are denominationally. Also, this shows visitors that the church plant is not some tiny sect but has many sister congregations and denominations.

Fifty Reasons Why Jesus Came to Die
This short devotional book by John Piper is aimed at a mass audience. Piper gathers fifty reasons from the New Testament that explain the gospel, answering the question of why Jesus came to die.

A Better Way
This book by Michael Horton addresses the subject of worship. Horton helps the reader see that worship is much more than just a debate of traditional versus contemporary worship. This is an excellent book on the subject of worship.

Jesus Loves the Little Children
This is a great book on the subject of infant baptism by Daniel Hyde. Many people who visit your church will have questions about infant baptism. This book helps the reader understand the biblical reasons we practice infant baptism.

An Unexpected Journey
This is the autobiographical account of how, as a high school student, Dr. W. Robert Godfrey, president of Westminster Seminary California, discovered the Reformed faith and why he considers it to be the purest expression of the Christian faith.

Modern Reformation Magazine
This bi-monthly periodical is an excellent resource to give to anyone who is inquiring about the Reformed faith. Also consider *New Horizons, The Outlook,* and other denominational magazines devoted to the propagation of Reformed theology.

Print Your Own Pamphlets
In the day in which we live, it's quite easy and inexpensive to make your own pamphlets.[4] Have a pamphlet on the table explaining why you worship the way that you do or why your children remain in the worship service with you. The OPC website (ww.opc.org) has many printable essays. Other pamphlets might cover subjects such as the sacraments,

---

4. Many URC, OPC, and PCA congregations have excellent resources on their websites. Also, don't neglect the work other church plants and churches have already done in producing pamphlets and website resources.

Sabbath practices, the use of catechisms and confessions, and the importance of church membership.

Explain the Service

This is a matter that primarily involves the church planter/pastor. When my family first went to a Reformed church—even though I had been through seminary and had spent a few years as an associate pastor—I had no idea why the pastor would raise his hands at the beginning of the service and say something like, "Grace, peace, and mercy to you, from God the Father and the Lord Jesus Christ." I had no idea why the law of God was read every Sunday morning or why the Apostles' Creed was confessed every Sunday evening. I certainly had no idea what a catechism was. I'm not suggesting that the pastor needs to explain every element of the worship service every Sunday. I typically pick one element of worship each week that I will take just a few moments—maybe thirty seconds—to explain. I have found, surprisingly, that a number of people come to me who grew up in the Reformed faith or who have been in a Reformed church for years and say, "Thanks for explaining that. I had no idea that is why we do that in worship." This also makes the members of the church feel more comfortable in inviting their friends or neighbors or co-workers to church, because they know that the pastor is going to explain why we do what we do in worship. It will also help members to be able to talk to their friends after church when visitors ask them, "Why did your pastor raise his hands?" or "Why did he read the Ten Commandments?" When they ask questions like that, they will be able to give them an answer.

Be Patient with People

We have to face the fact that people from a non-Reformed or unbelieving background who visit our church will not be at the same level of understanding as someone who has spent years in a Presbyterian or Reformed church. They might think that infant baptism is a Roman Catholic practice. They might think that we place our catechism on the same level as the Word of God. They probably won't know why we treat the Lord's Day the way we do. In fact, they might just walk in with a Starbucks cup on Sunday morning. How sad it would be if we expect visitors to be on the same page that we are! How sad it would be for us to gather in a huddle and whisper about the guy with the Starbucks cup: "Hey, did you see the

Sabbath breaker over there?" The idea is to be patient with people. Think about your own walk with the Lord. Hopefully, you are further along today than you were two years ago, and hopefully, two years from now, you will be further along than you are today.

The point is don't expect your visitors to come in knowing all (or any) of the finer points of Reformed theology and worship—or even anything about the Christian faith. They probably don't know what a church plant is. Be patient with them, lovingly teach them, and warmly welcome them into your congregation, no matter what they look like or where they are from. Starting a plant on a welcoming note will alleviate a problem some church plants have had with unexpected growth. A core group sometimes wants the church plant to consist of people like them, and when the plant becomes more culturally diverse, for example, the core members are uneasy and sometimes outright annoyed because it isn't "their church" anymore, or they don't have the pastor's full attention—like when a new baby comes into a family and the older brother sometimes resents his younger sibling's "intrusion." If the plant *starts out* welcoming all kinds of people, this "big brother" problem can be avoided.

Not long ago, I read of a tragic story. A young man named Gordon came from Nigeria to a large city in North America, was introduced to the Reformed faith, and started attending a Reformed church. He was excited about the Reformed faith and enthusiastic about his new church. But one day, after church, he mentioned to a few of the members that he still admired the teaching of certain televangelists that the members of the congregation considered false teachers. Instead of lovingly explaining the errors of the televangelists to this man, one of the members immediately lashed out at him and said, "How can you like those hell-bound heretics? All they're doing is leading people to their eternal death." Gordon left that church and never came back to it.

As we reach out to our communities, I pray that we would not only display love but that we would also display patience with those the Lord brings our way.

CHAPTER ELEVEN

∾

Flock and Family: A Biblical Balance

Shane Lems

By now I'm sure you are getting the picture—if you didn't see it already—that church planting is like one of those adventures you had as a child that was exciting and scary and agonizing all at the same time. Church planting is similar to sledding on an inner tube down a slushy hill: you start out laughing, and then you hit a few hidden fence poles that bang up your legs. Finally, after flipping around twenty-two times, you lie in the snow, bruised and shaken up, trying hard not to cry. Of course you limp back up the snowy hill to do it all over again. This is a metaphorical, weekly (sometimes daily) pattern for church planters.

Because we can't change the difficult realities of church planting, we need to remember the reason we plant churches. We have already seen that we plant churches because of Jesus' finished work. We are getting beaten up and bloodied while planting churches because of the message we are bringing to people: *Jesus Christ saves people from sin.* He is the source of our existence as a church, the reason we exist, and the purpose for which we exist: to praise and proclaim His name. We are taking up our crosses and denying ourselves so His name is magnified.

No matter how badly church planting goes—even if we are forced to discontinue a few months into the plant—the gospel will not fail to sustain God's people. Christ will firmly hold onto His sheep. The church planter needs to preach Christ to himself a thousand times a day, as Luther might say, or he will either sell out to the world or be driven into the deep night of depression and despair. So remember the good news!

In this chapter, we consider the church planter's family life as it relates to his core group, or congregation. As a husband, the church planter is called to love his wife as Christ loves His church (Eph. 5:25). As a father, the church planter is called to train his children in the fear of the Lord, with deep love and care (Eph. 6:4; Col. 3:21). As a pastor, the church planter is called to preach the gospel, administer the sacraments, teach the Christian faith, care for God's people, and do the work of an evangelist (2 Tim. 4:2–5; 1 Peter 5:2). The church planter's responsibilities often stack up well beyond these duties, but these are central in the church planter's life.[1]

If this chapter had to be summarized with a single sentence, it would be this: The church planter must maintain an intimate relationship with his wife, a close relationship with his children, and a pastoral relationship with the people of the church plant. We're really talking about a biblical balance. Perhaps one reason Paul said that singleness is a good thing is because the church/home balance is so difficult to maintain (1 Cor. 7:7–8). Since many church planters are married, however, it is necessary to wrestle through some church/home issues to prepare men for serving wife, family, church, and, ultimately, Christ. With these biblical themes in mind, we now turn to some specific and practical examples of what it means to labor in a church plant while loving your wife, raising your children, and caring for the flock.

Spend Much Time with Your Wife

A church planter must spend much time with his wife. John Piper explains,

> Oh, how crucial it is that pastors love their wives. It delights and encourages the church. It models marriage for the other couples. It upholds the honor of the office of elder. It blesses the pastor's children with a haven of love. It displays the mystery of Christ's love for the church. It prevents our prayers from being hindered. It eases the burdens of the ministry. It protects the church from devastating scandal. And it satisfies the soul as we find our joy in God by pursuing it in the joy of the beloved. This is not marginal, brothers. Loving our wives is essential for our ministry.[2]

Piper is right: the pastor's love for his wife is essential in his ministry. For church planters, this truth must be emphasized, because some people who attend church plants have seen few Christian marriages and don't

---

1. In *POPC*, the authors name four typical traits of a church planter: (1) he has a "special call" to church planting; (2) he is "gripped by the doctrine of the church"; (3) "he makes a deep commitment to a place and people"; and (4) "he serves without the promise of permanence" (35).

2. John Piper, *Brothers, We Are Not Professionals* (Nashville: Broadman, 2002), 245–46.

know what one looks like. It is essential for church planters to visibly display love for their wives. John Sittema points out, "You must be the one who holds before them the blessed joy and satisfaction of a marriage lived well under God's pattern and in God's presence."[3] By doing so, as we well know, we are portraying the gospel, Christ's love for His bride (Eph. 5:22–33).

Men, I can promise this: if you neglect your wife's needs, the church plant you pastor and your family will suffer sooner or later. Let me state this even more boldly: if your sexual and emotional intimacy with your wife is severely lacking or nonexistent, it will ultimately hurt your family and the church plant. Paul's command to nourish, cherish, and hold fast to your wife (Eph. 5:29, 31) means you must physically, emotionally, and spiritually do everything you can to protect, love, and care for your wife. Meditate on the gospel as you love your wife; follow Christ in His love for His bride.

I've read several accounts of pastors of church plants who work sixty hours or more every week. They leave early in the morning and get back late at night; this routine happens more often than not. The wife eventually becomes bitter but tries to hide it because she knows her pastor-planter-husband is doing work for Christ, and she doesn't want to slow him down. She submits, telling herself that when the church plant has deacons and elders, things will get better. Two years later, she finds out that things get worse when deacons and elders are ordained; now her husband has more to do.[4]

You will have to start the plant with the right habits or change now if you have bad habits. I can tell you from experience, as you unpack your books in your new study while facing the opening stages of a church plant, that you should not tell yourself, "For now, I'll do it this way and change it later." Do not say, "I'll study on Monday for now, and when I get settled in, I'll take it off." This does not work. Set realistic goals from

---

3. John Sittema, *With a Shepherd's Heart* (Grandville, Mich.: Reformed Fellowship, 1996), 101.

4. Karl Barth profoundly captured one of the grave characteristics of being a pastor that a church planter experiences profoundly. He noted that though a community surrounds the pastor, his pathway is solitary and exists in "uncanny isolation." Ironically, though the pastor is surrounded by likeminded people, "scarcely anyone can offer him a helping hand in the labor demanded of him, in the explication and application of the biblical message, and in his own theological work" (*Evangelical Theology* [Grand Rapids: Eerdmans, 1963], 110–11).

the beginning. For example, I found out that I need to do some work on Monday in case something comes up later in the week that demands my time. I work a few hours on Monday and take the rest of the day off to spend time with my wife and children. I have come to cherish and enjoy family time, and I do my best to guard it. Continue reading Scripture and praying with your wife habitually, communicate with her well and often, and spend time with her. These things will certainly help your spiritual intimacy and also positively affect your emotional and sexual intimacy.

If you are considering doing the work of a church planter or are called to plant a church, speak with your wife often and in detail about the rigors of church planting. Sit down together and write down several things you can do to protect your marriage and intimacy before you even pack the moving truck. As so many Christian marriage books rightly say, communication is vital in a marriage. Ask your wife what fears, excitement, concerns, and questions she has about planting a church. Exercise communication as you head into a church plant, when you're in the midst of one, and twenty years down the road. There are a few things you might not be able to tell your wife, but make sure you both talk about most things together, especially your relationship and family life.

When you talk to the elders overseeing the plant or the people of the plant, make it clear to them that they are not hiring two pastors for the price of one. Lovingly let them know, for example, that your wife might not have the time or gifts to play piano, lead women's groups, or other tasks that pastors' wives sometimes take on. Do not commit your wife to things that will soon weigh her down; "submission to husband" does not mean you can force your wife to be in charge of snacks after the morning service. She may assume that responsibility, but she is not obligated simply because she is a pastor's wife. In blunt terms, protect your wife from the church plant. Again, discuss all these things with your wife, and then with the elders and people of the church plant.

As I move on to the topic of children, let me exhort you again to love your wife. Work on your marriage! You can study waw-consecutives, aorists, Augustine, *attributa divina*, and commentaries during the week; study your wife and read books on marriage as well. Fight sexual impurity and lust; take serious steps to remain pure.[5] Build intimacy in your marriage

---

5. To protect yourself, your marriage, your church, and the purity of the gospel, the best thing you can do is have an elder or other church leader install a filter on your study/home computer. Also, find another pastor to keep you accountable in the area of purity,

while you plant a church. Spend time alone, where you can talk and listen, laugh, rest, discuss, and enjoy each other's presence. Ed Wheat gives four helpful areas of touching as we build intimacy with our wives: physically, emotionally, mentally, and spiritually.[6] Approach the daunting task of planting a church while holding your wife's hand tightly.

Spend Much Time with Your Children

Wayne Mack writes, "The ultimate responsibility for bringing up our children to know the Scriptures rests not with the church or school but with us as parents, and especially with those of us who are fathers."[7] You've probably studied the standard texts on raising children according to Scripture. As a review, remember one of the requirements of an overseer: he must "[rule] his own house well, having his children in submission with all reverence" (1 Tim. 3:4). We also remember Paul's instructions to fathers, that we are not to provoke our children to anger but love them and bring them up with discipline as well as Christian training (Eph. 6:4; Col. 3:21). We follow the Bible's lead as we raise our children.

One of the church planter's primary duties is to preach the Word and lead the public worship service. As a father, he is also called to lead private, or family, worship. As the *Westminster Directory for Family Worship* (1647) states, "The ordinary performance of all the parts of family-worship belongeth properly to the head of the family." I agree with the emphasis of *POPC*, which asserts, "Of all that is required of an organizing pastor, nothing is as important as utilizing all your shepherding skills in the care of your own family. You should consider your family to be your most treasured possession and their care to be your highest aim, as well as an opportunity to showcase the Reformed concept of covenant theology" (49). The minister should encourage other fathers to lead their families in worship by setting the pattern in his own home. While your wife is not called to be "assistant worship leader" at church, she is called to help you at home, and she may have to step up and lead family worship while you are at a Bible study, for example. However, you cannot completely trans-

---

and make sexual purity a discussion point in consistory meetings from time to time. Take every precaution to keep you and your church sexually pure.

6. Ed Wheat, *Love Life for Every Married Couple* (Grand Rapids: Zondervan, 1980), 135–50. Being familiar with the biblical principles of marriage and family is also helpful as we face counseling in the church plant. I've found CCEF (www.ccef.org) to be a helpful source for counseling.

7. Wayne Mack, *Strengthening Your Marriage* (Phillipsburg, N.J.: P&R, 1999), 159.

fer this duty to your wife, though she should hold your hand in training and raising children. Take care that family worship is not neglected; take time to teach your children about the great stories of the Bible, the great songs of the faith, and the fascinating lives of the saints who have gone before us. As it is in the pulpit, so it should be in the home.

How can you make sure that you do spend time with your children? There are quite a few ways. As you talk to your wife about her relationship to the church plant, also discuss certain times of day that will be devoted to family time. Some pastors help their wives wake the children up and get them ready for school. The family eats breakfast and has prayer time together, and then the pastor takes the children to school on his way to the study. Other pastors set aside Monday to spend time with children— the only reason they would be away is for a death or illness in the church. Personally, I devote as many evenings as I can to family time. I try not to schedule anything after 5:00 p.m. I have Bible study, consistory meetings, and other meetings a few times a month, but around twenty-five out of thirty nights of the month my children and wife can count on my being home at 4:30 p.m. Also, don't forget to zealously guard family vacation time; schedule certain days or weeks each year of family vacation time. Do not put these off because you are too busy. Most of the people in your church plant or congregation have hectic lives, so it is beneficial for the pastor to be a model for the flock in guarding family time. Be purposeful and self-disciplined when it comes to your schedule so you don't get caught up in the whirlwind that tears families apart.

This advice really is applicable to all pastors and church leaders: we want our children to grow up and love the church, not hate it for taking daddy away. Because it is probably more tempting to over-commit and overwork yourself in the first years of a church plant, these years are crucial in your family life. You want the children to know what you do and why you do it (remember the gospel), and you want them to experience the joy that comes from serving Christ and His church. However, if you often come home for the evening meal (if you come home at all) angry, frustrated, or too tired to talk, your children will eventually get the picture: daddy loves the church more than me. Your church plant may be growing and successful, but your family may be falling apart; do not let this happen! Guard your children, pray hard for them, and protect your time with them. Show them in your laughter, games, discipline, speech, and joy that the gospel you preach is the driving message in your family life.

Spend Much Time with Your Church Family

Thomas Murphy says that the pastor should "feel, and lead the people to feel, that he is one with them in heart, in sympathy and in those grand interests of the soul which bind men together the closest of all. The first thing…is for the minister to determine and earnestly strive to love his people."[8] Or, in John Nevin's words, "The more intimate a minister is with the character, relations, and circumstances of his congregation, the better."[9] In biblical terms, "Shepherd the flock of God" (1 Peter 5:2). Paul described his church-planting ministry in terms of motherhood: "We were gentle among you, just as a nursing mother cherishes her own children" (1 Thess. 2:7). He also uses paternal imagery: "We exhorted, and comforted, and charged every one of you, as a father does his own children" (1 Thess. 2:11–12). Paul loved the church and spent much personal time with its members; church planters today follow in these apostolic footsteps (Rom. 1:11; 2 Cor. 12:15; Gal. 4:19; Phil. 1:8, 4:1).[10] We are called to love the flock intensely, deeply, and visibly: do all you can for their spiritual good, even if it hurts.[11]

"Pastors," writes William Willimon, "are interesting characters on whom hands have been laid, a burden has been bestowed, and commu-

---

8. Thomas Murphy, *Pastoral Theology* (Willow Street, Pa.: Old Paths Publications, 2001), 269, 271. Dietrich Bonhoeffer also said it well: "[The pastor] will have to share the daily life of the fellowship; he must know the cares, the needs, the joys and thanksgivings, the petitions and the hopes of the others," in *Life Together* (New York: Harper and Row, 1965), 63. This book is a highly recommended resource for church planters.

9. John Williamson Nevin, *The Reformed Pastor: Lectures on Pastoral Theology,* ed. Sam Hamstra, Jr. (Eugene, Ore.: Pickwick Publications, 2006), 67.

10. One area concerning a pastor's relationship to a church that I do not have the space to discuss here is his role as servant. In many ways the pastor is the church's servant. Francis Turretin stated it this way, "Now the church is superior to pastors, not pastors to the church; the church does not belong to pastors, but the pastors to the church.... Pastors are called the servants and ministers of the church: 'We are your servants for Jesus' sake' (2 Cor. 4:5)" (Francis Turretin, *Institutes of Elenctic Theology,* trans. George Giger, ed. James T. Dennison, Jr., (Phillipsburg, N.J.: P&R, 1997), 3:227.

11. In *POPC,* we are reminded that a church planter "commits himself *without reserve* to the believers that God gathers around him" (emphasis mine). The OPC manual lists these examples of how to care for the people of a mission work: shepherd them, visit them, pray for them, and assimilate them (35, 37–38).

nal care is expected."[12] Elsewhere, he writes, "One of the great challenges of our pastoral care is to be present with people in need and not be overwhelmed by their need, to be available to our people as their pastor without being captured exclusively by them, to take their pain seriously and at the same time to take seriously our task to proclaim Jesus Christ and him crucified and resurrected."[13] Willimon continues, explaining that pastors—like Paul—care for God's people by sharing the gospel *as well as their lives* with God's people.[14]

We can lay down this principle as consistent with Scripture: men, get to know the people in the church plant you pastor. This is a major part of discipleship—not being part of a program but rather a people. Communicate with them often, with cards, emails, phone calls, text messages, or any way you can.[15] Your job in this area is probably easier than many pastors' because you have only about thirty or forty people to get to know. You can—and this is a great joy—pray for every single member of your church by name from memory.

You can go to the fair when two seventh graders from the church plant are showing their lambs; you can go to the high school gym when the eleventh-grade boy has his first varsity basketball game. You can visit the landscaping company where one man in the church plant works, and you can stop by the law firm of a lawyer who attends the church plant. You can visit the dental lab where another man from your congregation works. Pencil in time on your calendar to meet the people during the week where they are. Pray that the Lord would give you intense love for the people, and do what you can to befriend even those in the church plant who are completely different from you.

Again, one great thing about church plants is that they are usually small. This is good, because it forces the members and visitors to get to know each other. You can lead the way by including and welcoming visitors and new members at church events. Furthermore, you can actu-

---

12. William Willimon, *Pastor: The Theology and Practice of Ordained Ministry* (Nashville: Abingdon, 2002), 299.

13. Ibid., 108.

14. Ibid., 109. Tim Chester and Steve Timmis also emphasize this point well in chapter 8 ("Pastoral Care") of their excellent book, *Total Church* (Wheaton: Crossway, 2008).

15. "In the life of a maturing body of Christ, the need for good congregational communication is important and the opportunities for misunderstanding are many. As the organizing pastor of a mission work, you must work hard to ensure that communication is done well" (*POPC*, 43).

ally get to know your church family while you spend time with your children. The two are not at odds. I'm thinking simply of the church "hanging out" together, to use an old phrase. I suggest things more organic than the classic potluck—activities that all the members can participate in comfortably are best. Churches and church plants should not be so emphatically family oriented that they inadvertently leave out single people or those without children. This is something to be aware of in all churches, and especially in a church plant. A single person (unmarried, divorced, or widowed) should not feel like a lesser member of a church. The church can help paint each others' houses, remodel each others' basements, watch each others' baseball games, volunteer at the thrift shop together, or just have theme parties at different homes. The point is not to add more busyness to our already hectic lives but to integrate our lives as Christians to fight the frenzied individualism of our culture.

In the church plant where I pastor, several families frequently volunteer to watch our children while my wife and I spend time together. There are many different levels of friendships and relationships in the plant. Friendships can be messy and hard to maintain, but they allow us the opportunity to display forgiveness and love. An added benefit to knowing your church-plant members intimately is that it will certainly help in your preaching, teaching, and counseling.

A Word to the Church Plant's Workers and Overseers

If you have some oversight in coordinating the details of a church plant, make sure the pastor you call to be the church planter strives to maintain a balance among wife, children, and church. If the man you are considering to lead a church plant is not "a people person," one who is intimately involved in the lives of those around him, and if his family life is a shambles, you do not want to call him as a planter. If you are considering or have a church planter who does strive to maintain a balance, be sure to *help him* maintain that balance. As previously mentioned, don't put undue pressure on his wife to assume leadership positions if she prefers not to. The church planter's wife is called to be her husband's helper, not a co-pastor.

If your church planter-pastor has children, find families in the church who will babysit while he and his wife enjoy a walk or a date. Finally, be available for him. Make it easy for him to find you and talk to you during the week. Let him know when your children have a science fair or track meet. Let him know if you're having a birthday party for someone. Invite him to visit you at work; take him out to lunch or coffee. Send him emails to encourage him in his preaching; give his family little gifts of appreciation. Again, many of these things are applicable to any church's relationship with its pastor. Communication is not only essential in the home, but it is in the church as well. Church planters are under amazing stress because so many things can quickly shift the balance of wife, children, and church that a church planter is called to love and lead. Pray that your pastor-planter would love his wife, raise his children, and befriend you in a biblical, gospel-centered way.

Conclusion

This balance among wife, children, and church is a difficult one to maintain, and it should be a major part of your personal goals, daily prayers, and your church plant's prayers for you. Assume leadership in a church plant with the gospel as the "motor," or "engine," of your personal, family, and church relationships. Fall on the Scriptures for guidance in family and flock; love your wife better than yourself, cherish your children, and intimately know the sheep God has entrusted to your care.

By God's grace—by His gospel that has changed your life—you will make it through the bumps and bruises of a church plant. You'll even make it through the huge potholes, and when (not if) you end up hurting, bleeding, and crying, your wife and children will hug you and the people of the plant will shower you with loving prayers and care. In this way, outsiders will know you are disciples of Jesus by the way you love Him and share your lives.

CHAPTER TWELVE

∾

Declare His Praise among the Nations: Public Worship as the Heart of Evangelism

Daniel R. Hyde

Several years ago I was asked to speak at a missions rally in order to inspire my federation of churches to engage in evangelism, church planting, and missions. As I considered what to say, many things came to mind. I could have discussed missions in terms of how to increase a line item on annual church budgets. I could have discussed the necessity of church planting in large urban cities and the need for more young men to pursue this calling. I could have talked about starting up an evangelism program at the local church. I could even have lectured about my personal experience of church planting in terms of its need, its goal, and its execution. Instead, I decided to speak about public worship.

"Worship?" you wonder. Yes, worship. The Scriptures clearly envision that the center of the church's evangelistic ministry is not found in planned activities such as passing out tracts, street-witnessing, VBS, or any other program—as helpful as it may be—but in the public worship of the triune God of grace. I am convinced that if we as Reformed churches—and so much more church plants—start to view worship as the central theme of who we are, then things like evangelism will not be ominous topics but rather the effects of what we already are and do. After all, even John Calvin spoke of worship—not the doctrine of justification by faith alone—as the most important part of the reforming work of the sixteenth century in his 1544 treatise to Charles V, *The Necessity of Reforming the Church*.[1] The voluminous material that other Reformers such as Martin Bucer and Thomas Cranmer wrote in advocating and defending Reformed worship as the distinguishing mark of the Reformed churches also speaks this way.

To illustrate the importance of worship to the life of the church plant, think of the hub of a bicycle's wheel. Worship is the hub from which all

---

1. John Calvin, *The Necessity of Reforming the Church* (Audubon, N.J.: Old Paths, 1994), 4.

the spokes project and from which they derive the strength to do what they are supposed to do. From the hub everything else radiates, such as private and family prayer, reading of Scripture, fulfilling a calling in life, fellowship with other believers, assurance of salvation, good works, and evangelism in the world. These all should be the results of public worship as well as what we bring back to public worship as a part of our grateful "offering up of our desires unto God…with…thankful acknowledgment of his mercies" (WSC, Q&A 98).

Israel and the Temple

To demonstrate from Scripture that worship is the hub of the Christian church and life, I will trace the development of redemptive history and then provide a few applications from this topic.

Beginning with the call of Abram (Gen. 12), we see that the Lord brought salvation to one family and, eventually, one nation of the nations of the earth. At this point in redemptive history, the true worship of the Lord was the exclusive privilege of Israel for the purpose of eventually bringing the entire world to the Messiah, as such notable Gentile exceptions as Ruth illustrate.

With the command to construct the tabernacle, the Lord localized His gracious presence in the midst of His peculiar people (Ex. 25–31, 35–40). After Israel reached the Land of Promise, the Lord commanded that there be one central, permanent location where He would "put His name" (Deut. 12:5). The holy place of worship was no longer just in the midst of the people as they wandered in the wilderness. It now had a permanent place in the midst of the Holy Land. We read of this exclusivity in verses like Psalm 76:1–2:

> In Judah God is known;
> His name is great in Israel.
> In Salem also is His tabernacle,
> And His dwelling place in Zion.

Other verses extol the Lord for His exclusive work in the nation of Israel:

> He declares His word to Jacob,
> His statutes and His judgments to Israel.
> He has not dealt thus with any nation;
> And as for His judgments, they have not known them.
> Praise the LORD! (Ps. 147:19–20).

The Prophets and the Temple

With the coming of the latter prophets, the outlook of Israel and her worship was expanded to include the nations. Their anticipation was that a day would come in which the efficacious grace of the Holy Spirit would go out from Israel—for salvation is of the Jews (John 4:22)—to the entire earth (Joel 2), and people from every tribe, tongue, language, and nation would worship the Lord who had redeemed Israel and created them.

Isaiah 2:1–4

Central to this universal outlook of worship was the centrality of the temple in the center of Zion at the center of the earth. Isaiah 2:2–4 explains this future event: "In the latter days" the "mountain of the LORD's house shall be established on the top of the mountains" (v. 2). In Scripture, the "high places" are where the nations built their altars and temples to their gods, because the tops of mountains were closer to heaven. Yet in Isaiah 2 the vivid imagery is of Mount Zion being elevated above all other mountains. This imagery conveys that a day will come when the nations—not just Israel—will see the Lord of this holy mountain and come to Him, the King of kings and Lord of lords. And so Isaiah says,

> All nations shall flow to it.
>   Many people shall come and say,
> 'Come, let us go up to the mountain of the LORD,
> To the house of the God of Jacob;
> He will teach us His ways' (vv. 2–3).

Something new would happen "in the latter days" as the unclean nations would go up to the dwelling place of the Lord, where they formerly were not admitted, and be taught by the Lord Himself. We read in Isaiah 56: 1–8 of more than just admittance, as the prophet writes about the foreigner and the eunuch in priestly terms, saying that they are to be welcomed into the house of the Lord and given names better than those of the Israelite sons and daughters (v. 5). Then, in 56:6–8, the Lord says that He will gather these outcasts into His holy mountain and accept their sacrifices and prayer, for, "My house shall be called a house of prayer for all nations" (v. 7). A day would come in which the priests of the Lord would not be from one family line of one tribe of the nation of Israel but rather from all peoples, who previously were excluded.

The nations, then, would be drawn to Zion's worship and, through it, to Zion's Lord. This was a revolutionary way of thinking and a radical shift from how Israel had operated. In fact, so radical was this outlook that Isaiah again prophesied some of the most striking words of the Old Testament in chapter 19:

> In that day five cities in the land of Egypt will speak the language of Canaan and swear by the LORD of hosts; one will be called the City of Destruction. In that day there will be an altar to the LORD in the midst of the land of Egypt, and a pillar to the LORD at its border.... Then the LORD will be known to Egypt, and the Egyptians will know the LORD in that day, and will make sacrifice and offering; yes, they will make a vow to the LORD and perform it.... In that day there will be a highway from Egypt to Assyria, and the Assyrian will come into Egypt and the Egyptian into Assyria, and the Egyptians will serve with the Assyrians (vv. 18–19, 21, 23).

A day would come in which the enemies of the Lord, Egypt and Assyria, who made the Israelites their captives in a foreign land, would bring sacrifices and prayer to the altar of the Lord. A day would come when those who were far off would come near (Eph. 2:13), and they would all sing in the language of Zion as the one people of the Lord. The prophet Zephaniah says, "For then I will restore to the peoples a pure language, that they all may call on the name of the LORD, to serve Him with one accord" (3:9).

The prophet Zechariah foresaw the same glorious day in the future:

> Thus says the LORD of hosts:
> "Peoples shall yet come,
> Inhabitants of many cities;
> The inhabitants of one city shall go to another, saying,
> 'Let us continue to go and pray before the LORD,
> And seek the LORD of hosts.
> I myself will go also....'"

> Thus says the LORD of hosts: "In those days ten men from every language of the nations shall grasp the sleeve of a Jewish man, saying, 'Let us go with you, for we have heard that God is with you'" (Zech. 8:20–21, 23).

What do all these prophetical words have in common? They explain that in the days our Lord would usher in, the Gentiles would not only be converted but they would also join the people of God in worship, drawing near to the temple and offering sacrifices of praise and thanksgiving.

The means by which they would come to the Lord was through the worship of the Lord. Evangelism is firmly tied to corporate worship.

The Songs of the Temple
The reality that the Gentiles would join the Jews in worship was far from being just a theory or prophecy. It was a part of the piety, prayers, and songs of the people in worship. The Israelites not only heard this truth, they also sang about it and longed for it. Geerhardus Vos observes, "The mind of the Psalmist is not satisfied with holding the idea at the distance of objective contemplation, but translates it into an eager desire for witnessing the fulfillment of the prophecy. Thus a real missionary urge is born out of the eschatological vision of Jehovah and his kingdom. This desire projects itself into the future and breaks out into a direct missionary appeal conceived as addressed to the Gentiles from that standpoint."[2]

Throughout the Psalter, this hope is expressed in song. The sons of Korah sang of this day when they harmonized that the Lord Most High, who is to be feared above all because He is the king of all the earth, would sit upon His throne and be approached in worship by "the princes of the people" who would be "as the people of the God of Abraham" (Ps. 47:9). The choirmaster led the people in singing the opening words of Psalm 66, which many sing today in these words:

> All lands, to God in joyful sounds
> Aloft your voices raise;
> Sing out the honor of His Name,
> > And glorious make His praise,
> > And glorious make His praise.[3]

In yet another song, the priestly singers sang the praises of the God of Israel, who would number the nations with His people on His heavenly church membership list:

> I will make mention of Rahab and Babylon to those who know Me;
> Behold, O Philistia and Tyre, with Ethiopia:
> "This one was born there". . . .

---

2. Geerhardus Vos, *The Pauline Eschatology* (1930; repr., Phillipsburg, N.J.: P&R, 1994), 347.
3. *Psalter Hymnal* (Grand Rapids: Board of Publications of the Christian Reformed Church, 1976), no. 118.

The LORD will record,
When He registers the peoples:
"This one was born there" (Ps. 87:4, 6).

We also know well the words of Psalm 100, which we sing often to the tune of "Old Hundredth":

All people that on earth do dwell,
Sing to the Lord with cheerful voice;
Him serve with mirth, His praise forth tell,
Come ye before Him and rejoice.[4]

The shortest psalm, Psalm 117, opens by saying, "Praise the LORD, all you Gentiles! Laud Him, all you peoples!" (v. 1) Amazingly, this is one of the Hallel Psalms, which are traditionally sung at the Passover feast. It is as if the Israelites are singing, "The LORD has brought us out, and now it is your turn!" Even more telling is verse 2. After the psalmist calls the nations to worship the Lord, he gives the reason in verse 2: "For His merciful kindness is great toward us." The Lord keeps His covenant with His people, and we are to sing to Him for that; it is also a reason to call the nations to experience this same covenant love.

Finally, Psalm 96, which Edmund Clowney called "the doxology of the new mankind…heaven's Hallelujah Chorus,"[5] addresses the covenant people, but notice how its focus moves from Israel ("Oh, sing to the Lord a new song!" [v. 1]) to the nations ("Sing to the Lord, all the earth" [v. 1]), from the covenant community to the communities of the earth. This is a call to worship that extends to all mankind, for the chief end of man, not just our congregations, is "to glorify God and to enjoy him forever" (WSC, Q&A 1). This call to sing a "new song" is a theme in the latter prophets, which, Vos notes, "receives light from the idea of the 'new things' found in prophecy, especially in the latter part of Isaiah. There the 'new things' mean the great unparalleled events about to introduce the future state of Israel…the new name, the new creature, the new *diatheke*, the new Jerusalem.[6]

The psalmist calls all people to sing this new song of the new age to the Lord because of who He is. He is glorious (v. 3); He has done wonders

---

4. Ibid., no. 195.
5. Edmund Clowney, "Declare His Glory among the Nations (1976)," Urbana.org, accessed November 23, 2010, http://www.urbana.org/_articles.cfm?RecordId=879.
6. Vos, *The Pauline Eschatology*, 336.

(v. 3); He is great (v. 4); He made the heavens (v. 5); He is known for His honor, majesty, strength, and beauty (v. 6). Notice that verses 2–3 link the worship of this all-glorious and majestic Lord with evangelism. Synonymous with singing this new song is "[proclaiming] the good news of His salvation from day to day" and "declar[ing] His glory among the nations, His wonders among all peoples." As we sing to the Lord in heaven for all He has done, we are imploring the nations to join us and ascend the heavenly mountain in worship.

We see this in all the imperative verbs in this psalm: sing (v. 1); bless and proclaim (v. 2); declare (v. 3); give (vv. 7, 8); bring and come (v. 8); worship and tremble (v. 9); say (v. 10); be glad and roar (v. 11); rejoice (v. 12). It is as if the psalmist were saying, "In every way you know, bring the nations before the Lord with you in worship."

What I am describing is what has been called "doxological evangelism," that is, worship that is so focused upon the beauty and worthiness of God that it inevitably is also evangelistic.[7] Psalm 96 led Edmund Clowney to point out, "The gospel message is celebration before it is communication."[8]

New Testament Fulfillment

We see this nexus between worship and evangelism clearly illustrated in the New Testament. In Acts 2:5 "devout men" gathered to worship according to the Old Covenant feast of harvest. They did not yet believe in Jesus Christ, but, hearing the mighty works of God in the praises and proclamations of the disciples who were filled with the Holy Spirit in the Upper Room, they came together. As the church extols and lifts up the Father of our Lord Jesus Christ, the nations are drawn to the Lord through their praise and adoration.

To emphasize this point further, the apostle Paul speaks of the joining of worship and evangelism in 1 Corinthians 14:24–25, where he is correcting error in the Corinthian church. What is important to recognize regarding the evangelistic nature of worship is that Paul assumes the unbeliever, the outsider, would be in the midst of the covenant people in worship. What he points out so clearly is that the worship of the church must be intelligible. The gift of prophetic preaching in the language of

---

7. Edmund Clowney, "Kingdom Evangelism," in *The Pastor-Evangelist*, ed. Roger S. Greenway (Phillipsburg, N.J.: P&R, 1985), 23.

8. Ibid.

the people was to be desired more than speaking in foreign languages. In this way, the unbeliever who comes into our midst will clearly understand what is going on, who God is, and where he stands before Him. The result will be that he is without excuse, and he will fall down and confess the Lord's presence among His people (cf. Zech. 8:23).

Two Extremes

This is the biblical picture of evangelistic worship, which steers us clear of two problematic views of worship in our day, a subject that is especially important to think about for those who are planting a confessional church among non-confessional churches. On the one hand, the seeker-sensitive approach views worship *as* evangelism. Thus, everything is calculated to make the unbeliever feel comfortable. The congregation sings modern rock songs or praise songs set to rock tunes because they are familiar, the "preaching" is focused on how to live successful lives, and all types of activities abound to get children into the church. Yet, this type of worship does not build up the saints, who are simply there to bring in unbelievers.

This problematic approach may not affect us. Instead, there is another that does affect us. In Reformed churches, we tend to treat worship *as* edification and instruction of the saints. We think it is only for the covenant community, so we view our worship service as if only believers were there. What happens with this approach is that the lost in our midst are bored and do not understand what is happening. It prompts evangelicals like Jack Hayford to perceive Reformed churches in this way: "Reformed theology has…ended up creating a monster of theology that dampens the place of our passion and partnership with God."[9]

Outsiders view us this way because we have allowed the world to see us as the "frozen chosen." Rather, we need to let our theology reform our worship. Should we have passion for God? How can we not after reading question and answer 1 of the Westminster Shorter Catechism and the Heidelberg Catechism? Do we believe in partnership with God? Doesn't our covenant theology teach us that the infinite God has condescended to us and joined us in a covenant relationship with Him?

What, then, are we to do to both instruct the believer and lead the unbeliever to Christ in our worship at the same time? New York City

---

9. In Tim Stafford, "The Pentecostal Gold Standard," *Christianity Today* 49, 7 (July 2005): 27.

pastor Timothy Keller explains, "In summary, if the Sunday service aims primarily at evangelism, it will bore the saints. If it aims primarily at education, it will confuse unbelievers. But if it aims at praising the God who saves by grace, it will both instruct insiders and challenge outsiders. Good corporate worship will naturally be evangelistic."[10]

What Can We Do?

First, we must grasp the truth that public worship of God is the most important thing we do as a church plant. This is what God created us to do for eternity. Again, public worship is the hub of the wheel of the Christian life, including evangelism.

Second, we as Reformed churches must make our worship more celebratory. We do a great job of conveying reverence and awe for the Lord, yet we must also come with joy and praise. Jesus Christ is no longer in the tomb—He is risen indeed. Because He is risen, so are we. And as re-created people in the image of God, we have the Spirit in our hearts who cries out within us. The world must see that we are a transformed people who have been liberated from the bondage of sin. Our worship, as Keller says, must be focused on exalting the triune God of grace; in doing so, the world will be drawn into the wonder of worshiping the almighty yet merciful God. This immensely God-centered worship will set an excellent precedent for a new church plant.

Third, we must make our worship intelligible, as the apostle told the Corinthians to do. We can do this simply by having attractive bulletins that clearly set out the order of service in a way anyone can understand. Also, we need to have brief pamphlets available that explain what worship is, especially in a Reformed setting.[11] Even more, we ministers must teach our people about worship so that they are equipped to answer their unsaved neighbors' questions in an intelligible way. Week in and week out we can do so by simply explaining an element or two of the service, cycling through the entire liturgy over the course of a few months.

Fourth, our liturgies must proclaim the gospel. The progression of entering the presence of God at His gracious call, confessing our many sins and receiving His forgiveness, hearing the Word of the Lord as both law and gospel are preached, and seeing, touching, smelling, and tast-

---

10. Timothy J. Keller, "Reformed Worship in the Global City," in *Worship by the Book*, ed. D.A. Carson (Grand Rapids: Zondervan, 2002), 219.

11. See chapter 10, "Being a Welcoming Church Plant," by Kevin Efflandt.

ing that the Lord is good (Ps. 34:8) are necessary to teach and convey the drama of our redemption to us, our children, and the lost. One way we can do this in our church plants is in utilizing the historic liturgies of the church. We have a treasure that in many ways is gathering dust. Using the great prayers of Calvin, Luther, Cranmer, and others communicates the timeless truths of the Word in a way that lifts us up beyond ourselves and our time and place. The world longs for transcendence, and this is one way to engage in that.

Fifth, we, as the people of the Lord, must be salt and light in our daily lives. After developing relationships with our neighbors, we should invite them to join us in the house of the Lord to worship the God who made them and who has come to die for sinners. We need to be comfortable bringing the world to our church plants to worship, knowing that our worship will be meaningful, understandable, and, most importantly, saturated with the good news of the gospel. In doing this, we can be Reformed churches that are faithfully heeding the psalmist's call to sing the new song of Christ in the midst of an ungodly world. As we do so, the world will see us praising the unseen God, and, we pray, come among us and know that God is with us. May God make it so.

CHAPTER THIRTEEN

∾

"How's the Food?"
The Church Plant's Most Important Ingredient

Michael G. Brown

In some ways, a local church is like a restaurant; it is a place where people go to eat a meal. The pastor, like a chef, works with the finest ingredients and labors with his knowledge and passion to prepare something excellent. Guests arrive, sit down, and enjoy a meal that is served. Granted, the two belong to different kingdoms. A local restaurant belongs to the common kingdom; it is a business establishment frequented by customers. The local church, on the other hand, belongs to the kingdom of God; it is a manifestation of the body of Christ, created by His Word and Spirit.

Nevertheless, we should not dismiss the analogy too hastily. Before He ascended into heaven, Jesus told Peter, "Feed my lambs.... Feed my sheep" (John 21:15b, 17b). This command was from the same God who previously announced to His people,

> Ho! Everyone who thirsts,
>   Come to the waters;
>   And you who have no money,
>   Come, buy and eat.
>   Yes, come, buy wine and milk
>   Without money and without price.
>   Why do you spend money for what is not bread,
>   And your wages for what does not satisfy?
>   Listen carefully to Me, and eat what is good,
>   And let your soul delight itself in abundance.
>   Incline your ear, and come to Me.
>   Hear, and your soul shall live (Isa. 55:1–3a).

God compares hearing to eating. Just as the body needs nourishment from food, so also the soul needs nourishment from Christ, the Bread of Life, whom we receive in Word and sacrament. Feeding the sheep, therefore, is the chief part of Peter's exhortation to pastors in local churches to "shepherd the flock of God" (1 Peter 5:2a; cf. Acts 20:28). It is the fulfillment of God's promise in Jeremiah: "And I will give you shepherds according to My heart, who will feed you with knowledge and understanding" (Jer. 3:15; cf. 23:1–4; 31:10). As the eminent Puritan John Owen said, "This feeding is by the preaching of the gospel. He is no pastor who doth not feed his flock. It belongs essentially to the office."[1]

The church, then, is the place where the sheep go to eat. It does not merely consist of *people*; it is also the *place* where Christ, through His under-shepherds, feeds His flock publicly and corporately. The church plant is simply an infant manifestation of this people and place. And like a new restaurant, the church plant must serve excellent food. If it does not, it will stand little chance for survival and will fail in its objective of making disciples. It may have a solid liturgy, warm and friendly people, and a great location, but if the food is not top-notch, few people will be willing to drive long distances to worship each week and transplant their families to a struggling new mission work. Thus, as word of mouth travels about the church plant, the church planter must do all he can to give people a reason to offer a glowing report to that inevitable and most critical question, "How's the food?"

This chapter explores some of the essential ingredients of the food the church planter prepares each week for Christ's flock. It is by no means the final word on preaching and teaching. Rather, it is a brief description of several key features that must be present in the church planter's ministry of God's Word, pursuing the question, "What are we serving to our people in the church plant?" Since preaching and teaching are two different mediums, we will consider them separately.

Preaching

Kevin Vanhoozer notes, "The sermon is the best frontal assault on imaginations held captive by secular stories that promise other ways to the good life."[2] Curved in on ourselves in selfish introspection and idol worship, we need an external word, a voice that comes from outside of ourselves, to intrude our make-believe worlds and tell us the truth. The "lively preaching of His Word," as the Heidelberg Catechism puts it, is

---

1. John Owen, "Sermon V" in *The Works of John Owen* (Edinburgh: Banner of Truth, 1998), 9:453.
2. Kevin J. Vanhoozer, *The Drama of Doctrine: A Canonical-Linguistic Approach to Christian Theology* (Louisville, Ky.: Westminster, 2005), 456.

God's ordained means to accomplish this (HC, Q&A 98). God sends His appointed emissary to His covenant people in order to proclaim His covenantal speech from His canon of Scripture. It is an intrusive act, driving us out of ourselves and directing our faith to the promises of God, which in Christ are "Yes" and "Amen" (2 Cor. 1:20). The Westminster Larger Catechism gets at this precise point when it describes how the Holy Spirit makes the Word effectual to salvation:

> The Spirit of God maketh the reading, but especially the preaching of the word, an effectual means of enlightening, convincing, and humbling sinners; *of driving them out of themselves, and drawing them unto Christ;* of conforming them to His image, and subduing them to His will; of strengthening them against temptations and corruptions; of building them up in grace, and establishing their hearts in holiness and comfort through faith unto salvation (WLC, Q&A 155, emphasis added).

The Holy Spirit uses this external Word to accomplish an inward renewal. "Faith comes by hearing, and hearing by the word of God" (Rom. 10: 17). The preached Word redefines us as it redirects our gaze away from ourselves and to our Prophet, Priest, and King.

The sad reality, however, is that most who visit a Reformed church plant come from churches where preaching has not been understood in this way. Visitors lament hearing preaching that is more about them than Christ. They have been living on a diet of watered-down messages of moralism and therapy, which turn the gospel into good advice rather than good news. It is common for these visitors to come to our church plants beaten up and broken after years of hearing the law preached badly and being pointed back to themselves rather than to Christ. They are weary from their continual failure to live up to the so-called victorious Christian life, sick of narcissistic and anti-intellectual drivel, and often close to abandoning the church altogether. In short, they are starving for a good meal on Sunday. Their interest in Reformed theology may have been piqued by listening to radio programs such as *Renewing Your Mind* or *The White Horse Inn,* and, consequently, they have come to the Reformed church plant hoping to hear the preaching of Christ and Him crucified rather than, as William Willimon puts it, "humanity and it improved."[3]

---

3. William Willimon, *Peculiar Speech: Preaching to the Baptized* (Grand Rapids: Eerdmans, 1992), 9.

The Reformed church planter, therefore, is in a unique position to feed these weary sheep with a magnificent meal every week. These poor souls have been living on McDonald's, so to speak. The church plant, however, should be like a five-star restaurant. It may be tiny, it may meet in a school gym or rented facility, but it offers something that these tired and hungry people cannot find anywhere else.

With that in mind, it is highly recommended that the church planter focus on preparing his food with three essential qualities: First, his preaching should be redemptive-historical in nature. Second, it must always rightly distinguish between law and gospel. Finally, it must be served with clarity, simplicity, and passion.

Redemptive-Historical

The definition of "redemptive-historical preaching" often varies within Reformed circles. I have sometimes heard people caricaturize redemptive-historical preaching as preaching that ignores the imperatives of Scripture and leaves little place, if any, for application. This is an unfortunate misrepresentation. Redemptive-historical preaching, in its most simple definition, is preaching that preaches Christ from the whole Bible. It assumes that the Scriptures are not a collection of timeless principles in abstract but rather a coherent record of progressive revelation that tells the story of God redeeming a people for Himself through the person and work of Christ, His Son.[4] It takes seriously Christ's admonition to the Pharisees, who missed the point of this story: "You search the Scriptures, for in them you think you have eternal life; and these are they which testify of Me" (John 5:39). It is the kind of preaching that Christ delivered to His disciples on the road to Emmaus, where, "Beginning at Moses and all the Prophets, He expounded to them in all the Scriptures the things concerning Himself" (Luke 24:27). It applies biblical theology, which, as Graeme Goldsworthy notes, "is nothing more or less than allowing the

---

4. For basic resources on this theme see the following: for beginners—Derke P. Bergsma, *Redemption: The Triumph of God's Great Plan* (Lansing, Ill.: Redeemer Books, 1989); Graeme Goldsworthy, *According to Plan: The Unfolding Revelation of God in the Bible* (Leicester, England: InterVarsity, 1991); for intermediate—Michael Horton, *God of Promise: Introducing Covenant Theology* (Grand Rapids: Baker, 2006.); for advanced—Herman Witsius, *The Economy of the Covenants between God and Man: Comprehending a Complete Body of Divinity* (1822; repr., Grand Rapids: Reformation Heritage Books, 2010).

Bible to speak as a whole: as the one word of the one God about the one way of salvation."[5]

Most people visiting a Reformed church for the first time have never heard the Old Testament preached this way. They have heard characters such as Noah, Joseph, David, and Daniel preached as moral examples to imitate but not as sinners in the unfolding drama of redemptive history who foreshadowed Christ. Consequently, they have not really learned the Bible. Edmund Clowney observes, "It is possible to know Bible stories, yet miss *the* Bible story."

> The Bible is much more than William How stated: 'a golden casket where gems of truth are stored.' It is more than a bewildering collection of oracles, proverbs, poems, architectural directions, annals, and prophecies. The Bible has a story line. It traces an unfolding drama. The story follows the history of Israel, but it does not begin there, nor does it contain what you would expect in a national history. The narrative does not pay tribute to Israel. Rather, it regularly condemns Israel and justifies God's severest judgments. The story is God's story. It describes His work to rescue rebels from their folly, guilt, and ruin.[6]

Starving, weary souls need to hear this story line and unfolding drama. They do not need another topical series on how to be a better husband, father, or employee. Most visitors to our churches have heard those sermons preached ad nauseam. Rather, they need to learn the Bible as God gave it to us, hearing the redemptive work of Christ preached from all the Scriptures.

This is not to say, of course, that the Bible is silent about our roles as husbands, fathers, or employees or that the texts addressing those subjects should not be preached. But it must be understood that the Bible never addresses ethics abstractly or in a way that is detached from its central message of the redemptive-historical work of Christ. Paul's treatment of these very roles in Ephesians 5:22–6:9 is a perfect example. He preaches these imperatives only after and in vital connection to the indic-

---

5. Graeme Goldsworthy, *Preaching the Whole Bible as Christian Scripture* (Grand Rapids: Eerdmans, 2000), 7. This and the following titles provide good, accurate explanations of redemptive-historical preaching: Edmund Clowney, *Preaching Christ in All of Scripture* (Wheaton, Ill.: Crossway, 2003); Dennis Johnson, *Him We Proclaim: Preaching Christ from All the Scriptures* (Phillipsburg, N.J.: P&R, 2007).

6. Edmund Clowney, *The Unfolding Mystery: Discovering Christ in the Old Testament* (Phillipsburg, N.J.: P&R, 1988), 11.

ative he previously taught in the first three-and-a-half chapters. He first spends ample time telling us what God has done for us in Christ before he tells us how we should live as those whom God has raised to newness of life. Sermons on the imperatives in an epistle, therefore, should never stand apart from the gospel-based thrust of the epistle as a whole. As Geerhardus Vos says, our sermons should always be keyed to the gospel note: "Let us therefore be careful to key our preaching to such a note that when we stand as ministrants behind the table of our Lord to distribute the bread of life, our congregation shall feel that what we are doing then is only the sum and culmination of what we have been doing every Sabbath from the pulpit."[7]

Nor should we preach a New Testament text in a way that detaches it from its Old Testament promise. The structure of Old Testament promise and New Testament fulfillment is the Bible's prescribed method for our preaching (as demonstrated clearly in the sermon-letter to the Hebrews as well as the apostles' preaching in the book of Acts).

For this reason it is critical that the church planter preach *lectio continua* through whole books of the Bible and show how the gospel is central theologically in all the Scriptures. He must avoid the temptation to skip over significant sections of Old Testament books, such as the genealogies in Genesis, the ceremonial laws in the latter part of Exodus, or the apocalyptic imagery in the second half of Daniel, in order to emphasize the more "practical" parts of the book. Such picking and choosing of God's Word is irresponsible. We should not try to be wiser than God. He knows what we need far better than we do, and to that end He has given us the whole counsel of His Word—genealogies, ceremonial laws, and apocalyptic visions included. The truth is that these passages mystify most Christians. It is the preacher's job to explain these passages and show how they are a necessary part of God's redemptive-historical record that climaxes in the person and work of Christ. As R. L. Dabney explains, "The preacher's business is to take what is given him in the Scriptures, as it is given to him, and to endeavor to imprint it on the souls of men. All else is God's work."[8]

As any preacher faithful to this method knows, many people who hear the Bible preached and explained this way for the first time will

---

7. Geerhardus Vos, *Grace and Glory* (Edinburgh: Banner of Truth, 1994), 239.
8. R. L. Dabney, *Evangelical Eloquence* (1870; repr., Edinburgh: Banner of Truth, 1999), 37.

begin to develop a healthy and voracious appetite for God's Word. They become excited about learning how the Bible fits together and testifies of Christ in all of its genres. A thrilled sense of expectancy in the preached Word is cultivated in them. When they are asked, "Why do you go to that tiny little church that meets in the school?" it is not uncommon for them to answer with a smile, "Because, for the first time in my life, I'm learning how the Bible is all about Christ!"

Law-Gospel

An essential component of redemptive-historical preaching is the historically Protestant distinction of law and gospel. Rejecting the medieval hermeneutic of old law/new law, the Reformers adopted a covenantal hermeneutic to describe this distinction, equating the covenant of works to the law, which, as Zacharias Ursinus says in his Larger Catechism, "requires our perfect obedience to God" and "promises eternal life to those who keep it," and the covenant of grace to the gospel, which "shows us the fulfillment in Christ of the righteousness that the law requires" and "promises eternal life freely because of Christ to those who believe in him."[9] In the gospel, God provides to us in Christ what He demands from us in the law. The law says, "Do this and live," but the gospel says, "Christ did it for you." As Calvin's successor in Geneva, Theodore Beza, pointed out, the "ignorance of this distinction between Law and Gospel is one of the principal sources of the abuses which corrupted and still corrupt Christianity."[10]

Most visitors to our churches have been sitting under preaching that is ignorant of this distinction for some time. Instead of getting both law and gospel in their diet, they have been getting a compromised blend of the two, a sort of "go-law-spel" that is neither law nor gospel but rather a moralistic "law-lite" devoid of spiritual nutrients. "The law must be proclaimed in all of its force," says Michael Horton, "as God's unmasking of the 'spin' with which we have told the story of our lives, and the gospel must be proclaimed in all of its joy, as God's own act of clothing us in

---

9. Zacharias Ursinus, *Larger Catechism*, Q. 36, as cited in *An Introduction to the Heidelberg Catechism: Sources, History, and Theology*, ed. Lyle D. Bierma (Grand Rapids: Baker, 2005), 168–69.

10. Theodore Beza, *The Christian Faith*, trans. by James Clark (Lewes, England: Christian Focus, 1992), 41.

Christ's righteousness."[11] Anything less will have the effect of directing our hearers back to themselves rather than to Christ. Failure to distinguish law and gospel will inevitably cause the gospel to be presented as a new law, much as it was in the Middle Ages. It will be portrayed as a lighter version of Moses rather than proclaimed as the good news that motivates us to grateful obedience. This type of preaching will unavoidably produce one of two terrible responses in its hearers: either self-righteousness (that is, those who have fooled themselves into thinking they are keepers of the law) or despair (that is, those who know the painful reality of not living up to its demands but find no relief or hope in the message they are hearing).

The preacher, then, should take heed to the wisdom of our Reformed forebears who addressed this issue. William Perkins, for example, the father of Elizabethan Puritanism, urged new preachers to learn what he called the basic principle in application. In his 1592 book on preaching, *The Art of Prophesying,* he pointed out the importance of rightly distinguishing between law and gospel in sermon preparation: "The basic principle in application is to know whether the passage is a statement of the law or the gospel. For when the Word is preached, the law and the gospel operate differently. The law exposes the disease of sin, and as a side-effect stimulates and stirs it up. But it provides no remedy for it.... The law is, therefore, first in the order of teaching; then comes the gospel."[12]

Perkins recognized that a crucial part of the preacher's task in handling rightly the word of truth (2 Tim. 2:15) is identifying the difference between the indicative and imperative moods in Scripture. It is reckless to "preach the Word" arbitrarily without making this critical distinction, for it will only confuse law with gospel and consequently rob Christ's sheep of the one thing that offers them hope in this life and motivates them to joyful, godly living.

This does not negate the necessity of preaching the law in its "third use." As Horton illustrates, the law, for the Christian, functions like "sophisticated navigational gadgetry" on a sailboat, telling us the direction in which we are to travel. Yet, as important as such equipment is, it does not have the ability to move the sailboat. He points out, "You are

---

11. Michael Horton, *People and Place: A Covenant Ecclesiology* (Louisville, Ky.: Westminster, 2008), 50.

12. William Perkins, *The Art of Prophesying* (1592; repr., Edinburgh: Banner of Truth, 1996), 54.

thoroughly apprised of your location and direction, you know where to go, but you have no power."[13] Sailboats require wind in their sails if they are to move across the water. The gospel (the announcement of what God has done for us in Christ) is that wind. Horton concludes, "The problem is that apart from the gospel (indicative), the law (imperative) cannot actually accomplish anything in us but death and despair, 'because law brings wrath' (Rom 4:15)."[14] When we preach the third use of the law, then, it must always flow directly from the gospel, as the structure of the Heidelberg Catechism conveys so well.

Consequently, we cannot make the deadly assumption that our hearers already know the gospel and do not need to hear it preached regularly for their sanctification. If we do not preach the gospel regularly to our hearers, we will leave them dead in the water, or, to return to our previous metaphor, we will serve them food with empty calories. Concerned about consistency in this regard, Iain Murray offers an appropriate admonition to preachers: "It is true that the consequences of faithful preaching are with God and not with us, but are we sure that we are making salvation by Christ's righteousness as clear and prominent as it ought to be? Here is the only message truly relevant to the reality of the condition of fallen men and women. Every offer of hope to individuals which is based upon moral education, self-improvement, or religious devotion, is an empty hope."[15]

Only the gospel has the power to make the imperatives of Scripture our "reasonable service" (Rom. 12:1–2). But this message does not come to us by nature. It is not an inner word that arises from our own hearts; rather, it is a word that someone needs to tell us regularly. Again, Horton makes the point well:

> As the creature made in God's image for obedient fellowship, law is our native tongue. Although we suppress its truth in our own unrighteousness, we still know the law and the God who still requires this stipulated love of God and neighbor. As a surprising announcement that in Christ we have passed from death to life and from wrath from grace, however, the gospel is counterintuitive. So if we allow reason and experience—that which is inherent, familiar, and inwardly certain—not only to guide our access but also to deter-

---

13. Michael Horton, *A Better Way: Rediscovering the Drama of God-Centered Worship* (Grand Rapids: Baker, 2002), 73.

14. Ibid., 74.

15. Iain Murray, *The Old Evangelicalism* (Edinburgh: Banner of Truth, 2005), 95.

mine reality, we will be left with Kant to the 'starry heavens above and the moral law within.' The good news has to be *told*, and to the extent that it is assimilated to what we think we already know and experience, it will not be good news at all: perhaps pious advice, good instruction, and practical suggestions, but not good news.[16]

Invariably, by the Spirit's grace, people who sit under preaching that rightly distinguishes law and gospel will rediscover the liberating joy of Christianity. Pointed to their Savior and away from themselves, they will find grace surprising again.

Clear, Simple, and Passionate

I must address briefly the presentation of the food we serve, that is, the delivery of our sermons. Exploring the mechanics of good homiletics is beyond the scope of this chapter, but it should be duly noted that clarity and simplicity must be of the essence of a church planter's preaching. Preaching Christ consistently from all the Scriptures and rightly distinguishing between law and gospel will do us little good if our hearers find our speech unclear, convoluted, or overly burdensome to follow. As Bryan Chapell warns, "All preachers simply need to make sure that what they preach will communicate and not complicate the truths of God."[17]

The preacher in a church plant must pay careful attention to Chapell's warning. Preaching that is laborious to listen to may be (and perhaps, in some cases, should be) the hurdle that visitors cannot leap. Reformed church plants already have enough hurdles. In many cases (at least in the early stages), the congregation appears uncomfortably small, the singing sounds awkwardly inept, and the facility appears hopelessly unattractive. The church plant will probably not make much of a first impression on visitors, even though their perception may not be correct. When we add unclear or complicated preaching to these unfavorable circumstances, it becomes too much to ask visitors to consider uprooting their families and committing themselves to the church plant. Conversely, "people love to listen to what they can understand," says Chapell. "Speak plainly and people will listen."[18] We cannot overemphasize this point: the preaching in a church plant must be clear and simple.

---

16. Horton, *People and Place*, 73.
17. Bryan Chapell, *Christ-Centered Preaching* (Grand Rapids: Baker, 1994), 122.
18. Ibid., 325.

It is highly recommended, therefore, that the church planter use a sound, straightforward structure in his sermons: short introductions, three or four simple points that arise plainly from the text, strong conclusions that emphasize the redemptive work of Christ, and plenty of illustration and application where appropriate. He might consider providing sermon notes for the children in his congregation, which will foster their listening and stimulate discussion with their parents after the service.[19] Addressing the children directly at some point in his sermon is also a good practice. Clear and simple redemptive-historical preaching combined with application will not only increase the listener's appetite for God's Word but will also develop the listener's ear to follow the logical argument of sermons and thereby learn the meaning of the text that is preached. The church-planting preacher need not strive for originality and novelty; his clarity and simplicity in preaching Christ from all the Scriptures will cause his people to want to come back for more. They will be delighted in learning the Bible and understanding what they hear.

This is not to say that the church planter should avoid unfamiliar, theological terms in his sermons. Preaching is "peculiar speech," as Willimon argues. "We preachers need not be embarrassed by the distinctiveness of our speech."[20] As one must learn a new vocabulary when learning a foreign language (or new job, new sport, or new hobby), so also must a disciple of Christ learn the vocabulary of the church. Terms such as "justification," "sanctification," "Trinity," and "incarnation" take time to learn. The preacher is the appointed instructor to teach Christ's sheep this new vocabulary. His preaching should accomplish this in a way that encourages the congregation to learn more.

Finally, the food in the church plant should be served with passion. Though it is the Spirit of God who does the work in preaching, the Word preached should nevertheless grip the one who preaches it. "I think, truly," said Owen, "that no man preaches that sermon well to others that doth not first preach it to his own heart."[21] Such a statement contains wisdom and should not be written off as Donatistic. While God can use (and has used) a donkey to speak to people, He typically uses ministers who believe the gospel and are passionate to serve it to their flock. Owen explains further, "He who doth not feed on, and digest, and thrive by,

---

19. See "Morning Sermon Notes for Covenant Children" at the end of the chapter.
20. Willimon, *Peculiar Speech,* 8.
21. Owen, *Works,* 9:455.

what he prepares for his people, he may give them poison."[22] The church planter should be a preacher whom people expect to stand before them each week and say, "I have good news for you today. I have prepared something good for your souls, and I cannot wait to serve it to you!" A preacher who is excited about the gospel will invariably be excited to proclaim that gospel to others. Passion of this sort will not only be an ally to the church planter during tough times, but it will also be infectious to the growing congregation.

In sum, the church planter must strive to be an excellent preacher. There is a certain sense in which he really has nothing else to offer. He may be a great organizer, efficient administrator, or possess good counseling skills, but if he is not a faithful preacher who preaches Christ from all the Scriptures consistently and clearly and strives constantly to improve his craft, the church plant will be in jeopardy. Just as a new restaurant requires a good chef, a church plant requires a good preacher.

Teaching

People want to know what they believe and why. A recent study conducted by one of the largest evangelical megachurches in the United States, Willow Creek Community Church, revealed that the majority of their longtime members who felt dissatisfied with church and were tempted to leave desired in-depth theology classes, something their church had not offered previously. We should not find these results surprising. Created to love the Lord with our minds, we possess a natural desire to have our minds furnished with knowledge of God: who He is and what He has done.

This is one of the reasons people find Reformed churches attractive. Reformed churches are teaching churches.[23] Our tradition emphasizes catechetical instruction and encourages personal growth in the knowledge of God. While not as primary in importance as preaching, teaching is nevertheless a fundamental discipline of the church planter. Visitors to a Reformed church plant are presumably interested in Reformed theology, so they need a forum in which they can learn this theology and get a handle on it relatively quickly. The church planter, then, should provide his congregation and visitors with the opportunity to learn Reformed theology and have their questions answered and concerns addressed. At

---

22. Ibid.
23. For spiritual growth through teaching in church plants, see *POPC*, 58–61.

least four areas should be emphasized: Reformed confessions, covenant theology, worship, and membership matters.

Reformed Confessions

It is critical that visitors learn early on that our most important distinctive as a Reformed church is that we are a confessional church. That is to say, we stand with the Protestant Reformation and historic Christian faith by confessing certain doctrines summarized in ecumenical creeds and Presbyterian/Reformed confessions. Without those creeds and confessions, we are not a Reformed church.

Many visitors will find this somewhat strange. They want to know why we put such emphasis upon uninspired and fallible documents written by men. After all, if we have the Bible, which alone is the inspired Word of God and the only rule for faith and life, why should Christians bother with things like the Apostles' Creed, the Nicene Creed, the Heidelberg Catechism, the Belgic Confession, the Canons of Dort, or the Westminster Standards? This is a common (and valid) question. The church planter should offer a class, perhaps in connection with a membership class, in which he teaches the creeds and confessions of his church. This allows potential new members to read through, become familiar with, and receive instruction on the confessional standards that codify Reformed doctrine, preserve the church's unity, and protect it from heresy.

The church planter might also consider writing a pamphlet that explains the necessity of creeds and confessions that is readily available for visitors. Pamphlets or booklets, produced easily and inexpensively through software such as Microsoft Publisher, are an excellent way for the church planter to teach his growing congregation Reformed doctrine and practice. People who are new to a Reformed church will often ask the same questions. Providing free literature that anticipates these questions not only saves the church planter a lot of time in explanation but also allows him to instruct the flock on a broader basis.

Covenant Theology

Many church planters will soon find that many (if not most) of the visitors to their churches come from churches that taught dispensationalist theology. It is a regrettable fact that dispensationalism is the dominant theological system in the American evangelical church today. It is common to meet visitors who assume that Reformed theology consists of the so-called five points of Calvinism. These visitors are often amazed (and sometimes a little shocked) to find that Reformed theology has a different interpretation of the Bible from the one they learned and rejects the notion of two programs for two peoples of God—Israel and the church—culminating in a pretribulational rapture and premillennial return of Christ.

The church planter, then, should offer a regular class, perhaps midweek, that helps people learn the basics of covenant theology. The covenant of redemption, covenant of works, covenant of grace, and the differences between the Abrahamic, Mosaic, and new covenants can usually be covered in about six weeks. We should not underestimate the dividends such a class will pay. Learning to read the Bible with a covenantal hermeneutic is not only an exhilarating experience for the newly Reformed Christian but is also an indispensable discipline that reaps practical benefits throughout the believer's life. The subject of covenant theology should be a staple item on the church planter's teaching menu.

Worship

Like Reformed confessions and covenant theology, Reformed worship is often a foreign concept to visitors. Accustomed to praise bands with cutting-edge music, light and airy conversational speech in the sermon, and a tone of entertainment throughout the service, many visitors find Reformed worship austere and slightly strange. The minister raises his hands in the salutation and benediction; he reads the law and leads the congregation in confession of their sins and in proclaiming assurance of forgiveness from the Word. Even the songs in the service are unfamiliar. Instead of popular praise songs, the congregation sings psalms and sometimes reverent hymns rich in theology. Though these practices are old and have been present in Christian churches down through the centuries, visitors from evangelical churches will find them new and out of the ordinary.

The church planter should never be apologetic or embarrassed about Reformed worship, and many visitors will find the worship to be a refreshing change from the shallow and irreverent services they are used to. Still, the minister should take time to explain why we do what we do in our worship services. In either an adult Sunday school class or midweek study, the church planter should help his flock understand the purpose of the worship service (God serving us in the means of grace), the regulative principle, the difference between elements and circumstances, and the meaning of each part of the worship service. Teaching such a class early in the life of the church plant and on a regular basis thereafter will help lay a firm foundation in the new congregation's understanding of and love for Reformed worship.

There are many tools available to help the church planter accomplish this goal. *With Reverence and Awe: Recovering the Basics of Reformed Worship* by Darryl Hart and John Meuther, and *A Better Way: Rediscovering the Drama of God-Centered Worship* by Michael Horton, are both worthy books to consult for preparation. Daniel Hyde and Jon Payne have also produced helpful short books on worship: *What to Expect in Reformed Worship: A Visitor's Guide,* and *In the Splendor of Holiness: Recovering the Beauty of Reformed Worship for the 21st Century,* respectively, which are designed for laypeople thinking through these issues for the first time. Again, self-produced pamphlets are also an excellent resource to distribute that can address the particular questions visitors and new congregants ask: "What is the benediction?" "Why do we pray the Lord's Prayer?" "Why do we have an evening service in addition to the morning service?" Pamphlets addressing these particular questions allow the church planter to speak to his congregation personally and pastorally.

Church Membership
Finally, the church planter should offer a thorough membership class that, as already mentioned, takes people through the confessional standards of his church. This class should also be the opportunity for people to ask questions freely about Reformed doctrine as well as voice their concerns about joining a Reformed church.[24] As any Reformed pastor knows, visitors often come from churches that had no formal membership. Church discipline and accountability to elders for one's doctrine and life are new concepts. The church planter should be sensitive to this and take time to explain pastorally the nature of the local congregation as a visible manifestation of Christ's church. He should do all he can to explain clearly what is expected of members, while at the same time maintaining an environment where people feel comfortable in expressing their apprehensions. This class is a vital aspect to the life of any Reformed church plant.

---

24. For more on membership classes, see Daniel R. Hyde, "Teaching Membership Classes," *Ordained Servant* 14, 1 (March 2005): 11–14.

Conclusion

Serving Christ's ordained food to His flock is not a mere social event; it creates Christ's new society. The church planter has been entrusted with the message that creates and sustains the church. Nothing should give him greater comfort in his task than to know that the gospel, by the Spirit's grace, will do the work for which it was ordained. It will create faith, open and close the door to the kingdom, sanctify its hearers, create true community, produce mutual love among the members of congregation, and draw people to hear it. It is the engine that pulls the train. The church planter need only be faithful to preach and teach that gospel fully, consistently, and clearly from all the Scriptures. May God raise up more men who will make it their aim to labor in the kitchen and prepare exceptional food for the souls of His people.

Morning Sermon Notes for Covenant Children

These sermon notes appeared in a bulletin for the morning worship service at Christ URC in Santee, California, for a sermon on Exodus 17:1–7.

Covenant Children's Notes
(Parents: Please follow up with your children at home.)

Morning Sermon: "Water from the Rock"
This sermon is about how Christ took our punishment and how living water flows from Him.

From what book of the Bible did the pastor preach?

Which chapter?

What were the three main points of the sermon?

1.

2.

3.

Count the number of times you hear the pastor use these words in his sermon:

Judgment—

Mercy—

Living water—

Questions to discuss at home:

1. Why were the Israelites angry with Moses?

2. What did God tell Moses to do?

3. According to the apostle Paul in 1 Corinthians 10, who is the rock in this story?

4. When was Christ struck with God's rod of judgment? Why is this good news for you?

CHAPTER FOURTEEN

༁

Church Membership and
the Church Plant

Michael G. Brown

One of the greatest challenges for the church planter in the twenty-first century is the task of helping new parishioners come to an understanding of biblical church membership. This concept is foreign to many professing Christians today, and the church planter is bound to face objections. "Why do I need to become a member of a church? I am already a Christian and have a personal relationship with Jesus." Brought up in the radical individualism and pragmatism common to American Christianity, many find the idea of formal membership in an established church to be antiquated, unnecessary, and even legalistic.

Moreover, church membership goes against the popular notion in our culture that organized religion should be set against spirituality. The former is disparaged as passé at best and hatefully intolerant at worst, while the latter is readily embraced as chic and healthy. Organized religion is viewed as something very particular that manifests itself in narrow doctrines, liturgical customs, and exclusive tradition. Spirituality, on the other hand, is too often seen as something universal that can express itself in a wide variety of personal faiths and individual practices that generally seek a common goal of self-improvement. Influenced by this mode of thinking, many professing Christians believe they can have membership in the invisible church while opting out of membership in the visible church.

Things do not appear to be improving. Indicators show this sentiment to be on the rise, not the decline. According to market research guru George Barna, established churches are rapidly becoming a thing of the past. "Based on our research," says Barna, "I have projected that by the year 2010, ten to twenty percent of Americans will derive all their spiritual input (and output) through the Internet."[1] Why would someone be incon-

---

1. George Barna, *Revolution: Finding Vibrant Faith Beyond the Walls of the Sanctuary* (Carol Stream, Ill.: Tyndale House, 2005), 180.

venienced by attending (let alone becoming a member of) a church when he can get the same spiritual benefits in private? Says Barna: "Ours is not the business of organized religion, corporate worship, or Bible teaching. If we dedicate ourselves to such a business we will be left by the wayside as the culture moves forward. Those are the fragments of a larger purpose to which we have been called by God's Word. We are in the business of life transformation."[2]

Since "life transformation" can come from a multiplicity of methods in our fast-paced culture of technology and personal convenience, the church needs to update itself if it wants to remain relevant to spiritual consumers. Organized churches that require formal membership are not what the "experts" have in mind.

The confessional church planter, then, seems to be swimming upstream. He will find himself continuously explaining, often to those who are quite skeptical, why Christians must join a true, local church. Added to this challenge is the somewhat complicated scenario of membership in a church plant during the planting stage. Much is dependent upon the overseeing church until the plant organizes as an established congregation in the denomination or federation to which it belongs. With these challenges in mind, this chapter will pursue three questions: What is church membership? Why is church membership necessary? How does church membership operate in a church plant?

What Is Church Membership?

Church membership is a formal, covenantal relationship between a particular family or individual and a true, local manifestation of Christ's visible church. It begins with the understanding that Christ not only possesses an invisible church, that is, all the elect people of God whose names are written in the Lamb's book of life (Rev. 21:27), but He has also established a visible church on earth (Matt. 28:18–20; cf. WCF, chap. 25).

God first instituted this visible church immediately after the fall when He separated the seed of the woman from the seed of the serpent and established the woman's seed as a people united in His promise of salvation (Gen. 3:15). He further established His community when He made His covenant with the patriarch Abraham and his offspring (Gen. 15, 17) and fulfilled His promises, first in the nation of Israel and the Promised

2. George Barna, *The Second Coming of the Church* (Nashville: Word, 1998), 96.

Land of Canaan, but more fully in the person and work of Jesus Christ. Throughout the unfolding drama of redemptive history, from the days of Abraham to Christ, God kept His people as a visible covenant community marked by the covenantal sign and seal of circumcision.

With the completion of Christ's earthly ministry and the inauguration of the new covenant, however, God no longer confined His visible church to one people (national Israel) and one place (Palestine). Having satisfied the law of Moses in His life, death, and resurrection, Christ commissioned His apostles to preach the gospel, baptize, administer the Lord's Supper, and make disciples to the ends of the earth. As the book of Acts reveals, the apostles fulfilled this commission by planting churches (Acts 2:42). Beginning in Jerusalem, Christ added daily to His church those who were being saved (Acts 2:41, 47; 4:4). The visible, covenant community became a "chosen generation, a royal priesthood, a holy nation, His own special people" (1 Peter 2:9a; cf. Ex. 19:6), made up of people ransomed "out of every tribe and tongue and people and nation" (Rev. 5:9b).

After the apostles died, however, the visible church did not cease to exist. The New Testament makes clear that Christ has intended His visible church to continue until the end of the age. He ordained the office of pastor to feed His flock with the preaching of the gospel so that His sheep will be healthy and grow to maturity (Rom. 10:14–17; Eph. 4:11–16; 2 Tim. 4:1–5; Titus 1:5–9). He has supplied His church with the tangible elements of ordinary water, bread, and wine in the sacraments, which the Holy Spirit uses to nourish our faith (1 Cor. 10:16; 11:17–34; cf. John 6:41–58). He gave the office of elder so that His people will have guardians over their souls and governors keeping order (Acts 14:23; Phil. 1:1; 1 Tim. 3:1–7; 5:17; Heb. 13:17; 1 Peter 5:1–4). He maintains the purity and peace of His church through the exercise of discipline (Matt. 18:15–20; 1 Cor. 5; 2 Thess. 3:6, 14–15; Titus 1:10–14; 3:9–11). He has provided the office of deacon to ensure care for the poor and needy in the congregation (Acts 6:1–7; Phil. 1:1; 1 Tim. 3:8–13; 5:3–15). He pours out gifts upon His church so that each believer uses his or her gifts for the benefit of others (Rom. 12:3–8; 1 Cor. 12; Eph. 4:15–16). Everywhere, the New Testament reveals to us a church established by Christ that is an observable, identifiable society made up of real flesh-and-blood members and real organization and structure.

Church membership, therefore, is about belonging to this visible, identifiable community as it is manifested in the local congregation. The church is not a store frequented by loyal customers. Nor is it a voluntary association of individuals loosely united by consumer preferences or cultural practices. Rather, the church is the people who belong to Christ and the place where Christ meets them through the means He has ordained.

When families or individuals pursue formal church membership, they are saying, "We are Christians; therefore, we belong to Christ and His body." They and their children pass through the waters of baptism, acknowledging that they are part of something much larger than their own private, spiritual experience. They recognize that Christ has set them as living stones in His one temple (Eph. 2:19–22; 1 Peter 2:4–5) and gathered them as sheep in His one flock (John 10:1–29; Acts 20:28). They take public vows in the holy assembly of God's people in which they profess their faith in Christ and their willingness to submit to His lordship and the government of His church. Likewise, the congregation receives them and acknowledges their obligation to them as fellow members of God's family.

Why Is Church Membership Necessary?

"All of this sounds great," a visitor might say, "but I just want to attend your church. Why is it necessary that I become a member?" Frequently, the church planter will encounter people who recognize the visibility of Christ's church and enjoy attending worship services but view membership as little more than an unnecessary formality. In fact, it is common for a visiting family or individual to attend worship services regularly for more than a year without expressing any desire to join the church. What is the church planter to do in such situations? Either in his new-members class (which should also function as an orientation class for inquirers and visitors) or in private conversations with the family or individual, the church planter will need to provide reasons membership is necessary. The following three may be helpful to consider.

Submission to Christ

Christ is the head of His church (Eph. 1:22–23; 4:15) and the king of His kingdom (Matt. 28:18; 1 Cor. 15:25; Heb. 2:8–9; cf. Ps. 110:1). Christ was not only crucified and raised from the dead but He also ascended into heaven and was exalted at the right hand of the Father. In other words, He not only saves, He also rules. And the way He rules His citizens is through His Word and Spirit, chiefly through the officers He has appointed at the local congregation. Consider the exhortation the writer to the Hebrews gives at the end of his sermon-letter: "Obey those who rule over you, and be submissive, for they watch out for your souls, as those who must give account. Let them do so with joy and not with grief, for that would be unprofitable for you" (Heb. 13:17). This is Christ's design. As His subjects and possession, we must submit to what He has ordained.

Church membership is part of this submission. It allows the leaders in a local congregation to keep watch over our souls. As Michael Horton has pointed out, "We are commanded not to become self-feeders who mature beyond the nurture of the church, but to submit ourselves to the preaching, teaching, and oversight of those shepherds whom God has placed over us in Christ."[3] It has been the historical practice of Reformed churches to require a public vow to that end. For example, the fourth and final vow of the public profession of faith in the *Psalter Hymnal* that is used by the United Reformed Churches in North America asks: "Do you promise to submit to the government of the church and also, if you should become delinquent either in doctrine or in life, to submit to its admonition and discipline?"[4]

This practice, however, is precisely where the proverbial "rubber meets the road" for many people. Prizing their freedom to roam where they please, they simply cannot bring themselves to submit to Christ's delegated authority in His visible church. Kim Riddlebarger has appropriately labeled these folks "spiritual drifters": "Spiritual drifters…make little or no commitment to a particular congregation (much less express loyalty to a particular denomination and specific doctrine). These drifters will move from one church to another just as soon as something offends their fickle sensitivities, or when the preaching and music fail to keep them in rapt attention."[5] Spiritual drifters need to be confronted with texts such as Hebrews 13:17. One simply cannot claim to love Christ while despising His body. One cannot have Christ as Savior while refusing Him as Lord.

---

3. Michael Horton, "No Church, No Problem?" (chapter 4), 51.

4. *Psalter Hymnal* (Grand Rapids: Board of Publications of the Christian Reformed Church, 1976), 132.

5. Kim Riddlebarger, "The Fruit of Righteousness and Peace: On Church Discipline" in *Called to Serve: Essays for Elders and Deacons*, ed. Michael G. Brown (Grandville, Mich.: Reformed Fellowship, 2007), 199.

Accountability and Discipline

One of the ways Christ watches over our souls through the leaders in the local church is by the exercise of church discipline. Church discipline is the practice of applying the Word of God to members of the congregation who are in rebellion (that is, unrepentant of a particular sin) or involved in some public scandal that affects the health of the church as a whole. The goal of church discipline is the restoration of erring disciples, the preservation of the church's doctrine, the peace and purity of the congregation, and the protection of the church's reputation in the eyes of the unbelieving world.

Christ gave His church the authority to exercise discipline when He said to Peter, "I will give you the keys of the kingdom of heaven, and whatever you bind on earth will be bound in heaven, and whatever you loose on earth will be loosed in heaven" (Matt. 16:19). Reformed churches have understood these keys to be the preaching of the gospel and the exercise of church discipline (see WCF, chap. 30). The Heidelberg Catechism (1563) puts it like this:

> *83. What is the Office of the Keys?*
> The preaching of the holy Gospel and Church discipline; by which two things the kingdom of heaven is opened to believers and shut against unbelievers.

> *84. How is the kingdom of heaven opened and shut by the preaching of the holy Gospel?*
> In this way: that, according to the command of Christ, it is proclaimed and openly witnessed to believers, one and all, that as often as they accept with true faith the promise of the Gospel, all their sins are really forgiven them of God for the sake of Christ's merits; and on the contrary, to all unbelievers and hypocrites, that the wrath of God and eternal condemnation abide on them so long as they are not converted: according to which witness of the Gospel will be the judgment of God, both in this life and in that which is to come.

> *85. How is the kingdom of heaven shut and opened by Church discipline?*
> In this way: that, according to the command of Christ, if any under the Christian name show themselves unsound either in doctrine or life, and after repeated brotherly admonition refuse to turn from their errors or evil ways, they are complained of to the Church or to its proper officers, and, if they neglect to hear them also, are by them excluded from the holy Sacraments and the Christian communion,

and by God Himself from the kingdom of Christ; and if they promise and show real amendment, they are again received as members of Christ and His Church.

Reformed churches confess this because it is what the New Testament teaches. Jesus gave instruction on discipline and public excommunication in Matthew 18:15–20. Paul wrote a whole chapter to the church in Corinth describing how sexual immorality among Christians defiles the church and that the offender, if unrepentant, is to be excommunicated and delivered to Satan (1 Cor. 5). Other examples abound (1 Tim. 1:18–20; 6:3–5; 2 Tim. 2:14–18; Titus 1:10–14; 3:10–11).

Without church membership, however, the church cannot fully use the keys Christ has given her. The elders cannot excommunicate an unrepentant offender who was never in communion with the church in the first place. Church membership, therefore, provides every member of the congregation—including the minister and elders—with accountability. It allows the elders to fulfill their duty of ensuring that purity of doctrine and holiness of life are practiced; it permits the deacons to care for the needy within the church (Acts 6:1–7; 1 Tim. 5:9); and it makes every member in the congregation responsible for his doctrine and life. The person who does not join a true congregation of Christ's visible church, however, is accountable to no one but himself. He opts for a life of "Lone Ranger Christianity," acting as his own pastor, elder, and deacon.

Spiritual Nurture through the Sacraments
Church membership allows a disciple to participate in the sacraments and thereby receive the spiritual benefits that the Holy Spirit provides through them (1 Cor. 10:16). The spiritual drifter often presumes that he has a right to participate in the sacraments at any worship service he chooses to attend, simply by virtue of his personal relationship with Jesus. What he has yet to understand, however, is that Christ's sacraments are inseparably related to church membership.

One does not have the right to be baptized without joining the visible church. Christ instituted Christian baptism as a one-time, initiatory sacrament that not only signifies the washing away of sins with His atoning blood but also identifies the baptized person as a member of God's visible covenant community, much as circumcision did in the old covenant (Matt. 28:18–20; Acts 2:39). Thus, one is baptized into church membership and under the oversight of a local body of elders.

Likewise, one does not have the right to partake of the Lord's Table without church membership. Christ established the Lord's Supper as a holy meal for the members of His church. It not only signifies His body and blood offered on the cross but also nourishes the faith of repentant sinners (1 Cor. 10:16; cf. John 6:22–60). As the governors and overseers of the church (Rom. 12:7; 1 Cor. 12:28; 1 Tim. 3:1–7), the elders have the responsibility of supervising participation in the Lord's Table and ensuring, as much as possible, that people do not partake in an unworthy manner (1 Cor. 11:17–34). The Heidelberg Catechism summarizes the New Testament's teaching in this way:

81. Who are to come unto the table of the Lord?
Those who are displeased with themselves for their sins, yet trust that these are forgiven them, and that their remaining infirmity is covered by the passion and death of Christ; who also desire more and more to strengthen their faith and amend their life. But the impenitent and hypocrites eat and drink judgment to themselves.

82. Are they, then, also to be admitted to this Supper who show themselves to be, by their confession and life, unbelieving and ungodly?
No; for by this the covenant of God is profaned, and His wrath provoked against the whole congregation; wherefore the Christian Church is bound, according to the order of Christ and His Apostles, by the office of the keys to exclude such persons until they amend their life.

Reformed churches have sought to apply this teaching by requiring a public profession of faith and membership in good standing from all who come to the Lord's Table.[6]

The bottom line is that participation in the sacraments requires biblical church membership. While Christ has appointed the sacraments as visible signs and seals of the gospel for the nourishment of our souls, He did not design them to be individualistic practices. The sacraments are

---

6. For example, the *Directory for Public Worship of the Orthodox Presbyterian Church* says, "No one shall be allowed to take part in the celebration of the sacrament of the Lord's Supper who has not first made public profession of faith in Jesus Christ as his Savior and Lord" (chapter V.4). Article 45 of the Church Order of the United Reformed Churches in North America states: "The Consistory shall supervise participation at the Lord's Table. No member shall be admitted to the Lord's Table who has not first made public profession of faith and is not living a godly life. Visitors may be admitted provided that, as much as possible, the Consistory is assured of their biblical church membership, of their proper profession of faith, and of their godly walk."

acts of divine service to His assembled people on the Lord's Day. He condescends to His flock so that He can feed them with His means of grace.

The spiritual drifter, however, who is not accountable to a local congregation or in submission to Christ's authority, as it is delegated to church officers, seems to think he knows what is best for his spiritual well being, even if it is contrary to what God has revealed. Refusing to join Christ's visible church and submit to Christ's authority, he disqualifies himself from participation in the sacraments to the injury of his own soul.

Thus, Reformed churches confess in article 28 of the Belgic Confession: "We believe, since this holy assembly and congregation is the assembly of the redeemed and there is no salvation outside of it, that no one ought to withdraw from it, content to be by himself, no matter what his status or standing may be." The fact that in this life the visible church is imperfect and mixed with hypocrites gives no Christian the right to depart from it. As the church leader Cyprian explained in the year 251, "You cannot have God for your father unless you have the Church for your mother. If you could escape outside Noah's ark, you could escape outside the Church."[7] Except in otherwise extraordinary cases, a person cannot belong to the one, holy, catholic and apostolic church without also belonging to a visible manifestation of it as well, which, according to the New Testament, is the local congregation that preaches the gospel, administers the sacraments, and exercises church discipline.

A Pastoral Approach

But suppose a family or individual attends the church plant for an entire year and completes the new members' class but still does not want to join the church. What is the church planter to do? In such cases, there are at least three important things he must do.[8]

---

7. Cyprian, *The Unity of the Catholic Church*, in *Early Latin Theology*, ed. S. L. Greenslade (Louisville, Ky.: Westminster, 1961), 127–28.

8. One difficult issue in a church plant is turning someone away from church membership. For example, suppose someone visits the plant for eight months and seems like a solid Christian. The pastor and elders have gotten to know this person but realize he is overbearing on some theological points that the church plant's confessions are quite clearly against. He wants to join, but since some of his beliefs are contrary to the confessions and he is unteachable in these areas, the elders and pastor would have to refuse membership. There are several effects of this:

> 1. Some of the members or other visitors of the plant might disagree with the elders' and pastor's assessment.

First, become acquainted with the visitors and find out their circumstances as well as their hang-ups. Ideally, the church planter will begin doing this from his earliest contact with the visitors. Over time, however, he should come to know about these visitors and their ecclesiastical background. Do they presently have membership in another congregation? If so, what type of church is it? Is it a confessionally Reformed or Presbyterian church and member of the North American Presbyterian and Reformed Council (NAPARC)? If they do not hold membership in any congregation, from what gathering of professing Christians have they come? Perhaps they are completely new to the Christian faith. Whatever the case, the church planter must do all he can to learn their circumstances and, to the best of his ability, understand their background. For example, the church planter may discover that a person is hesitant to become a member because of a bad experience in a previous church with tyrannical leaders. He must do all he can to help that person work through those issues and restore his or her confidence in Christ's authority as head of the church.

Second, the church planter, with the help of the overseeing elders, must ensure that the Lord's Table is fenced properly. While fencing the table is a case-by-case matter, it should always exclude those who refuse to submit to Christ's authority as it is delegated to the officers of a local congregation. Those who do not possess biblical church membership or have abandoned the congregation in which they previously were members are not eligible to come to the Lord's Table. At times, the church planter will need to explain to a regular attendee—even one who has attended for several months or even years—that he must abstain from the sacrament until he has biblical church membership and is under the oversight of elders.

---

2. The person/family may have added much-needed numbers and finance to the plant, and the loss will be devastating to the church plant.

3. Turning this person away may seriously hurt the momentum and morale of the plant.

In the long run, the elders and pastor have made the right decision.

Another worthwhile note: Some families will come to a plant from another confessional Reformed or Presbyterian church and want to join, but their reasons for wanting to join are not biblical (such as they don't get along with their old pastor or they like a smaller church). Sometimes you have to tell such people, "Go to your elders and talk to them; we will accept you only if your elders give approval." Again, as with the other case, it can be hard turning a family like this away.

Third, the church planter must be patient with such visitors. Almost every church plant will have its share of nonmember attendees. If the church planter is doing his job in explaining the biblical case for church membership, getting to know visitors and their backgrounds, and fencing the Lord's Table properly, then he should be able to rest and allow visitors whatever amount of time they need to familiarize themselves with the confessions, liturgy, and people of the church. He may feel frustrated that some visitors are taking a long time to become members or "just don't get it," but dealing with such frustrations can be expected for the church-plant pastor. While remaining firm in his convictions, persistent in his instruction about membership, and pastorally sensitive to his flock, he must continue to be longsuffering toward those who take an extra long time to join. Perhaps no fact is more helpful for him to remember than that the church is not his, but Christ's.

How Does Church Membership Work in a Church Plant?

There remains one more important question: How does church membership operate in an infant congregation before it is organized with its own elders and deacons? This is a challenging setting for the church planter as he seeks to educate new parishioners and visitors on the importance of biblical church membership.

The Overseeing Church[9]

Suppose a family commits to the church plant and desires membership. Since a church plant is not a self-started, autonomous entity but rather a mission work of an already established church or, in some cases, group of churches, their membership will reside with the overseeing church.[10] Throughout the entire church-plant process, the elders of the overseeing church are obligated to govern and care for this family attending the church plant as much as the families attending the overseeing church. They are part of the congregation until the church plant organizes as a church with officers of its own.

---

9. See also chapters 16–17, "Shepherding toward Maturity: Parts 1 and 2" by Spencer Aalsburg as well as chapter 3 of *POPC*, along with the other relevant sections.

10. See the OPC *Book of Church Order* XIII.8 and XVI.2; the OPC BCO applies to members "worshiping with a mission work" who should be kept on membership rolls.

The Church Planter

Through his preaching and teaching, the church planter has the responsibility of educating people that the church plant is under the oversight of a body of elders from another church. This is critical for helping those in attendance from misinterpreting the church plant as an independent body or the sole endeavor of the church planter. The church planter might consider such detailed practices as stating before every worship service, "Welcome to North Church. We are a church plant and mission work of South Church," as well as having the same statement printed in the bulletin and posted on the website. Another helpful habit is for the church planter to walk with the visiting elder to the pulpit just before the worship service begins and shake the elder's hand before the announcements and call to worship. Such practices will communicate to those in attendance that biblical oversight is in place, and membership is with the overseeing church.

It is also imperative that the church planter ensures that those desiring membership fully understand the binding nature of their membership vows before they make them in public. Ideally, this instruction will occur in the new members' class and will be reiterated by the elders in the membership interview. While bylaws may vary from church to church, typically there are only four ways for a member to end his or her membership in a Reformed church: 1) by transfer of membership by the elders to another Reformed or Presbyterian church; 2) by death; 3) by excommunication; 4) by non-disciplinary dismissal to affiliate with a different Christian church.[11] Again, the church planter must explain this carefully to those pursuing membership, and the elders should restate it briefly in the membership interview. This helps the new member in understanding better what he or she is doing by taking vows and joining the church. It also provides some protection for the church—both the leaders and the congregation—from any excommunicated persons who would attempt to take legal action against it.

Finally, the church planter should do all he can to encourage the members of the church plant as they submit themselves to the elders of the overseeing church and await the day when elders will be ordained in their own church. He should be sensitive to the fact that they have taken some

---

11. Many churches retain this as an option for certain non-disciplinary cases in which a member desires to have his membership transferred to a Christian church that is not in ecclesiastical fellowship with the church to which he currently belongs.

risks committing to the church plant and are in a somewhat irregular situation. A wise church planter will keep a shepherd's eye on the needs of his parishioners and stay in close contact with his overseeing elders until the time of transitioning from church plant to organized church.

The Transition from Church Plant to Organized Church[12]
While each case is different, typically a church plant should organize as a church sometime within three to five years from its inception.[13] If after five years of labor the church plant still does not possess the critical mass, qualified leaders, and financial stability to organize as a church, the overseeing elders may need to take a closer look at the work to determine its suitability as a future church. But in those cases where a church plant is ready to organize, the memberships accumulated over that period will need to be transferred from the overseeing church to the newly organized church. This can be done in three stages.

First, new elders and deacons need to be nominated, trained, and elected. While the elders of the overseeing church will nominate suitable men for office, the members of the church-plant congregation should be given the opportunity to elect their new officers by vote. This is vital for the encouragement and maturity of the new congregation.

Second, the members of the church plant will make request for their memberships to be transferred from the overseeing church to their newly organized church. This can be done by producing a list with all the members' names, having the members sign the list, and attaching a letter addressed to the clerk of the overseeing body of elders requesting transfer. The church planter and elders from the overseeing church should explain this process to the members who are being transferred so that everyone fully understands what is happening.

Third, after the new officers have been elected and the overseeing church has acted on the transfer of memberships, an installation/organization service should be held. Also, the new officers would then elect

---

12. For more details on the topic of transition from church plant to an established church, read chapter 6 of *POPC*. Page 80 notes that an organized congregation is "a definite membership organized as a distinct congregation with its officers." Also read the OPC BCO XXIX and the PCA BCO V, which deal entirely with the organizing of congregations.

13. The OPC manual for church planting lists these characteristics of a mature church plant that is ready to organize: self-sustaining, self-governing, self-propagating, and self-consciously a church (*POPC*, 11–12).

to call a pastor, most often the man who has planted the church. This is an appropriate time for the new congregation to hear the charges given to their new leaders, receive a charge as a new congregation, and give thanks to God for His faithfulness.

Indeed, few things are more joyful and exciting than seeing the birth of another local manifestation of Christ's true church. May the Lord of the harvest continue to bless us with that sight as we seek to be faithful to His commission to make disciples to the ends of the earth.

A Sample List of Questions for Membership Interviews

1. Tell us about your background. Where are you from? How did you come to faith? Where have you attended church? What brought you to our church?

2. What are the confessional standards of this church?

3. Have you read these? Do you agree with them? Is there anything that you disagree with or are struggling to understand or affirm?

4. Are you a Christian?

5. Can you explain what it means to be a Christian by referencing the main three parts of the Heidelberg Catechism?

6. What do you believe about the authority of the Bible? Is it the Word of God?

7. What do we mean when we say God is a Trinity?

8. What is the meaning of calling God "our Father?"

9. Did God make people sinful and wicked?

10. Where did your sin come from?

11. What shows you your sinfulness?

12. Can you keep the law of God perfectly? Why or why not?

13. Will God allow sin to go unpunished? Why or why not?

14. What do you need in order to escape the wrath of God and be made right with Him?

15. Who is Jesus Christ?

16. What did Jesus do?

17. How do you receive the righteousness of Christ and become justified?

18. What is true faith? What are its three parts?

19. Who is the Holy Spirit?

20. What does the Holy Spirit do?

21. What are the main ways the Holy Spirit sanctifies you?

22. What is the difference between justification and sanctification?

23. How does preaching sanctify you?

24. What are the sacraments?

25. What does your baptism signify? Why is it important for you?

26. What does the Lord's Supper signify? Why is it important that you, as a Christian, partake of the Lord's Supper?

27. How do baptism and the Supper sanctify you?

28. If you have been saved by grace alone, through faith alone, because of Christ alone, why do you need to do good works?

29. Tell us about your prayer life. Do you pray and read Scriptures with your family (if applicable)? Do you catechize your children (if applicable)?

29. What is the church?

30. What are the marks of a true church?

31. What does it mean to be a member of the church?

32. Are you willing to submit to the elders and take public vows?

33. What do you understand about the importance of attending the means of grace regularly? Are you willing to attend our worship services regularly?

34. Are you comfortable being a member of a Reformed church?

CHAPTER FIFTEEN

∾

Shepherding toward Maturity, Part 1:
The Authority in Church Planting

Spencer Aalsburg

When a consistory has the God-given opportunity to plant a church, where do they begin? Does every consistory (or session[1]) need to reinvent the wheel of church planting? It is my hope that these two chapters will provide a helpful starting point for planting confessionally Reformed churches by addressing some issues involved in shepherding a church plant toward maturity.[2] These chapters are written from personal experience in church planting, combined with much wisdom from other church planters throughout my own denomination, the United Reformed Churches in North America (URCNA), as well as sister denominations such as the Orthodox Presbyterian Church (OPC).[3] Can one church-planting model work in every situation? While details will vary among specific churches and their church plants, the principles of authority and maturity expounded here will serve to guide and guard confessionally Reformed church planting.

The consistory is unquestionably called by Christ to shepherd the church entrusted to it and, consequently, any church-plant work that church undertakes (Acts 20:28–31; 1 Peter 5:1–4).[4] This foundational prin-

---

1. The terms "consistory" and "session" are synonymous for the purpose of this essay; they can be used interchangeably throughout.

2. Since differences exist among confessionally Reformed church orders, the reader needs to consult his respective form of church government. Vocabulary may differ between church orders even where there is agreement on principles. The URCNA and OPC church orders are referenced in this essay, though primarily the former.

3. Much insight in this article is taken from the OPC's insightful church-planting *POPC*. A hearty thank-you goes to the OPC for its profitable labors in producing this book and making it freely available online.

4. Cf. Church Order of the United Reformed Churches in North America, article 21: "In each congregation there shall be a Consistory composed of the minister(s) of the Word and the elders, which shall meet at least once a month. The Consistory is the only assembly in the church(es) whose decisions possess direct authority within

ciple must be fully embraced and its crucial implications developed so that all persons involved are in agreement about the nature of a church plant and its proper leadership. Regardless of the events leading to its inception, a church plant will most likely be threatened by an unstable vacuum of leadership.

Temptations exist for all human beings, regardless of their age, yet young people do face a peculiar set of temptations. Likewise, young church plants face their own intensified set of struggles. This is due in part to the reality that the work of planting churches is perhaps the most intentional and volatile attack on the gates of hell itself.[5] Therefore—as in all warfare—effective, strategic leadership becomes all the more crucial to the work of church planting. It is imperative that planting consistories understand their roles and responsibilities, communicating those effectively to the whole congregation—members at home and at the church plant alike.

While it is at least conceivable that a church plant can be overseen by a relatively "hands-off" approach, I will argue for a more "hands-on" approach. This approach follows naturally from the nature of a church plant: a group of believers that is distinct—yet not separate—from the mother church.

The Church Plant

At times, established congregations—whether or not they are affiliated with a denomination—seek entrance into a confessionally Reformed denomination. In the URC, for example, this congregation would come under the care of a neighboring consistory—a situation addressed by article 32 of the URCNA CO. Given that the elders and minister of the aspiring church subscribe to the Three Forms of Unity and the Church Order, article 32 allows that "any such church shall be provisionally accepted into membership in the federation by the classis, pending ratification by the following synod." This scenario does not describe a church plant but rather what could be called an adopted congregation. This organized congregation has office bearers in place and a certain level of

the congregation, since the Consistory receives its authority directly from Christ, and thereby is directly accountable to Christ" (Church Order of the United Reformed Churches in North America, 4th ed. [2007], http://urcna.org/ [accessed December 1, 2010]). All subsequent references will be to the URCNA CO.

5. *POPC*, 12.

maturity.[6] The OPC welcomes another congregation into the denomination following a certain order as well, finally under the oversight of presbytery (BCO XXIX.B.1).

A church plant, on the other hand, is a daughter congregation that grows from and with an established congregation. Article 22 of the URCNA CO describes a church plant: "When a congregation is organized within the federation, this shall take place under the supervision of a neighboring Consistory and with the concurring advice of the classis."

A Word about Broader Assemblies

While we will focus primarily on the consistory's responsibilities in church planting, it is fitting to determine the role of classis (or presbytery) early in the process. No doubt this will differ somewhat in every federation or denomination; each must consult its specific church order. In the URCNA CO, article 22 requires classis's concurring advice with the consistory's recommendation before a church plant can be organized as a separate congregation; the OPC and Presbyterian Church in America (PCA) both note that a new church can be organized only by the authority of presbytery.

And yet if that concurring advice is the first time a classis evaluates a church plant—right before the final step of organization—then surely the consistory has missed out on valuable input from classis in the years leading up to the church plant's organization. If classis is asked to give concurring advice, then, ideally, it would have been involved on some level in the preceding years. Doctoral candidates don't begin seeking advice from their advisors on the same day they publicly defend their dissertation. Similarly, a diligent consistory will seek the advice of classis even before it begins church-planting work. In fact, the OPC BCO, in chapter XXVII, wisely notes that mission works must ordinarily be initiated at the level of presbytery or general assembly.

Will the consistory seek classical advice concerning the start of a church plant out of necessity? No, not strictly speaking—in the same sense that belonging to a federation is not mandatory, or necessary, to

---

6. Accordingly, they will most likely (though not necessarily) need a lesser degree of shepherding. Parents who adopted a fourteen-year old (cf. URCNA CO, art. 32) wouldn't need to shepherd in the same way that they would if they adopted a two-year-old (cf. URCNA CO, art. 22). We need to remember, however, that years of age don't always correspond to maturity in the faith.

being a church. Belonging to a broader assembly is, however, necessary for the well being of the local church.

According to the letter of the URCNA CO, a local congregation may begin a church plant wherever and whenever they deem fitting, without any input from the classis. They could petition the churches of classis—or even the whole federation—to help with the finances of this new plant. And yet this is not the wisest course of action, as wisdom is found in a multitude of counselors (Prov. 11:14).[7]

Working with classis before the start of a church plant will provide significant help for the consistory. First, the consistory can obtain more objective advice offered by those who are not immediately associated with the situation. Like many circumstances in our lives, the closer we are to a situation, the blinder we can be to obvious pitfalls. Classis can review a proposal and provide helpful feedback.

Not every church plant opportunity that appears possible should be embarked upon. Are there other North American Presbyterian and Reformed Council (NAPARC) congregations in the proposed area? If a group has approached a URC consistory about starting a church plant, what are their motivations? Did they recently embrace Reformed theology? Or did they perhaps leave disgruntled from another Reformed church?

Getting answers to these questions is necessary before beginning a plant; careful consideration of the group's responses may help prevent a disaster for the churches. Since many consistories have never planted a church, they may not be aware that they need to ask insightful questions like these. Moreover, there is a tendency for a planting consistory to "reinvent the wheel" when they do not dialog with the broader assembly. Novice consistories that work with classis avoid duplication of work as they gather indispensable advice from other consistories that have experience with church planting.

Second, as a consistory works with classis from the inception of a church plant, they will encourage mutual appreciation for the work that will be demonstrated with financial support from classical churches. When classis has given its concurring advice (however informal that may be) to begin a church plant, those who have provided advice develop a sense of ownership and responsibility for the work. Involving the other churches in this way is different from sending a letter that requests financial assistance for a new church plant with a need. Churches that have

---

7. Cf. URCNA CO, foundational principle no. 9.

benefited from the advice and approval of their classis will have more credibility with churches in a different geographical region when they send out financial requests. For example, a church in California receiving a request for financial assistance from a church on the East Coast would be assured that the particulars and viability of the church plant have been assessed by the whole classis.

A planting consistory does well to solicit the feedback of classis before embarking on church-plant work, and throughout the plant process, the consistory should foster a fruitful, edifying relationship between its church plant and the rest of the classis. This relationship will be nurtured as the consistory gives regular updates to the other churches of classis in order to ensure that they're offering informed prayers and as it continues to gather valuable advice from a multitude of counselors.

A Church Plant: A Parent/Child Relationship

The illustration of mother and child works well to describe church plants. God knits together a child in the womb of his mother (Ps. 139:13). He providentially uses the flesh and blood of the mother to "build" this young person from conception onward. This unborn babe necessarily stays close inside his mother, growing up to maturity. Not only are mother and child in close proximity, they are organically connected. They share the same lifeblood. The mother's heart pumps for the baby. The mother's liver purifies the blood they share. Where mothers go, babies go along. Then comes the day that the mother delivers the baby, and the cord is cut (often today by a happy father).

Mother and child become two separated people, no longer connected to one another by an umbilical cord. They are still connected, however, in that enduring bond of filial love and affection. This relationship continues to grow as the baby is nursed. The infant develops, continuing to grow physically and in his relationships with his parents and siblings.

From their toddler years to their teenage years—when parents' God-given authority is often tested—children need to have their hearts shepherded. In a real way, the life of a covenant child is one of constant shepherding, to the end that he may take his place among God's people as a professing adult. Then comes the day when he is married and the "apron strings" are cut.

While all analogies are imperfect, a mother-and-child analogy is nonetheless fitting for church planting. Church plants are to be shepherded and edified by the mother church. The two bodies are distinct but not separate entities—especially while the plant develops in the first months of existence "in the womb." And while the mother church and the plant are not identical, mother and child do have a similar DNA.

Parents are quite simply the God-given authorities in the child's life. While children do have a means of input (varying with age), parents ultimately and necessarily decide what is best for maturing children. Children live under their parents' nurturing care. Parents have the authority, and thus the responsibility, to "train up a child in the way he should go, and when he is old he will not depart from it" (Prov. 22:6).

If we are to "raise" church plants into God-honoring, confessionally Reformed and Presbyterian churches that take their place among their sister churches, we must begin shepherding them when they are young. And this process will take time, usually somewhere between two and five years.[8] The consistory has the authority and the responsibility to shepherd the church plant toward maturity, teaching its members what maturity is and how to attain it. We don't want immature children thinking they are adults, ready to get out from under their parents for the sake of independence. We need to shepherd our children to trust and obey, preparing them to live on their own in a God-honoring home. We don't want our children to leave home prematurely just so they can listen to their own kind of music—music that doesn't follow the house rules.

A Church Plant Is Not a Separate Congregation

An established church births a church plant that is organically and organizationally connected—a body that is distinct but not separate. All members of both the mother church and the church plant have the same leadership, the same God-ordained office bearers to shepherd them.[9] Accordingly, the best way to perceive a church plant is as *a select group of the mother congregation meeting in another location.* The whole church has a vision, namely, that the Lord would spiritually and numerically develop a mature congregation that would one day take its place among

---

8. *POPC* maintains a timeframe of somewhere between two to four years (57, 71). While two years may be close to a minimum, we must recognize that the four-year figure is generalized. It could take longer than four years to organize, depending on the providential bumps in the road.

9. If several families are present at the inception (conception, to use our analogy) and want to be official members of the church plant, then they will join the mother church.

the churches in the denomination or federation. Geographic distance can often distort this view of a church plant; nevertheless, a church plant is exactly this. How could it be any different, biblically or church orderly? A church plant is not merely a group of individuals that meet independently, conducting the affairs of the church as a democracy that is rubber-stamped by the "overseeing consistory."

The careful reader will notice the avoidance in this chapter of the "overseeing consistory" terminology—a phrase that seems to have arisen from the renowned "Dept. of Redundancy Department." Using this phrase is like referring to our *"merciful* deaconate." Is there a kind of deaconate that is not merciful? Is there a kind of consistory or session that does not *oversee?* Shepherding oversight is built in to the very fabric of eldership (Ezek. 33:1–11; Acts 20:28; 1 Peter 5:1–4). The phrase "overseeing consistory" is problematic because of the misconceptions that may accompany its use: "Well, they're just the overseeing consistory." The phrase needs clarification. Does it mean the church plant will conduct its own agenda while the mother church simply watches from a distance? This certainly would not be appropriate.

The misconception finds clarity when we realize that the church plant has a consistory that oversees those who worship at the church plant, just like it oversees those who worship at the mother church. Parents do not let children raise themselves from the crib; they nurture them toward maturity. And a consistory will not turn a church plant loose to be a law unto itself, to operate as a remote island in a vast sea.

In church planting, essentially one local church has a district, or parish, that meets in another location for one or two worship services a week. A church plant is an intimate part of an established church shepherded by the consistory. Understanding this not only allows the elders to be faithful to their office but also provides clear answers to church-planting questions that frequently arise. There is really no need for a church plant to ask the following questions: "Where are we actually members?" "What is our music policy?" "Who are our office bearers?" "Whom do we list as the session or consistory in our bulletins?"

This biblical and church orderly understanding of a church plant will not be readily realized without manifesting that organic unity in a visible way. Depending on the driving distance between the mother church and the plant, they should share church activities: monthly fellowship meals, Bible studies, and seasonal worship services are all good examples. When the location of a church plant is a significant distance from the mother church or already has two worship services, there will obviously be fewer opportunities for the mother church and the church plant to manifest their close, saintly communion.

In either situation, the dutiful consistory will not only educate itself on this fundamental relationship but also will teach and cultivate this vitally important bond among the congregation. Ideally, this instruction would happen long before the church plant begins meeting for worship services so that the great privilege and duty of church planting will less likely serve as the source of uninformed conflict, and the congregation can joyfully support the church plant work with their prayers, finances, and time. In short, the consistory and all mother church members need to own their church plant.

The Goal of Church Planting

We must be very clear concerning the goal of a church plant. Formal organization (or particularization) of a church plant certainly is one goal of church planting. This must not, however, be the main goal—no more than a godly parent aims primarily at getting his child out of the house and into his own apartment as quickly as possible. While a child may be eager to get a place of his own, simply putting a teenager into an apartment does not make him mature enough to live alone without parental shepherding. Children need to be spiritually ready to live on their own. A child needs to be mature.

Accordingly, the goal with which we plant a church is to establish a mature congregation that wields the keys of the kingdom of God—through which God's people can grow up in every way "into Him who is the head—Christ" (Eph. 4:15). It is Christ "from whom the whole body, joined and knit together by what every joint supplies, according to the effective working by which every part does its share, causes growth of the body for the edifying of itself in love" (Eph. 4:16).

Christ would have His church attain maturity, "to the measure of the stature of the fullness of Christ" (Eph. 4:13). It is for this reason that Christ gave the church gifted leaders—"for the equipping of the saints for the work of ministry, for the edifying of the body of Christ" (Eph. 4:11–12). This glorifies our Father in heaven. When we lose sight of this goal in church planting, church planting ceases—at least, in a way that honors God and blesses His people while at the same time serving as a witness to the watching world. Maturity is the goal—"until Christ is formed in you" (Gal. 4:19).

At the outset of the church-plant work, everyone at the plant and in the mother congregation must agree to be patient, bearing with one another in love (Eph. 4:2). Everyone signs up for the "long haul." In our Father's eyes, simply having a separate church entry in the denominational directory pales in comparison to having a church community that is rooted and established in love for Christ and His people (Eph. 3:17; cf. also Rom. 12; 1 Cor. 12; Eph. 4).

Too often churches have the sad misunderstanding that organization is the primary goal, and it is hastily pursued at the expense of being knit together in brotherly love for Christ. The point of these two chapters is not how to organize but rather how to shepherd the church plant toward maturity in Christ. Organization is a byproduct—though important, it is less important than the church plant's mature unity in Christ (Eph. 4:1–3). Sessions and consistories must be cautious of those who seek autonomy for the church plant as quickly as possible.

Elders Who Shepherd

Shepherding Authority

The consistory is composed of a minister(s) of the Word and elders.[10] We believe it is "the only assembly in the church (es) whose decisions possess direct authority within the congregation, since the consistory receives its authority directly from Christ, and thereby is directly accountable to Christ."[11]

Indeed, the church is the possession of Christ—who is the mediator of the new covenant (Acts 20:28; Eph. 5:25–27) and thus the head of the church (Eph. 1:22–23; 5:23–24; Col. 1:18). Therefore, the principles governing the church are not a matter of human preference but of divine revelation (Matt. 28:18–20; Col. 1:18).[12] As the OPC *Book of Church Order* so eloquently explains:

> There is therefore but one King and Head of the church, the only Mediator between God and man, Jesus Christ, who rules in his church by his Word and Spirit. His mediatorial office includes all

---

10. URCNA CO, article 21; see also the OPC Form of Government I.2–3.

11. URCNA CO, article 21.

12. URCNA CO, "Foundational Principles of Reformed Church Government." Cf. principles 1–3.

the offices in his church. It belongs to his majesty from his throne of glory not only to rule his church directly but also to use the ministry of men in ruling and teaching his church through his Word and Spirit, thus exercising through men his own authority and enforcing his own laws. The authority of all such ministerial office rests upon his appointment, who has ordained government in his church, revealed its nature to us in his Word, and promised his presence in the midst of his church as this government is exercised in his name.[13]

The office of elder (*presbyter/episkopos*) is clearly local in authority and function. Thus, Reformed church government is presbyterial, since the church is governed by elders, not by broader assemblies or congregational majority (Acts 14:23; 20:17, 28; Titus 1:5).[14] The duties of elders arise out of the truth that Christ cares for His church through the office bearers whom He chooses (Acts 6:2–3; 1 Tim. 3:1, 8; 5:17).[15]

As those who are Reformed, we necessarily adhere to the principles of Reformed polity. We hold to the scripturally high view of the office of elder. We're not congregational, where "the majority says, so let it be." Christ calls the elders to shepherd the flock lovingly according to His Word (1 Peter 5:1–4). The elders are called to be the watchmen on the walls of Zion (Ezek. 33:1–11). They are called to be the overseers (Acts 20:28).

Especially when they are establishing a church plant, the consistory and the whole congregation must be unified regarding whom Christ has publicly ordained to the authoritative office of elder. The church is not a democracy; it is a theocracy where Christ is king—a king who publicly ordains leaders. A church plant finds its God-given leaders in the consistory of the mother church.

It is the organized church that has been entrusted with the official administration of the Word and sacraments. And the church functions through the structure of office bearers, which Christ gave as a gift to His body (Eph. 4:7–16). Martin Monsma concludes, "Consequently, the organized church functions through the offices and does not even exist without the offices."[16] When God gives authority, it is always to be used

---

13. OPC *Book of Church Order*, I.2.

14. URCNA CO, principle 4.

15. URCNA CO, principle 6.

16. Martin Monsma, *The New Revised Church Order Commentary* (Grand Rapids: Zondervan, 1967), 159. The full context of this citation aptly states the important and essential character of the offices for the organized church of Christ on earth: "To the institute of organized churches the administration of Word and sacraments has been entrusted. This significant task has not been committed by God to unorganized groups of

to serve the body of Christ (cf. Eph. 4:11–13). Ministers and elders are not given authority to stroke their ego or lord it over others (1 Peter 5:3) but to employ it in discharging the duties of the shepherding office.

Accordingly, we come to an inescapable conclusion: an office bearer cannot and may not pass on his God-given shepherding responsibilities to someone else. Therefore, a consistory cannot and may not pass on its God-given shepherding responsibilities to another group of people (such as a steering committee or leaders of a Bible study). While a consistory may use a steering committee, it does not—and may not—do the work that properly belongs to elders.[17]

Shepherding Duties

There are no advantageous shortcuts to shepherding a church plant. It involves much work for the consistory. However the church plant begins, as diligent shepherds, the session or consistory must be prepared for necessary, time-consuming labors. For elders, there will be long nights, sweat, and tears; but remember, the crown awaits your eager and exemplary service (1 Peter 5:4).

Generally speaking, elders' duties are clear: praying, ruling the church under Christ and His Word, and maintaining pure doctrine and holy living (cf. 1 Tim. 3:1–7; Titus 1:5–16).[18] Elders, along with the minister(s), are

believers. Nor has it been left to the initiation of individual believers. Not as if the believers have no rights and duties regarding the gospel of salvation.... But the administration of the Word in its official sense and the administration of the sacraments pertain only to the organized and authorized Church of God. This authorized church has the charge to go with divine authority proclaiming the Word and will of God, and to signify and to seal the same by means of the sacraments. And the church must discharge itself of this beautiful and important task through the duly appointed office-bearers. Likewise, the churches govern themselves, under Christ, through the offices, and engage in the world of Christian mercy through the offices. Consequently the organized church functions through the offices and does not even exist without the offices. Hence it follows that only when the offices have been instituted can it be said the Church of Christ has acquired a definite and authoritative form. Wherever the offices have been instituted there the Church has been organized" (ibid.).

17. See appendix C, "The Steering Committee." Note that church planting doesn't require a steering committee. It is perfectly appropriate for the consistory to be the steering committee.

18. The URCNA CO, article 14 details thirteen specific duties of elders: "The duties belonging to the office of elder consist of continuing in prayer and ruling the church of Christ according to the principles taught in Scripture, in order that purity of doctrine and holiness of life may be practiced. They shall see to it that their fellow-elders, the minister(s) and the deacons faithfully discharge their offices. They are to maintain the purity of the

the overseers of the whole congregation, which includes the church plant. Since the duties particularly pertaining to the church planter are covered elsewhere in this volume, this section will particularly focus on the consistory's duties as a whole. And since there are many resources to enrich ministers and elders in the diligence of their shepherding obligations, the following discussion will address these duties as they relate specifically in a church-plant context.[19]

Prayer

The work of establishing a new church is from first to last the work of God in storming Satan's stronghold and finding His chosen people.[20] Therefore, in this spiritual assault, purposeful and persistent prayer is a must, for God gives His grace and Holy Spirit only to those who ask ceaselessly (HC, Q&A 116). We should remember that our church-planting God ordains not only the ends but also the means—which include the prayers of His people (Rom. 15:30–32; Eph. 6:10–12).

It is important that we do more than talk about prayer. It would be reckless for the consistory to rely on its own abilities, the abilities of a zealous planting pastor, or the abilities of members who worship at the plant. Simply because we are confessionally Reformed and embrace our doctrinal distinctives does not ensure spiritual growth toward maturity. Especially since church plants will be faced with many temptations and trials, the consistory must labor in believing prayer for its church plant. The apostle reminds us: "For we do not wrestle against flesh and blood, but against principalities, against powers, against the rulers of the darkness of this age, against spiritual hosts of wickedness in the heavenly places" (Eph. 6:12).

Word and Sacraments, assist in catechizing the youth, promote God-centered schooling, visit the members of the congregation according to their needs, engage in family visiting, exercise discipline in the congregation, actively promote the work of evangelism and missions, and insure that everything is done decently and in good order."

19. See books such as Gerard Berghoef and Lester De Koster, *The Elders Handbook* (Grand Rapids: Christian's Library Press, 1979); *Called to Serve: Essays for Elders and Deacons*, ed. Michael G. Brown (Grandville, Mich.: Reformed Fellowship, 2007), 199; John R. Sittema, *With a Shepherd's Heart* (Grandville, Mich.: Reformed Fellowship, 1996); and the series by Nelson D. Kloosterman, *Visiting Members*. This is a DVD series containing ten sessions for office-bearer training and is available directly from the author at ndksales@gmail.com.

20. *POPC*, 54.

The members of the consistory must take the initiative and lead by example. The obvious minimum for elders would be specifically praying for the church plant at monthly consistory meetings and, of course, in their private prayer closets. The consistory will want to ensure that the whole congregation (at home, at the mother church, and on-site) prays, seeking sustaining grace for the church-plant leadership and members in the challenges they face and thanking God for the progress in maturity and increases He gives.

Weekly prayer meetings at the church-plant site will not only unite the members of the church and church plant but also strengthen them as a formidable force against the kingdom of darkness. Moreover, striving to keep the bond of peace in the Spirit of unity includes faithful, frequent, and fervent prayers (Eph. 4:1–3; 6:18–20). The distribution of prayer cards for the church plant would be fitting to remind prayer warriors of the duty and necessity of prayer. These cards could even be distributed to neighboring congregations.

Ruling to Ensure Doctrine Is Preserved and Practiced
The authoritative duties of elders include the great responsibility to rule in the name of Christ, for His honor and the edification of His church.[21] The apostle Peter orders overseers to "shepherd the flock of God which is among you, serving as overseers, not by compulsion but willingly, not for dishonest gain but eagerly; nor as being lords over those entrusted to you, but being examples to the flock" (1 Peter 5:1–3). This is not mere advice for elders but a divine command.

The consistory is not left without concrete direction; it has God's sufficient Word. The principles taught in Scripture must be the church plant's guide—not private agenda, personal opinion, or nonessentials. The consistory is shepherding a confessionally Reformed plant toward

---

21. The opportunity to plant a church is a great time for the elders of the mother church to review their own roles. The following books are recommended for review or study—and for the future elders in the church plant: *Called to Serve: Essays for Elders and Deacons*, ed. Michael G. Brown (Grandville, Mich.: Reformed Fellowship, 2008); Thomas Smyth, *An Ecclesiastical Catechism of the Presbyterian Church* (Fellsmere, Fla.: Reformation Christian Ministries, 2006); *Order in the Offices: Essays Defining the Roles of Church Officers*, ed. Mark Brown (Duncansville, Pa.: Classic Presbyterian Government Resources, 1993); and John Sittema, *With a Shepherd's Heart* (Grandville, Mich.: Reformation Fellowship, 1996).

maturity, not a group of Christians with some extra-confessional emphasis that makes them distinct.

All of the duties of the elder could be grouped into two categories: ruling according to doctrine and life. In other words, there is a purpose for the elders' praying and ruling—to ensure that doctrine is preserved and practiced. If a church plant will grow to maturity as a confessionally Reformed church, it must be unashamedly Reformed from the beginning—in doctrine and practice. Therefore the elders are to pray and rule in such a way that Reformed theology is propagated. They are to "[hold] fast the faithful word as [they have] been taught, that [they] may be able, by sound doctrine, both to exhort and to convict those who contradict" (Titus 1:9).

To ensure purity of doctrine, it is important that consistory members be intimately familiar with the teaching of Scripture and its faithful summary preserved in the Reformed confessions.[22] Even churches that the apostle Paul planted—like Corinth—later fell into doctrinal error. We must not think that simply because the sign says "Reformed" and we have heard doctrinally robust sermons all our life that we are somehow immune to doctrinal error.

Furthermore, we must not assume that only confessionally Reformed persons will find the church plant. Indeed, we pray to reach the underfed, misled, and spiritually dead.[23] Because of its potential vulnerability, a church plant can be appealing to those with particular theological axes to grind and specific agendas to propagate. Elders must be on guard like watchmen of Zion, ready to blow the warning trumpet (Ezek. 33:1–11). They must, with sound doctrine, exhort and convict those who would contradict or go beyond the confessionally Reformed teaching of the church plant (Titus 1:9).

Paul warns all church-planting consistories when he writes: "For I know this, that after my departure savage wolves will come in among you, not sparing the flock. Also from among yourselves men will rise up, speaking perverse things, to draw away the disciples after themselves. Therefore watch, and remember that for three years I did not cease to warn everyone night and day with tears" (Acts 20:29–31).

---

22. See Cornelis P. Venema, "Why the Elder Needs to Know, Love and Defend Reformed Doctrine" in *Called to Serve*, 85–101.

23. *POPC*, 46.

Since the elders are duly responsible for maintaining the purity of preaching, they must carefully oversee the pulpit. This would include the important task of securing pulpit supply. Pulpit supply usually is planned months in advance by a forward-looking consistory so that the whole consistory and church know who will be preaching, whether at home or at the plant. In an established congregation, it is fitting to have an assigned elder secure the pulpit supply for the church plant. This overseeing task should not be assigned to a layperson who might merely find a preacher that everyone will like. Church members may provide assistance by showing hospitality to visiting preachers, but the elders are the ones divinely commanded to maintain the pure preaching of the holy gospel. Even when the church plant has the steady pulpit supply of a minister who has been called to serve, the elders' work on overseeing the pulpit is not suspended. The consistory should set aside a time at their meetings to allow elders to give helpful feedback on the church-plant minister's sermons, as they would for any minister.

The same principle of oversight follows for ensuring the purity of teaching. While a well-meaning layman may be zealous about teaching a study at the church plant, the elders will do their best to ensure that a consistory member teaches both catechism classes and weekly Bible studies. If consistory members are not available to teach or at least be present at the various studies, then a serious question arises: How can the consistory fulfill its responsibility to ensure the purity of doctrine taught in the church plant? This question is all the more important with a church plant, as the developing group is more susceptible to doctrinal error, and even factionalism.[24]

The sacraments also should be administered at the church-plant location. Elders from the mother church should be present to provide the proper fencing of this sacred meal. For example, the elder(s) and minister can interview prospective communicants by having them fill out a communion request card, appropriately labeled with the name of the mother church.[25] The consistory determines the frequency of the Supper as well as the elements used, based on what best nourishes the church plant. Along with the Lord's Supper, the sacrament of baptism serves as a vis-

---

24. *POPC*, 27.

25. I recognize that not all churches follow this particular practice. On the issue of fencing, see Daniel R. Hyde, "Table Manners: Whom We Welcome to the Lord's Table," in *Called to Serve: Essays for Elders and Deacons*, ed. Michael G. Brown (Grandville, Mich.: Reformed Fellowship, 2007), 135–43.

ible means of grace that signifies and seals God's covenant. How fitting
for both sacraments to be administered in church plants, ensuring that
they bear the marks by which the true church may be known and the
false church rejected![26]

In short, the consistory oversees the worship services of the mother
church and the church plant. Worshiping our triune God forms the foundation and focus of all that is done in the life and ministry of a Reformed
church plant. Therefore, as the shepherds of God's people, the elders will
oversee this grand privilege and duty of corporate worship.

Not only do elders ensure the purity of doctrine, but they also
shepherd the flock toward holiness of life. Pure doctrine, when rightly
understood, manifests in godliness (2 Tim. 3:16–17). An ungodly church
is not a positive witness "in the midst of a crooked and perverse generation" (Phil. 2:14–16). Holy lives of sacrifice, lived in response to God's
grace, demonstrate the only right reaction to the grace of God for us in
Christ Jesus (Rom. 12:1–2).

Elders must have contact with those whom they shepherd, spending one-on-one time with them. They should visit the members of the
congregation according to their needs. While the church planter may
visit members often, it does not excuse the elders from their duties. For
instance, they should be available for family visiting with the minister.

How awkward it would be for a member family that attends the
church plant if they meet their God-given elder for the first time at their
annual family visit or if the visit is one of the few times they have ever
talked to or prayed with those called to shepherd them. Church-plant
attendees must know and have a relationship with their elders if they are
to eagerly trust and submit to them (Heb. 13:17). Likewise, elders must
know the flock entrusted to them by Christ in order to eagerly shepherd
them (1 Peter 5:2).

These relationships will be cultivated at worship services and during weekly Bible studies as well as through the practice of hospitality,
to which God calls elders (1 Tim. 3:2). Dutiful elders will set an example of inviting church-plant visitors to their homes or by arranging for
fellowship meals at the church-plant meeting place or by talking with
church-plant members over a cup of coffee during the week.

---

26. Belgic Confession, article 29. See also Michael Horton's lecture, "Why the Marks
of the Church Need the Mission" (lecture, Westminster Seminary California, Escondido,
Calif., January 18–19, 2008).

Timid church members will be encouraged and emboldened when they see their shepherds—both pastor and elders—being quick to greet and initiate fellowship with visitors. Moreover, watching their elders actively promote the work of evangelism and missions will affirm the godliness and obedience of the elders to whom they are called to joyfully submit.

To ensure that doctrine is practiced, the consistory has been commissioned by Christ to exercise discipline toward repentance. If a church plant will bear all the marks of the true church, the consistory must obediently exercise discipline when necessary (Matt. 18:17–18; 1 Cor. 5). Indeed, given the intense spiritual warfare involved in church-planting work, you can expect that the consistory will be called upon to exercise discipline toward repentance. The POPC reminds us that the "session should anticipate that problems of a disciplinary nature will arise as the mission work develops and matures, and should be prepared to take the time required to instruct and correct effectively."[27]

If any individual bearing the Christian name continues to show himself unsound either in doctrine or life, he ought to be lovingly shepherded by official discipline toward repentance (1 Cor. 5; HC, Q&A 83–85). A loving consistory will be prepared to take the time required to patiently instruct and humbly admonish those sheep that are erring. It is the members' privilege and right to have their consistory fulfill this authoritative duty of correction according to the Word (2 Tim. 3:16).

Whether or not a consistory is planting a church, it would be highly beneficial to the body of Christ for the elders to work through a book on church discipline.[28] How critical church discipline is in a church plant as it grows and matures! Church plants are by their nature vulnerable, and it is necessary (as it is in the mother church) to deal appropriately with divisive persons and the threat of schism: "Reject a divisive man after the first and second admonition" (Titus 3:10). Jay Adams comments on this verse: "This is vital direction. There should be provision to speed up the disciplinary process in cases of divisive persons. If you linger too long over the process, you may find your church divided. Paul is clear:

---

27. *POPC*, 33.
28. Two excellent, biblical books on this subject are Ken Sande, *The Peacemaker: A Biblical Guide to Resolving Personal Conflict* (Grand Rapids: Baker, 1997); and Alfred Poirier, *The Peacemaking Pastor: A Biblical Guide to Resolving Church Conflict* (Grand Rapids: Baker, 2006).

if the divisive person does not cease his divisive ways after one or two confrontations, remove him."[29]

On the front lines of the kingdom battle, the church wields the keys of the kingdom of God. A consistory that neglects or ignores discipline damages the church work by dishonoring God, failing to remove the stain of sin, and declining to use this key of the kingdom of God to reconcile believers to Christ and the church. Ralph Pontier explains, "It is not easy work but it is commanded and it is necessary if the church is to be built up and obtain the goal for which Christ died. If the elders do not engage in such work, they rob the pulpit of much of its power."[30]

God calls elders to ensure that everything is done decently and in good order (1 Cor. 14:40). To do this faithfully they must be intimately involved in the church-planting work. Shortcuts and indifference are simply not an option for a healthy, God-honoring church plant.

Shepherding in Person

The overwhelming implication of the biblical duties of elders is an obligation to be physically present in the church plant in order to discharge those duties faithfully and effectively. To rule and shepherd the flock of God *among* them (1 Peter 5:2; Acts 20:17–38), the conscientious consistory necessarily will have a delegation present at every worship service—both at home and at the church plant. The elders need to be present so that the attendees can recognize and esteem the leadership in the church and submit to those who are called to shepherd (1 Thess. 5:12–13; Heb. 13:17).

It is especially important that church-plant members have a relationship with their elders so that the church-planting pastor does not become a lone "point man." When church-plant members deal with consistorial authority only through the pastor, in the event of disagreements,

---

29. Jay Adams, *Handbook of Church Discipline: A Right and Privilege of Every Church Member* (Grand Rapids: Zondervan, 1974), 109. Adams also summarizes: "Discipline is not easy to do correctly or even to do at all. It involves courage and fortitude. It requires care and precision. It must be done in neither a sloppy nor a careless manner. Therefore the process must be carried on with the knowledge and assurance that what is being done is right in God's sight. But even though discipline is difficult and runs many risks, churches dare not run the greater risk of withholding a privilege and blessing provided by Christ, thus depriving sinning members of all the help He has provided for them. Nor dare they disobey Him in refusing to follow His program for church discipline—lest, in the end, they find themselves disciplined by Him (cf. 1 Cor. 11:31–32)" (ibid., 75).

30. Ralph Pontier, "The Duties and Tasks of the Elders and Deacons" in Michael Brown, ed., *Called to Serve*, 20.

his ministry to the saints could be compromised. Especially in a church plant, conflict is common. If the pastor is in the middle of the disagreement, he is in a precarious situation—just as he would be in an organized congregation. However, having hands-on elders from the mother church will help to relieve the pastor of becoming a target in the event of disagreements.

It is helpful to have one or two elders and deacons specifically assigned to work with the church-plant members. These elders not only directly supervise the worship services, but they also serve on the steering committee. Of course, all elders, as members of the consistory, are involved with the church plant, but these elders are specifically assigned to the church-plant labors. Since the church plant is essentially a district of the mother church, these assigned elders will have a district like their fellow elders—the district consisting of members who attend the church plant. Consistories or sessions may want to anticipate the increased workload by adding an elder or two to the consistory.

Shepherding at a Distance

The preceding advice has assumed a feasible driving distance.[31] What do we do if elders cannot drive to the church plant every Lord's Day to fulfill the scriptural duties laid out in the church order? These situations need to be evaluated carefully. The consistory will need to consider if and how they can rightly supervise the church plant when weekly driving is not feasible. They will need to make decisions based on biblical principle, not on pragmatism, expediency, or convenience. If a consistory cannot put in the time required to shepherd appropriately, it may be best to pass on the opportunity. Yet an insightful consistory will realize the need for extremely weighty reasons to pass on overseeing the work of the kingdom of God in their midst. Our God equips those whom He calls for obedient service (Eph. 4:1–16; Phil. 4:13).

At the same time, we must realize that situations providentially arise that are less than ideal. And when a church embarks on a distant church plant, much more work will fall upon the ordained church planter. As the home missionary, he will largely carry out the duties of the consistory at

---

31. One URC sent an elder 150 miles (one way) every Sunday for five years. The elders took turns driving down each Sunday for worship, spending the day with one of the families, and attending the evening service before returning home. While less than ideal, literally going the distance can be accomplished with determined elders.

the church plant until a time when elders from within that group may be properly elected and installed to serve on the consistory. Not unlike Pastor Titus, the church planter will be directed to "set in order the things that are lacking" and identify possible elders to eventually recommend and submit to the consistory for consideration (Titus 1:5).[32]

There are obvious concerns with a church planter who does not have ordained elders to shepherd alongside of him. These matters are not always insurmountable. The consistory entering into such a scenario will want to ensure the closest possible contact with their church-planting minister, even allowing for a feasible frequency of elder visits to the church plant. Also, the church planter—who, as a minister, is a member of the consistory—should attempt to attend all monthly consistory meetings. Whatever label the church-planting pastor is given (e.g., "church planter" or "associate minister"), he is a minister of the mother church with duties pertaining to the church-plant district.[33]

Conclusion

A church plant, no less than an established congregation, has God-given office bearers to shepherd it. I have demonstrated that a church plant is really *a select group from the mother congregation meeting in another location.* The relationship between mother church and church plant is not unlike the relationship between a parent and child. Not unlike parents caring for their children, a church plant needs to be shepherded toward maturity—the most significant goal of church planting.

This shepherding is the responsibility of the consistory, comprising men whom God has publicly authorized. These praying elders and ministers are called to ensure that biblical doctrine is preserved and practiced. Elders must not neglect their office-bearer duties, even where willing parties would gladly help out. Christ has ordained the consistory to shepherd His church plant to maturity, which inescapably requires an intimate involvement with the church plant. All persons must clearly recognize the biblical authority structure and submit to one another out of the fear of our church-planting Lord. The church, with its many faithful church plants, is Christ's.

---

32. *POPC*, 36–37.

33. The URC Church Order recognizes only a "Minister of the Word and Sacraments" without any subcategories such as "evangelist" or "church planter."

While all the applications of shepherding authority are not fleshed out in this chapter, the principle of the organic unity between mother church and plant should guide the decisions of the consistory. It will be up to consistories to apply these principles to their varied situations and to the issues that arise in the course of church planting.[34]

So when is the appropriate time for elders to be installed from within the church plant? Who knows the prospective elder candidates to attest to their life and doctrine? Who should vote on these men? And where would they have authority as elders—in the mother church or in the church plant only? Even though organization is not the ultimate goal, when and how does it happen? We address these and other questions in the next chapter.

---

34. For instance, the understanding that the church and church plant comprise one congregation with a group meeting at another location has implications for finances. While offerings from the church plant will be distinctly recorded, perhaps even placed in a different account, these monies are not ultimately separate from the mother church. The deacons are responsible to care for the finances of all the districts in *the* church. Accordingly, it would be wise to have deacons assigned to a steering committee (if there is one). See appendix C on the steering committee.

CHAPTER SIXTEEN

∾

Shepherding toward Maturity, Part 2: Identifying a Mature Church Plant

Spencer Aalsburg

Just as direct parental responsibility is temporary (usually around eighteen years), so also the consistory must recognize the temporary nature of its task in church planting. The Lord willing, the church plant will be organized one day under a new consistory of men from within the group—when the "apron strings are cut," so to speak. Then the church plant will be an organized congregation and will take its place as a confessionally Reformed church among sister congregations.

The temporary nature of this mother/child relationship should not detract from the reality of the shepherding task, which was described in the preceding chapter. Our parenting is shaped by the reality and hope that our children will someday leave home. We want to dutifully train our children in the ways of the Lord, preparing them to live as kingdom citizens and to be future leaders in Christ's church. This process of maturation requires God's grace through time.

The same applies to the maturing of a church plant into an organized congregation, which is the culmination of a long process. From the first time people meet each other at a Bible study, to joining the same church plant, to electing their leaders, to becoming an organized congregation—this development entails a lengthy time of maturing together.[1] It cannot be overstated that the main goal of church planting is not formal organization (or particularization), but maturity. The following discussion will help a mother church to identify what that maturity looks like.

Identifying a Mature Congregation

This process of maturation is ultimately not the work of the consistory or church planter but rather Jesus Christ. The King of the church, by His

---

1. *POPC*, 71.

Word and Spirit, molds and fashions His people together after His image. "Until Christ is formed in you" describes what the consistory must look for in a mature church plant (Gal. 4:19).

Since this maturing process is God's work, it comes in His time. The growth of a church plant to organizational maturity can take anywhere from two to five years, possibly longer. However, where a proper, godly relationship exists between church plant and mother church, there will be no undue rush to sever the parental ties and hastily organize into a separate congregation.

All people involved need to ask loving and honest questions when they are discerning the church plant's maturity and readiness to organize as a distinct congregation. Here are a few questions that we need to prayerfully consider and openly discuss when we seek to identify a mature church plant. [2]

Do members of the church plant love, respect, and defer to one another in the Lord? If they do not, it will be difficult for them to stand together as an organized congregation in the years to come.

Do members respect, submit to, and obey their God-given leaders on the consistory? Or do their attitudes reflect impatience, as though they are simply waiting to be organized in order to get out from under a perceived intrusion and the interference of "outsiders"? If such attitudes are prevalent, the patterns are not yet set for church-plant members to embrace and follow their leaders, whom God has ordained.

Are members united in their worship of God at the church plant? Does the worship there edify and encourage their hearts? Proper unity can be hindered by significant differences of opinion about the order and practice of corporate worship. If there is simply a reluctant toleration of one another, then the members may not yet be ready to walk together as a unified body of Christ.

Are the members growing in spiritual maturity as a result of the ministry of the church? Are they reaching out to their neighbors, relatives, and friends, and is God using their efforts to gather more of His elect into the church? Are the members demonstrating a proper concern for the needs of those in their community, and are they involved in ministries of mercy? It is vital to hear positive answers to these questions about the ministry of the church that God is building. Hearts will be knit together in gospel fellowship where the gospel is faithfully preached and received

---

2. Many of the ideas for the following questions are taken from *POPC*, 72.

in faith. This will necessarily produce springs of mercy for those around them in the community. If the answers to these questions are not evidently positive, those who are involved in the church plant are little more than participants in a theological club or a group with the same interests.

Do the members know what it means to be confessionally Reformed, and do they understand the fundamentals of the federation (or denomination) they are joined with as a church plant? Do they share the denomination's interests and concerns, or is the denomination a means to the end of a particular agenda? Is the church plant actively involved in praying for the churches of the federation and in financially supporting home and foreign missions?

Back at the mother church, is the consistory worn out by all the work involved, and might it be prematurely looking to organize for the sake of convenience? Are the church-plant members working with artificial or unrealistic expectations and timeframes? Do they fear that they will be looked down upon because their church plant is taking too long to mature?

The consistory needs to use these criteria to render a judgment concerning the church plant's basic readiness to be organized as a new and separate congregation. If Christ is not formed within the church plant, it is certainly not ready to become a God-honoring, healthy, organized church. The consistory must seek and acknowledge honest answers to these questions so that it can be properly confident "that the hand of God has produced both a group of mature believers and a unified congregation that can vow, 'In reliance upon God for strength…[we] promise to walk together as a church of Jesus Christ according to the Word of God.'"[3] Organization is a righteous goal, yet it must be pursued for the right reasons in the right time, for the honor of Christ's name and the edification of His church.

Identifying Mature Leadership

The consistory must shepherd its church plant to maturity, and that involves identifying and training men to be elected as elders and deacons. A church plant will not be ready for organization until elders and deacons from the church plant are in place. Furthermore, readiness for

---

3. The OPC Form of Government XXIX, A, 3, d, as cited in *POPC*, 71–72.

organization under a new consistory must be determined by the consistory and corroborated by classis.[4]

While training and installing office bearers is a significant step for a maturing church plant, this goal—like formal organization—should not be viewed as an end in itself. The *POPC* expresses this well: "Too often, the training of officers is seen as the most urgent work performed by the organizing pastor, and the plan is to get the church organized as quickly as possible. However, the church is much more than its elders. *A word of caution is therefore issued in this discussion of the training of office-bearers, that their roles and responsibilities must be kept in proper perspective within the overall process of organizing the mission work into a new congregation.*"[5]

With this perspective in mind, the church plant needs to be educated about the nature and qualifications of office bearers. There may be people in the church plant who, because of their backgrounds, are unaware of what an elder or deacon is and does. An office-bearer class open to the entire congregation accomplishes at least two things: it teaches members about proper biblical expectations for their servant leaders, and it educates them on what qualifications candidates must evidence when we vote on them to lead the church. Other ways of instructing church-plant members about this doctrine is through sermons and midweek Bible studies. Also, notes in bulletins that remind both seasoned Christians and newcomers to the faith of the New Testament texts that teach about these offices may be helpful as well.

Furthermore, *POPC* reminds any church-planting consistory that choosing leadership must be careful and deliberate: "A new mission work is a place of great need, which often has a vacuum of leadership. Those who help to start them are often unqualified or not yet ready to assume leadership in them. Additionally, those who want to lord it over others often gravitate to newly established churches. And even when mature, qualified men are part of the group, it takes time for the church to recognize them as such."[6] The process of identifying and installing leadership must be conducted biblically and deliberately, and it should not be short-circuited in the name of convenience. Paul specifically warned Timothy

---

4. See URCNA CO, article 22. See also Martin Monsma, *The New Revised Church Order Commentary* (Grand Rapids: Zondervan, 1967), 165ff.

5. *POPC*, 73 (emphasis added).

6. *POPC*, 28.

not to lay hands hastily on a man, presumably referring to the ordination of an elder (1 Tim. 5:22).

Aspiring to the office of elder is a noble task (1 Tim. 3:1), yet the Belgic Confession states, "Every one must take heed not to intrude himself by improper means." Moreover those who aspire to office are "bound to wait till it shall please God to call him; that he may have testimony of his calling, and be certain and assured that it is of the Lord" (BC, art. 31).

Some will argue that Acts 14:23 necessitates appointing elders immediately: "So when they had appointed elders in every church, and prayed with fasting, they commended them to the Lord in whom they had believed." A closer look at this verse in context does not support the immediate, unrestricted appointment of elders. The focus in Acts 14:23 is on the apostles committing the local churches to the Lord, not on meeting a specific timeframe. We gather that Paul and Barnabas came back from Lystra, Iconium, and Antioch to strengthen and exhort the church groups (Acts 14:21–22). Finally, when they were ready to be commended to the Lord, Paul—a divinely inspired apostle—appointed elders in those places.

Acts 14:23 does indeed reveal something about elders: the necessity of eldership in local churches. From that we can conclude that an organized local church exists where elders are installed. We have been discussing the concept of church plants, but we must remember that these already have elders since they are part of a local church. This text cannot be used to support a demand for immediately naming elders from within the church plant. Moreover, Paul would not transgress his own divinely inspired command that the elders must be 1 Timothy 3 men.

The consistory needs to ensure that it leaves the church plant in the care of godly, competent men who are called by God to serve the newly organized church. Accordingly, those who aspire to the office of elder and deacon should undergo a period of training and preparation prior to their election and installation as the first officers of a newly organized church. This goes for any elder and deacon candidate, regardless of his past ordination and experience in the church, even in a Reformed denomination.[7]

---

7. Cf. *POPC*, 75. Sometimes it is argued that once a man is ordained to the office of elder, he is always an elder and therefore an elder in the church plant. We must remember that an elder's power and authority is local, while a minister's is global (BC, art. 31). In other words, that individual may have served as elder in another congregation, but that doesn't mean he is an elder in every congregation he visits.

The consistory must set the high standard of leadership for this future organized congregation (mirroring its own lofty standards) by training the prospective leadership. The training should be intense and last long enough to cover a wide range of material, usually for a duration of six to nine months.[8]

Identifying Mature Decisions

Questions inevitably arise at the point when the church plant is ready to elect and ordain office bearers from among its members: Who will vote on these men? Only those from the church plant? Do only members from the mother church vote? Or do both? Because the church plant is a district of the mother congregation, the answer is that the whole congregation should elect these men, including both those worshiping at the home church and those who are part of the church plant. Members of both the home and plant are members of one local church with one consistory.

Accordingly, church-plant attendees who join the church can and should vote on elders for the mother church because, after all, the mother church is their local church, and these men will be their elders too. Likewise, mother-church attendees are called to vote on elders from within the church plant since those elders will serve on *the* consistory, which is their consistory. Because there may be church-plant members who have not had experience in electing office bearers, there should be solid instruction on how to vote. In his church polity catechism, Thomas Smyth gives a good description: "In a spirit of meekness, humility, peace, and prayer; with a supreme regard to the glory of Christ and the spiritual interests of the church; and without partiality or respect of persons."[9]

Perhaps members from the mother church are unfamiliar with the men who are nominated for office from the church-plant group.[10] By the

---

8. Cf. *POPC*, 75. It is beneficial for the mother church to inform the church plant when officer training is happening—not only to keep the church plant members informed but also to show them that confessional churches take the training of office bearers seriously.

9. Thomas Smyth, *An Ecclesiastical Catechism of the Presbyterian Church* (Fellesmere, Fla.: Reformation Christian Ministries, 1996), 36.

10. Those elders already assigned to the church plant can help guide the council, who "shall present to the congregation nominations for the offices of elder and deacon" (URCNA CO, art. 12). Of course, as in any office-bearer election, "the council may give the congregation opportunity to direct attention to suitable men" (URCNA CO, art. 12). Also, it is the council that determines the length of term for service (URCNA CO, art. 13). In nominating an office bearer from the church plant, six to twelve months may be fitting for the first office bearer(s).

time the local church is ready for elders from the church-plant group, ideally (depending on the distance between plant and mother congregation) the whole congregation has gotten to know these men, at least to some extent. As with any election, church members can trust their council to put forth names of 1 Timothy 3 men for office.[11]

It is understandable that the idea of having a man on the consistory who lives two hours away and who rarely attends the mother church for worship may generate some questions. How would this man vote on a matter not directly related to the church plant, such as a discipline case in the mother church? Or how is he supposed to vote on recommending an expensive addition to the mother-church building? The questions dissipate when we remember that there is one consistory for the entire local church, even with part of that church meeting in another location. Keeping this truth central will begin to simplify answers to questions that arise.

Accordingly, elders vote on matters as elders, whether they live two hours away or ten minutes. An elder is an elder of both the local church and the church's church plant. It may not be wise to send an elder from the church plant on family visiting in the home congregation when there are other closer elders who know the people better. However, for him to go would be entirely permissible since he is an elder in the consistory of that one local church.

If formal discipline is being applied to a member who worships at the home location, the church-plant elder would function like the other elders: using his God-given gifts in the discussion and voting accordingly. In this situation he would surely lean much on the wisdom of those fellow elders who are closer to the situation. Discretion would dictate that he not take charge of a discussion about which he knows little. Men who by God's grace meet the standards of biblical eldership—noble men, above reproach, sober-minded, self-controlled, respectable, not violent but gentle, not quarrelsome (cf. 1 Tim. 3:1–7)—will conduct themselves suitably.

In short, elders are elders, with all the authority and responsibilities of elders to the whole congregation. Although they may be specifically assigned to work primarily with the church plant, this does not negate the authority or responsibility of the office of elder. Those who have concerns about an elder from the church plant holding a position of authority in

---

11. These men may or may not already be on a steering committee. Being a member of that committee does not "secure" him a position on the consistory.

the mother congregation have a serious question to answer: Why would this man be considered suitable to shepherd the church plant but not the mother church?

Likewise, congregation members are congregation members—whether they worship at the mother church or at the church plant—and as such they are entitled to the rights and responsibilities of membership. Godly wisdom will dictate solutions to the various situations that arise. For instance, a church-plant attendee may choose not to vote on the building addition at the mother church because he thinks that decision would be better decided by those who regularly attend the mother church.

This reality underscores the need to have open and honest discussions about a church plant from the beginning. There must not be suspicion, aggravation, or competition within a local church that has the great privilege and joy of planting another church. There should be no "us and them" mentality between mother church and church plant because all share in one local congregation that God has chosen to plant.

Rightly rooted and grounded in love—which suffers long and is kind…does not seek its own…is not provoked, thinks no evil…bears all things, believes all things, hopes all things, endures all things—the whole congregation will have a mutual vision for loving God's work of church planting in their midst (1 Cor. 13:4–7; Eph. 3). The dutiful consistory will ensure that this vision is fostered within the whole congregation.

Church-Plant Decisions

We have been discussing the unity of the whole congregation—mother-church worshipers and church-plant worshipers alike—and decisions that affect them both as members of the same congregation with the same office bearers. And yet there are decisions that are peculiar to the church-plant group. Where should the church plant meet for services? Should there be a coffee time after the morning service, the evening service, or perhaps both?

In shepherding the church plant toward maturity, the consistory will need to specifically foster unity within the church-plant group. The consistory "should recognize that congregational decision-making in the life of a mission work is often a difficult matter."[12] Again, the OPC offers experienced guidance: "In the early days of its life, the mission work

---

12. *POPC*, 33.

may often become polarized if asked to make decisions about secondary issues, such as a change of name or meeting location. And even on primary issues, such as the selection of an organizing pastor or the purchase of land, the group often has not yet formed sufficiently deep relationships with one another in order to make mutual decisions."[13]

Accordingly, the OPC Form of Government does not make provision for a mission work to decide these kinds of matters formally. While the session or consistory will arrange for informal discussion between themselves and the members of the church on significant matters, it often is the consistory that will settle potentially divisive decisions.

The consistory must promote godly communication. Practicing open, honest communication facilitates trust and fellowship and is important in both established churches and church plants. A good means of communicating important information is "town hall" meetings once a month, perhaps after the weekly church-plant prayer meeting. Meetings of this sort will help ensure adequate communication between church-plant members and their consistory. It could be a time when the consistory (perhaps making use of the steering committee) could gather corporate feedback. Members would have the opportunity to communicate with those appointed to make decisions for the church plant. This should be a time of mutual encouragement and edification, discussing how to effectively serve Christ, one another, and the community in which they live. This would not, however, be a time for destructive gossip, airing grievances, or other unbecoming speech. So that they do know what to expect, it is wise to teach the church-plant members about the different types of congregational meetings that will occur and how they work. Make sure they understand who runs the meetings and why, if women may vote, and how many votes are needed to carry a motion.

It is important to realize that the church plant will eventually develop a distinct (though not separate) identity as the members there grow together and the Lord adds others. Understanding that there can be variations on nonessentials, the consistory must be sensitive to this and shepherd the church plant accordingly. For instance, a church plant may be blessed with musicians that can play elaborate arrangements of certain psalms and hymns. The music may not be the same the mother church uses in her services, but there is room for nonessential variations. The phrase "That's the way we've always done it" can be an unbiblical

---

13. *POPC*, 33.

excuse for not properly considering other equally valid interpretations of biblical principles.

Appropriate variation between mother church and church plant can be permissible, especially as the church plant matures. The goal of church planting must not be the creation of a cookie-cutter duplicate of the mother church.[14] Using the parent/child analogy, a father wouldn't normally insist that his son get the exact haircut he wears. If the father were to insist, then the son would be duty-bound to submit—even though the father would probably not be making the best choice on this nonessential. But there are different haircuts that can be equally appropriate (or equally inappropriate).

Parents grant a child more freedom as he matures and shows that he is ready for it—yet he remains subject to his parents' authority. Indeed, in order to prevent a child from struggling when he leaves home and gains many new kinds of responsibility, he needs to be granted increasing freedoms as he becomes ready. The consistory will shepherd (not lord it over) the church-plant members accordingly as they mature together, for the glory of Christ and His church. And the church plant will lovingly honor those in authority who are shepherding them for their good.

Toward Organization

The emphasis of this essay has been the goal of shepherding a church plant toward maturity, with organization being an outcome of that maturity. The URC Church Order, article 22, reads: "When a congregation is organized within the federation, this shall take place under the supervision of a neighboring consistory and with the concurring advice of the classis."[15] The OPC BCO says, "A group of believers may be organized as a separate congregation of the Orthodox Presbyterian Church only under the supervision of presbytery" (XXIX.2; cf. PCA BCO V.8).

The church plant can organize only when Christ is formed in it (Gal. 4:19). Spiritual maturity manifests in a holy unity—a growing in the grace and knowledge of our Lord Jesus Christ that is demonstrated by bearing with one another in love. This maturity can be seen in a growing unity of purpose and mind within the church plant. In fact, the OPC BCO asks

---

14. For further discussion of this subject, see chapter 20, "The Cultural Factor in Church Planting," by Mitchell Persaud.

15. For a discussion of this article, see the section "A Word about Broader Assemblies" in the previous chapter.

the church plant an essential question as it makes the step toward organization: "In reliance upon God for strength do you solemnly promise to walk together as a church of Jesus Christ according to the Word of God and the constitution of the Orthodox Presbyterian Church?" (XXIX.3.d; cf. PCA BCO V.8.3). Spiritual maturity also brings forth trained leadership from within the church-plant group—men who have been serving as elders and deacons on the council of the mother church (which is the council of the church plant).

While spiritual maturity is necessary, it is not sufficient for the consistory to seek the concurring advice of classis to particularize the work into a separate congregation. The church plant needs a fitting number of families and sufficient financial resources to stand as an organized congregation. Also, the bylaws of the proposed new congregation will need to be ratified by the consistory, along with any other paperwork like a budget, insurance, articles of incorporation, and 501(c) 3 status. The church plant can slowly work on these items as it gains momentum.

Since varying contexts dictate the required numbers of families and necessary finances, it is difficult to assign general numbers that would apply to every church plant. As a rule of thumb, it is fitting to have no fewer than ten church-plant families with the ability to meet most of their budget. Again, if the proper biblical relationship exists between mother church and plant, there is no need to rush the formal process of organization.

When the consistory has determined that the church plant has grown to maturity, it is time to organize. Ideally, the elders from within the church plant would be members of the first organized consistory of the church plant. This facilitates a healthy continuity for the new consistory; however, one or more elders from the church plant may need to be added to comprise the appropriate number for the new church's first consistory.

Once the consistory receives concurring advice from classis, a special service can be held where the office bearers are installed as the first consistory of the church plant. And what a glorious service for all from the mother church and church plant to attend! In keeping with proper procedure, the newly organized congregation needs to call the church planter to be its pastor since he is a minister in the mother church. A fitting installation service for a minister follows—giving another opportunity for the saints to rejoice in our gracious, church-maturing God.

Conclusion

Godly maturity is the mark of a church ready to be formally organized into a separate congregation. This maturity needs to be shepherded by the office bearers in order that the church plant can grow up to adulthood as the body of Christ (Eph. 4:7–16). The leadership vacuum must be filled intentionally with biblically qualified men to serve as elders. While training and installing office bearers is a goal, it is not the main goal in church planting.

The mother church/plant relationship needs to be nourished to ensure that there is unity in the vision of church planting. The consistory also must foster the bond of unity among church-plant attendees. This process of maturing will take time, and unduly rushing it is neither necessary nor helpful. Working with the churches of classis will enrich church planting while also edifying the rest of the churches.

Authority can be a divisive issue. Differing views can be divisive. Nonessentials can be divisive. Yet church planting does not have to be a divisive endeavor; in fact, it must not be. God's grace working in the consistory will prevent division as the elders fearfully remember that Christ has placed them in authority to shepherd the church with its church plant (Acts 20:28; 1 Peter 5:2–4). Likewise, God's grace working in us all to help us submit accordingly to one another in love will prevent division (1 Thess. 5:12–13; 1 Peter 5:5a; Heb. 13:17).

May we all remember that church planting is about Christ building His church to the glory of God and the enjoyment of the saints, who delight in Him. It's about Him. It's not about us. "Yes, all of you be submissive to one another, and be clothed with humility, for 'God resists the proud, but gives grace to the humble'" (1 Peter 5:5). "Walk worthy of the calling with which you were called, with all lowliness and gentleness, with longsuffering, bearing with one another in love, endeavoring to keep the unity of the Spirit in the bond of peace" (Eph. 4:1–3).

> How good and pleasant is the sight
> When brethren make it their delight
> To dwell in blest accord;
> The Lord commands His blessing there,
> And they that walk in love shall share
> In life that never ends.[16]

---

16. *Psalter Hymnal* (Grand Rapids: Board of Publications of the Christian Reformed Church, 1976), no. 278:3.

CHAPTER SEVENTEEN

Motivation: The Planting Church and the Planted Church

Eric Tuininga

How does a planting church motivate her members to get excited about planting? How does a planting church motivate the church plant to stay together and build true Christian fellowship? This chapter covers these two important aspects of the church plant. First, we deal with the planting church (sometimes called the mother church or supporting church). Second, we focus on the church that is being planted.

Training and Motivating the Supporting Church

It is easy for one or two visionary members to get the idea of planting a church, run with it, and leave their congregation behind. This often causes friction, disunity, and lack of support. Perhaps you are experiencing this: you want to plant a church badly, and you feel God wants you to be planting a church, but getting others motivated seems difficult. Maybe you are tempted to echo the words of Jesus—that others are foolish and slow of heart to believe in your great idea to plant a church (Luke 24:25). But church planting is not an individual or small-group task. It requires the united support of a sending church. As much as you might be tempted to do this on your own, you can't. Even the apostle Paul left for his journeys only after his supporting church prayed and fasted (Acts 13:1–3).

So if it is Christ's will for a church to be planted, how can you train and motivate the supporting church? How can you get people on board? Enthusiastic support for church planting is not automatic. Many churches are reluctant to sponsor a daughter church or mission work. But here is your hope: God is in the business of changing hearts and lives, and if He has the power to plant a church, He also has the power to motivate and train a supporting church. Remember, it must be God's work, not yours. You are simply the instrument. God cares most about heart attitudes, and so should you. Seek, by God's grace, to change the heart attitudes of people in your church. What follows are the heart biblical attitudes you should display, cultivate, and pray for.

Heart Attitudes to Cultivate

A Yearning for God to Receive Glory

People say that they desire God's glory, but it must become a *real* desire in their hearts. Set before your congregation the awesome grace of Christ and that everything must be centered on Him. Set before them the life-changing truth that their lives are not about themselves—not their marriage, their friends, or their American dream of a house and job and family—but the glory of God (1 Cor. 10:31). If the primary motive of their life is God's glory and they know that God is glorified by planting a church, then they will eagerly support the church plant.

A Love for God's Kingdom

Many people are familiar with Matthew 6:33, "Seek first the kingdom of God," but the truth of this verse must become a *real* desire in their hearts. If you ask members, "What is the purpose for our church? Why are we here?" what kind of answers do you get? Let people know the purpose of the church is not to be inwardly focused—concerned with how we can be happy, comfortable, and content,—but rather kingdom focused: concerned with how God's kingdom can grow. There should be a yearning and hunger for the kingdom of God to move forward—not just within the walls of the church but everywhere. Ask, "How can we build the kingdom in a community that is, perhaps, fifty or a hundred miles away?

A Love for People in Other Communities

People say that they care about the lost, who are daily being plunged into eternal hell to suffer the wrath of God, but their concern must become a *real* love. Cultivate such a love for people from all nations and races and tribes and tongues. And even more, cultivate a love for those who are saved but who are spiritually starving because they lack a solid church home. Then you can point out, "Anyone in our town who desires a solid church can come to ours, but the neighboring communities have nothing. Do we love God's people there?" There are people calling out for truth. Do we love them? Do we have mercy? Paul did, and he told the Thessalonian church that he was "affectionately longing for you,... well pleased to impart to you not only the gospel of God, but also our own lives"

(1 Thess. 2:8). Let us cultivate an "affectionate longing" for Christians to be blessed with solid churches and for unbelievers to be saved.

The Importance of the Local Church

Many people yearn for God's glory, love God's kingdom, and have great concern for the lost, but they don't support church plants because they don't realize the importance of the local church. We need to help people realize that the local church is the best way for God to receive glory, for God's kingdom to grow, and for people to be saved and encouraged. We can teach the importance of the local church by using the book of Acts. In Acts, Paul plants churches everywhere, ordains elders, and writes letters to the new church plants. This is how the kingdom grows—planting churches. Remind people that the church is not our idea—it's God's idea. Christ loves the church (Eph. 5:22–33). The church is the gift the Father gives to the Son and is therefore to be cherished by God's people (John 6:37–40). The biblical emphasis on the local church is summarized well in the Westminster Confession and Three Forms of Unity, so make use of these valuable teaching tools.

An Eagerness to Give

Cultivate an attitude of willingness to suffer for others—to give away our time, our energy, our money, our lives (2 Cor. 8–9). One of the greatest areas in which the sponsoring church must suffer is prayer. Prayer is hard work, but a sponsoring church should be devoted to prayer, much like Antioch was filled with prayer before sending out Paul and Barnabas (Acts 13:1–3). Overseeing and funding a church plant is a sacrifice—it is hard work that requires suffering. Cultivate an eagerness to suffer for Christ. There are churches that do not have their own buildings, but instead of saving money for a new building, they give their money away to other church plants. This is an example of willingly choosing to suffer for Christ's kingdom.

These are the heart attitudes you should cultivate in your congregation. If these heart attitudes are alive and well, then the members of your congregation will enthusiastically support the idea of church planting. But be aware that there are bad motives as well and watch for them. Avoid the following wrong motivations for church planting.

Wrong Motives for Church Planting

One wrong motive for planting a church is congregational pride; a congregation plants a church to prove that it is a great congregation. Pastors must kill pride wherever they find it—especially in themselves—and should preach repentance. Pray for God to humble you and your congregation.

Guilt is another wrong motivation. A congregation plants a church because otherwise the members feel guilty for not doing enough for Christ. It is true that we are all horribly guilty, but planting a church is not the solution. We must take our guilt to the cross and plant a church out of joy over Christ's forgiveness and our yearning for others to experience that joy.

Finally, we should not plant churches if we are motivated by a "party spirit," in which we simply want our group or denomination to advance. Don't plant the "Apollos" church to compete with the "Paul" church and the "Cephas" church. Don't define yourself by what you are *not* (for example, we are not seeker-sensitive/Baptist/Lutheran). Define yourself by who you are—part of the one holy catholic church of Jesus Christ, seeking to honor His name and advance His kingdom. I would humbly suggest for your consideration that we take care with the language that we use and avoid speaking too much of the "Reformed faith" as though it were opposed to the "Lutheran faith" or the "Presbyterian faith" or the "Baptist faith." There is one faith—and it is faith in Jesus Christ for salvation. We are here to preach Christ! I firmly believe that the Reformed faith is both biblical and true, and I am not saying that you should compromise on what is true. Don't compromise on the confessions. But preach Christ. Beware of the danger of preaching "salvation-by-being-Reformed."

How Do I Motivate My Church?

Now that you've seen the heart attitudes that need to be cultivated, you may wonder how you can cultivate them. You can't, but God can. He can use you through these means.

Pray continually and earnestly for the members of your congregation. Only God can change their hearts. Pray for Him to work these changes.

Preaching is a powerful tool to change attitudes. So preach a vision of God's glory, God's kingdom, love for others, the importance of the local church, and a life of sacrifice and mission work. Preach the gospel thoroughly, and don't give up.

Lead your church in sponsoring a conference. Call a church planter or missionary to come in and speak. This can encourage a passion for evangelism that will motivate the congregation to plant a church.

God can use your conversations with the people of your congregation to help them develop a motivation for church planting. Speak of the essential heart attitudes over a cup of coffee, in informal discussions, in family visits—whenever you can.

A desire for church planting must begin with the church leadership. Share with the elders and deacons the glorious truths that shape the necessary heart attitudes and encourage them through leadership training, devotions at elders' meetings, and informal conversations while driving to family visits.

Be Reformed in your approach to evangelism. Both the Westminster Standards and the Three Forms of Unity stress the fact that the gospel must go out. For example, the Westminster Larger Catechism discusses the truth that the covenant of grace includes people from all nations (WLC, Q&A 35). Emphasize the truth that Reformed Christianity is necessarily evangelistic.

Be patient. Take seriously Paul's word to Timothy, to "exhort…with all longsuffering and teaching" (2 Tim. 4:2). Do not become angry, bitter, or jealous of other congregations. Do not grow weary in doing good, for in due season you will reap.

Practical Steps to Take

So by an amazing work of God's grace, your congregation has these heart attitudes in place—there is real growth in zeal for God's glory, His kingdom, and a love for others, along with all of the other necessary heart attitudes. Praise the Lord! What are some practical ways to train and motivate the supporting church, once church-planting efforts are underway?

It is important to communicate effectively with the congregation of the planting church. Make sure the people understand the overall process of church planting—what they can expect to happen, what the long-term commitment is, what will be required in the first few months of starting the plant. Once the plant is started, keep them informed with regular announcements, a newsletter, bulletin reports, prayer suggestions, emails, and blogs and website updates. Share the work that Christ is doing with as many details as possible.

Encourage the people of the planting congregation to know the members of the plant congregation and get involved. Make a small photo directory of the church plant members and their families so that people in the planting church can see their faces when they pray for them. It is easier to love people when you can see their faces and know something about who they are. Encourage the members of the planting church to attend the Bible studies and services of the church plant on occasion. In my own experience, those who traveled the fifty miles from the planting church to attend our Friday evening church-plant Bible study even one time were much more excited and eager throughout the process than members who didn't visit. They had personally met the core group and seen their excitement. They caught the vision.

Be patient if you are faced with opposition or congregational hesitation. Avoid mentally dividing the congregation into camps of supporters versus opponents. Satan will use anything to cause disunity, including overseeing a church plant. Many sources of disagreement can arise in mission work, such as how best to move forward, as even Paul and Barnabas discovered (Acts 15:39). Remember, God is sovereign over hearts and minds, so don't give up! Lay every discouragement before the Lord in prayer. Christ is king, and He will build His church. He can use you and your congregation. He has the power! Press on in serving Him.

Training and Motivating the Core Group

Perhaps you have four or five interested families who would like to begin a Bible study. But what should you study? How should you train them? This will depend on your own local situation. Are these families already members of an OPC, URC, or PCA? Are they recent converts? Have they even heard of Reformed or Presbyterian churches? In the church plant where I was pastor, most of the families had never heard of the URC before we began the Bible study. They simply loved the doctrines of grace and the "solas" of the Reformation. Here are some pointers to remember as you plan a Bible study and prepare to begin worship services:

- Base all your training solidly on Scripture. Don't assume that "everyone knows" that the traditions or doctrines you hold are biblical. Prove them from Scripture.

- Distribute and use the confessions. Show how they explain Scripture. Encourage people to read them and think deeply about them. Make free copies of the Westminster Standards or Three Forms of Unity available.

- Have a book table. Distribute other solid Reformed literature.

- Keep it simple enough for people who know nothing of Reformed theology yet in-depth enough to provide real meat.

- Make your training spiritually refreshing, addressing both the mind and the heart. For example, focus not just on what the doctrines of grace are but why we love them and the difference they make in daily life and spiritual experience.

- Saturate your training in prayer. Let the foundation for this church be rooted and grounded in helpless dependence on Christ—as evidenced in prayer.

- Train people about the hardships of a church plant. Be real about the pain, the hard work, the commitment, and the sacrifice. Are they ready for this? Help them think seriously about what they are getting into. Remind them it could take three, four, or five years, for example.

- Take people through at least the equivalent of a membership class in your planting church. Be sure to cover topics such as the doctrine of God, the doctrine of Scripture, justification by faith, the doctrines of grace, the "solas" of the Reformation, covenant theology, the doctrine of the church, sacraments, church leadership, church membership, and worship.

- Continue to train people once worship begins. Be sure Sunday school and catechism curriculum are in place. The training never ends! Teach them to observe all that Christ has commanded them.

Motivating the Core Group

A core group should be self-motivated. If motivating the core group is proving to be difficult, there are serious problems, and it is probably not the right core group for planting a new church. Hopefully God has been working in their hearts for years already, and they are excited and willing to jump in with both feet. Again, if this is not the case, be very careful. One of the purposes of a Bible study should be to ascertain if there is a core group motivated enough to hang on for the long haul. Satan will go after them at some point. Will they press on? If so, remember, even the most self-motivated core group needs encouraging. So encourage them! Here are several ways to do that.

- Give members the big picture. Let them know Christ's love for the church, Christ's power, Christ's unlimited resources, and Christ's promise to give what we ask. Remind them that this is Christ's church, not theirs, and the gates of hell will not prevail against it. It must be His work, not ours.

- Keep communication open. As in any good relationship, communication is vital. The mother church needs to let the plant know what is going on and why. Likewise, the plant needs to let the mother church know what is going on and why. This will not only motivate but also ensure against the problems that come from miscommunication. Some church plants have failed, humanly speaking, simply because they did not properly communicate.

- One of the best ways to motivate the core group is to show love and support from the mother congregation. It is a great encouragement to know you have a church solidly behind you financially, spiritually, and in every way.

- Be sure to send up elders, deacons, and members regularly to join in the Bible studies and worship services. Be there for them literally. Also, another way to keep plant morale up is to invite the members to the planting church's fellowship events.

- Encourage plant members to support each other. Once services begin, remind them of the need for all of them to attend regularly and help in any way possible. Sporadic attendance is a discouragement to a new group. You could also plan potlucks and other types of social gatherings for fellowship.

Conclusion

Realize that the Holy Spirit must be at work. Training and motivating the congregation and core group isn't something you can do. You are not adequate to the task. Christ must do it. So move forward in helpless dependence on Him. Ask Him, trust Him, and seek to be used by Him. Then, whether the plant succeeds or fails, you will have hallowed His name and given Him glory. That is what matters most.

PART FOUR

ↄ

The Context of
Planting Churches

CHAPTER EIGHTEEN

∾

Church Planting in a Melting Pot

Shane Lems

In essentials unity, in non-essentials liberty, in all things charity.
—Augustine

Churches are planted in an existing cultural situation. This statement is obvious, but it is one that church plants—pastor-planters, consistories/sessions, and church plant members—must weigh carefully. In this chapter, we deal generally with the church plant as she relates to her cultural surroundings. This chapter could be considered a sort of appendix or footnote to several other helpful chapters in this book that address how church planters and missionaries are to engage the people with whom they are working. If their chapters were about people engaging people, this chapter is about church plants engaging the broader cultural context. By "culture" I simply and broadly mean the habits, lifestyles, beliefs, and traditions of a local people group.

Many of today's teachers and theologians have spoken loudly and clearly about the huge cultural shift that we find ourselves on the tail end of. Thirty or forty years ago, American churches were still modern, though modernism was starting to crumble at the corners a little. Today it has crumbled to the center; though there are epistemological parallels between modernism and postmodernism (and post-postmodernism), culturally it seems as if we're in a different world. From David Wells to Michael Horton to Kevin Vanhoozer to Don Carson and others, evangelical and confessional teachers have been pointing out this gigantic paradigm shift.[1] As these authors have explained, we can see the cultural shift even by looking at the changes in church life over the

---

1. I also recommend that the church planter and elders read and discuss several of Lesslie Newbigin's books, since his perspective on the gospel as it relates to Western culture is worthy of consideration as we move forward in planting churches. See especially

last thirty years. From seeker-sensitive to megachurches to emergent to house churches, a big part of American churches rises and falls with the cultural ebbs and tides.

This chapter is limited in its scope and is unable to address this matter thoroughly. The discussions of contextualization, Christ and culture, and worship wars have been covered over and over in print and in the blogosphere. While I am aware of these debates, this chapter is not an attempt to settle them. I mean it simply to be a sort of catalyst for further thinking and discussion as we plant confessional churches in a tidal wave of cultural shifts. More could be said on all the areas that follow; my hope is that the readers will take culture more seriously than they may have before, yet less seriously than the confessions.

What are some differences between the old school and the new school, between modernism and postmodernism? They are many—too many for us to discuss here. But the following are a few examples: Modernism affirmed an absolute truth, at least to some extent, while postmodernism affirms local truths and questions absolute ones. Modernism had some vestiges of a Judeo-Christian sort of worldview, including rules, ethics, and morals, down to the way people dressed. Modernism said there were norms for what one could wear and say; postmodernism is not so quick to say such things. Modernism would—at least sometimes—call sin what it is, while postmodernism hesitates to do so. Modernism said there were right ways to do things that were applicable to the American culture; postmodernism again hesitates to make such sweeping statements.

We could certainly add many to this list. At the risk of being reductionistic, we might think about that dear little eighty-year-old grandmother who is entirely set in her ways and compare her to the postmodern twenty-something, for whom almost anything goes. Communication tools like Facebook and Twitter are not appealing to a grandmother, while a twenty-something might not recognize the value of a carefully handwritten letter. A study of popular culture alone would reveal the vast difference between modernism and postmodernism.[2]

Truth to Tell: The Gospel as Public Truth (Grand Rapids: Eerdmans, 1991) and *The Gospel in a Pluralist Society* (Grand Rapids: Eerdmans, 1989).

2. For more information, read Ken Samples's helpful evaluation of postmodernity in *A World of Difference* (Grand Rapids: Baker, 2007), 219–31.

Preliminary Postmodern Notes

Before considering the church plant and culture, we will briefly note the "spirituality" of postmodernism. David Wells's "The Supremacy of Christ in a Postmodern World" summarizes some aspects of postmodernity's spirituality.[3] First, Wells notes that America is perhaps the most multi-ethnic and religiously diverse nation in the world.[4] Mosques are not just in the Middle East; there are many in American cities and towns. Second, this means that the United States is a melting pot of traditions, religions, languages, and customs. You name it, we have it! The once-isolated rural areas are no longer bastions of old-school American Christianity and morals. Mormons, Jehovah's Witnesses, Scientology, UFO cults, and many more such religions are pervading even the rural areas of America. To put it bluntly, odd and false religions are not "out there" anymore—they are here, next door, even in rural America. It is almost impossible to stay in a Christian bubble in the twenty-first century.

What accompanies this diversity is a blending of spiritualities and traditions. Wells notes that around 44 percent of Americans think the Bible, the Koran, and the Book of Mormon contain the same truths expressed in different ways.[5] Another thing for church plants and planters to know is that "the self" is the forceful influence for many people in the United States. This has always been the case to some extent, but it has morphed into a much greater force. Self-esteem, self-awareness, and self-actualization—these are engines of today's spirituality.[6] People will do nearly anything to bolster these self-cravings and needs, from expensive laser surgery to Zen Buddhism to a "Jesus diet." Self-empowerment is the fuel that drives the religious markets today, from Joel Osteen to Oprah to Deepak Chopra. As Wells writes, many Americans "say that in life's crises they look within themselves for answers rather than to an outside power like the Christian God. They are in search of a new *conscious-ness…transformation…connectedness*," and so on (author's emphasis).[7] This

---

3. David Wells, "The Supremacy of Christ in a Postmodern World," in *The Supremacy of Christ in a Postmodern World*, ed. Justin Taylor and John Piper (Wheaton, Ill.: Crossway, 2007).

4. Ibid., 23.

5. Ibid., 26.

6. For example, Deepak Chopra opens one of his books with this: "The purpose of life is the expansion of happiness. Happiness is the goal of every other goal" (*The Ultimate Happiness Prescription: 7 Keys to Joy and Enlightenment* [New York: Harmony Books, 2009], 11).

7. Wells, "The Supremacy of Christ," 26.

therapeutic moralism does not fit well with authority, specifically church authority. All of this is really paganized spirituality of the inner self. The capitalistic, self-centered economy only throws gallons of fuel on this inner fire. If it feels good and helps me, I'll pay a ton for it (and I'll return it if I'm not happy with it).

This is the culture in which our church plants find themselves. As the reader may have noticed, it is both good and bad. The situation is bad because confessional churches will not be attractive in such an individualistic pagan culture because they don't offer things that cater to the American self and because many people in our culture refuse to submit to church authority.

On the other hand, it is a great place in which we find ourselves. This clash will help distinguish the confessional church from American culture and spirituality. It is good because the comfort the church offers is neither temporary nor self-centered; people at the end of the postmodern rope may see beauty in true hope. It is good because postmodernity's rejection of authority is like a time bomb; authority is needed or anarchy results. Solid church leadership will be like an anchor in the postmodern storm.

This changing and difficult cultural context is an exciting one in which to preach the gospel because it is so foreign to the American way of thinking. As old-school American morality crumbles, the gospel will stand out all the more. Perhaps this culture shift we're in will once for all divorce Christ from America—it will be a painful divorce, perhaps, but painfully good for the church.

Furthermore, only the church has a viable, living, breathing, close-knit group of people bonded by something greater than themselves, their wants, or their choices: the electing love of God and the gospel of Christ. The postmodern floater might be liberated by such a truth. Wells points out that the postmodern self—while loaded with goods and comforts—is the loneliest self in the world.[8] While many Americans are gaining the world, they are losing their souls. Through His church, Christ can turn that around so that self is killed and souls are gained by a cross and death. Rather than hunker down in traditional trenches and long for a return to the "golden age" of modernity, the church plant should stand on the tallest building in town and herald the sound of the gospel that

---

8. Postmodernity "denies that anything can be ultimate because ultimately nothing is there" (Wells, "The Supremacy of Christ," 40).

will shake the world and bring some home. In today's cultural landscape, church isolationism, a ghetto mindset, or sectarian withdrawal will not do. "To the end of the earth" is a biblical call against withdrawal (Acts 1:8). We don't plant churches just to reach the underfed; we plant churches to also reach those who have *never* been fed, who need to be led—like the Samaritan woman—to the well of Jesus.

What about *Our* Church Plant?

In order to be good missionaries, church plants need to be abundantly aware of such a cultural shift. Not everyone needs to be a sociologist or Barna expert to plant a church, but those involved in a church plant should study the culture and read the authors associated with postmodern thought to attain some general knowledge of the cultural landscape of the day. We're not planting in a cultural vacuum; there *is* a cultural context. We follow Paul, who engaged the ideas of the day (Acts 17:22–23). Church planters and sessions should be aware of larger cultural changes, which can be deduced by reading political blogs, noting which TV shows and movies bring in the most viewers, and skimming the books (fiction/nonfiction) at the top of the *New York Times* Best Seller list. These are little clues to show the church plant what makes people "out there" in the plant's surrounding area tick. Church plants would do well to think like missionaries by gaining a basic understanding of the culture around them.

Confessions and Traditions

Many traditional churches over the years have established cultural norms that go along with being a generational Christian. Many lifelong Christians who are children of Christians are accustomed to doing certain things a certain way, either intentionally or unintentionally. This is not necessarily a terrible thing; a problem occurs when tradition gets mixed in with confessionalism or doctrine. Similar ethnic groups tend to have similar customs or traditions as well as religious beliefs, and over time the two can become mixed.

For example, the men in one ethnic group do not wear—and never have worn—anything but slacks and a tie to church. When this practice mixes with the confession, the ethnic group thinks the Christian thing to do is wear dress pants and a tie to church functions.[9] Again, it may not be a bad thing if the men wear dress pants and ties to church functions, but it is important for us to realize this is a tradition and is not confessional. Even if we prefer ties, we wouldn't force people to wear them to church. Other examples include methods of raising children, hobbies, and politics. What often happens when traditions get changed, dropped, or questioned is that many overreact and cry, "Liberalism!"

Here is where the postmodern shift is a teacher for the discerning and diligent church plant. The church plant has a great opportunity to keep traditions and the confessions separate.[10] Church plants can be a diverse group when it comes to traditions and a unified group when it comes to the confession. A session or consistory could try to plant another church that shares the traditions and customs of the mother church, but that church plant would not draw in people with different traditions and habits. It would be what some call a "ghetto" church plant.

I firmly believe that the church plant should be open to all sorts of peoples, traditions, and customs, and it should not try to force everyone into the same traditional mold. What should bind the church plant (and all churches) together is the common confession of faith in Christ.[11] Or, in the words of Paul, a chief duty of the church is to hold firm to apostolic

---

9. A brief summary of what I mean by confessions in this essay is Scott Clark's helpful description of the Reformed confession: "It is…a theology, piety, and practice of the gospel, of the Father's love for sinners, of the Son's saving acts for sinners, of the Spirit's work within sinners applying to them Christ's work for them, operating through the preaching of the holy gospel and the holy sacraments" (R. Scott Clark, *Recovering the Reformed Confession* [Phillipsburg, N.J.: P&R, 2008], 218–19).

10. Jim Belcher, a pastor/planter in the PCA, says we should look beyond our own experiences to the formative eras of church history—the apostolic and patristic days—as we seek to be biblical in our cultural context (*Deep Church* [Downers Grove, Ill.: InterVarsity, 2009], 135). Though I may quibble with several aspects of *Deep Church*, I do think it is a good book for church planters to consider. I also suggest wrestling with some church-planting books and lectures from other traditions. I strongly recommend Tim Chester's and Steve Timmis's *Total Church*, which is much more helpful than *Deep Church*. Several of Ed Stetzer's works are also worth pondering: *Planting New Churches in a Postmodern Age; Planting Missional Churches;* and *Lost and Found: The Younger Unchurched and the Churches That Reach Them.* Other examples are *Vintage Church* by Gerry Breshears and Mark Driscoll and *Church Planter* by Darrin Patrick, as well as some publications from 9Mark (www.9marks.org). Even though we may not agree with every doctrine or method, we can certainly learn from these resources.

11. As Mitch Persaud notes in chapter 20, "The Cultural Factor in Church Planting," some cultural traditions are in conflict with Scripture; these must be lovingly addressed and confronted.

tradition—that is, the *teaching* of the apostles (1 Cor. 11:2; 2 Thess. 2:15). While we become "all things to all men" (1 Cor. 9:22), we do so holding firmly to apostolic doctrine.

A church plant is also a great place to show what election is: God chooses whom He will put in the pew or chair next to us. We don't get to choose. Michael Horton says this well: "I did not choose these people for my sisters and brothers; God did. If I am to be God's child, I must accept these others as my siblings, coheirs in Christ. A local church…is not free to develop its identity in continuity simply with the givens of racial, ethnic, socioeconomic, generational, or consumer affinities. Each particular expression of the church must seek to exhibit the catholicity that is grounded in God's electing choice rather than our own."[12] We shouldn't try to funnel people like us into our plant. We should preach hard, pray hard, and let the Lord surprise us with the people He brings to worship with us. God's "surprises" keep the church plant from lukewarmness and instead ever amazed at the power of His electing grace.

Perhaps a few examples would help. In a church plant, there may be some people who are accustomed to calling the preacher "Reverend." Those with other backgrounds may be accustomed to calling him "Pastor." Either is fine—our confessions do not show a preference for which of these titles we use. Or, as I have experienced, some Christian traditions call the Lord's Supper "Breaking of the Bread" while others call it "the Holy Supper." The careful consistory or church planter would notice this and use both terms—in the bulletin, sermons, and liturgy—since both are certainly biblical. One final example: some Christians enjoy coming to church early on Sunday with a cup of coffee, sitting in the pews, and reading over the Scripture passage and hymns for the service. Other Christians enjoy chatting at the back of church with others who are coming to worship. Either of these is acceptable. These examples could be multiplied, to be sure, and the church plant should discuss these things. The main point is this: we must be careful as we deal with customs or traditions on which the Bible and confessions are silent.

Specifics for a Church Plant

As we discuss more specifics, it is important to remember the regulative principle of worship stated in the Heidelberg Catechism (Q&A

---

12. Michael Horton, *People and Place* (Louisville: Westminster, 2008), 201–202.

96–98), the Westminster Confession of Faith (chap. 21), and elsewhere. The Reformed/Presbyterian distinction of *elements* (those things the Bible explicitly commands for worship services) and *circumstances* (those things that Christian wisdom and the implicit truths of Scripture dictate) is a good way to engage this discussion of the church plant and culture.

The culture doesn't trump the elements, but it can become the occasion to evaluate and tweak the circumstances of worship. In other words, even though the culture doesn't like the confession of sins, we cannot take it out of the service because it is biblical (cf. Ps. 51). On the other hand, if the culture is more relaxed, it may be best to meet for worship at 10:30 a.m. instead of 9:00 a.m. The matter of the confessions is elemental and confessional; the issue of meeting time is not. Here are a few more examples to help us wrestle with the relationship between church plant and culture.[13]

Meeting Place

Church plants may want to consider renting a building other than a traditional steeple-tipped structure. To many people in culture, spotting an old-fashioned steeple-tipped building is equivalent to spotting a dentist's office—it evokes a shudder. Also, many Mormon and Jehovah's Witness church buildings look similar to traditional church buildings. Sometimes the best place for a church plant to meet is the abandoned storefront of a business that failed a few years back. The location alone might make for a few visitors and walk-ins. Budget is an issue, but the plant and elders might want to think about the surrounding culture when selecting a location to worship.

Name

Church plants also may want to consider names that an average American can deduce something from or remember. For example, there are many false churches and cults with "united" in their names (United Church of Christ, United Unitarians, United Church of Religious Science). If a

---

13. On the subject of being missionaries to people in our culture, I've found it helpful to read a variety of resources on what some missionaries call "contextualization." This is a discussion too vast to discuss here, but along with the Newbigin books previously mentioned, I suggest reading chapter 9 ("What Is a Missional Church?") of *Vintage Church* by Driscoll and Breshears, chapter 15 ("Contextualization") of *Church Planter* by Darrin Patrick, as well as some discussions of this topic by evangelists from Eastern countries who have planted solid Christian churches in their own culture. It will benefit church plants to be students of missionary theology and history, at least to some extent.

URCNA plant was in the same area as one of these types of churches, the members may want to consider what "united" means to those in the broader community. They would probably want to distance themselves from these "united" churches and use a different primary name. While the name of a church plant isn't overly important, it should be a name that conveys something historically Christian to the broader culture.[14]

Language

Church plants should also consider the culture when selecting songs, Bible translations, and forms for the sacraments while keeping the regulative principle in mind. If the church plant is in an area of low literacy, it is best to use a simple but sound translation.[15] Our confessions do not name a translation we must use; it belongs to the circumstances of worship.

While the words of the music we use should always be clearly biblical and Reformed, the grammar, syntax, and music style should be easy to sing and understand. Our grandparents may know what "hither to thine own, from henceforth unto endless age" means, but the average American does not. In a church plant, the gospel is a difficult enough "language" to learn; using Shakespearean lingo makes it all the more difficult to understand. I also believe our creeds and confessions should be updated to reflect modern syntax and grammar, making them easier to read. Many people the church plant comes in contact with have little or no Christian training, and they also have a very difficult time with the older grammar and syntax of the creeds and confessions.

Older grammar and syntax may sound more reverent and conservative to us, but it is not the same for other cultures; in fact, it may be a hindrance to worship for some people. Another way to summarize this is

---

14. Names such as Emmaus Way Church (Luke 24:13) or Desert Road Church (Acts 8:26), with their biblical allusions, are gospel centered. In other words, when you explain the name of your church, you have the clear opportunity to do so by explaining who Jesus is and what He has done. For example, in these two instances, you'd be able to talk about how the risen Christ opened the eyes of two disciples and told them He was at the center of the Bible and how Philip told the good news about Jesus to the questioning Ethiopian who was reading Isaiah.

15. Church plants have to be prepared to deal with two types of illiteracy: biblical and general. Not only are many people ignorant of biblical truths, they are also quite incapable of reading anything complex. Church plants might want to check the statistics of the literacy rate of the city in which they are located. Because of the decline in literacy rate, for example, I often use a simpler translation in our church's prison Bible study.

to say that confessional language (i.e., redemption, justification, sanctification, repentance) should stay, while cultural language should be flexible.

Acceptance
Church plants should be accepting places. I realize the term "accepting" is thrown around in mainline churches, implying that gays or lesbians are welcome, with no questions asked, but this is not what I mean by the term. "Accepting" simply means that if someone who looks, talks, or acts differently comes to our church plant, we should be warmly welcoming him or her.[16] Church plants should let visitors get to know them through worship, friendship, and fellowship in a welcoming and patient way. We shouldn't pressure someone to join the church after he visits for five or six weeks, for example. The best way is to let him experience the community for a while and then start to discuss membership and commitment.

While we won't be accepting of someone who lives in unrepentant sin or unbiblical doctrine, we will be accepting to those people who are vastly different from us in background, culture, and tradition. In this we can experience a tiny foretaste of the great heavenly chorus made up of every tribe, tongue, and language (Rev. 5:9). Church plants shouldn't want to make people middle-class patriotic Republicans; instead, we are making disciples of Jesus who are united by the gospel and publicly confess it together.

One man in a church plant invited his unbelieving co-worker to church. He knew his co-worker would probably not dress up, so he dressed for church the way he knew his co-worker would so that his co-worker would not stand out. This is what "accepting" means.

Christian Liberty
These things may take some discussion and training for those involved in a church plant. While some who are accustomed to living around many cultures and traditions are already tolerant of different kinds of people, others who are less tolerant of other cultures may have to be instructed in Christian liberty, explained clearly in WCF 20 and BC 32. In fact, confessional church plants should preach Christian liberty just as soundly as justification by faith alone, because liberty is an "appendage" of justification, as Calvin described it.[17] "Unless this freedom [liberty] be comprehended, neither Christ nor gospel truth, nor inner peace of soul,

---

16. See chapter 10, "Being a Welcoming Church Plant," by Kevin Efflandt.
17. John Calvin, *Institutes,* 3.19.1.

can be rightly known."[18] God forbid we mix our traditions in with *sola gratia* so as to make them laws.[19]

It might be a good idea to have a brief sermon series on Christian liberty at some point early in the life of a church plant. The elders and planter should model this liberty and freedom in addition to teaching and discussing it. At the risk of oversimplification, clear gospel preaching will instill this in people—that in Christ there is neither male nor female, rich nor poor, slave nor free, and so forth; we are all one in Christ (Gal. 3:28). As James says, when it comes to the "assembly" (our worship), we should show no partiality (James 2:1–9). Instead, out of love we make no distinctions between the CEO and the homeless, between the mechanic and the woman recovering from drug addiction.

Obeying the First and Great Commandment
I once read a preacher's explanation of how to love your neighbor as yourself in the pulpit (Matt. 22:39). What this means is when he is in the pulpit, the pastor should look out for the interests of others by thinking about how they receive the message (cf. Phil. 2:4).

We can also apply this commandment to the church plant. It can be tempting for the core group or the consistory to do the plant their way. In other words, *they* want the pastor to dress a certain way; *they* want slow and somber music; *they* want an organ and not a piano; *they* want to be a home-school or Christian-school plant.

However, several things chasten this selfish view of church planting: primarily *the first and great commandment* (Matt. 22:37–38). Loving God and obeying Him comes before our wants and desires. The church plant is not our plant but God's plant. It does not exist to fulfill our church plant wants according to our ways but rather God's wants according to His ways. Keeping this in mind will naturally lead to loving our neighbors as ourselves by being flexible about the circumstantial elements. We love our neighbor so much that we sometimes adjust the circumstantial elements in a way that helps him better love the Lord.

---

18. Ibid.

19. Many people who visit your church plant will have an "American" view of religion. They'll think religion is about morals—doing things to make God happy (i.e., not cussing, not drinking, and being nice). Preaching and teaching Christian liberty clearly—and living it—will fight all unbiblical forms of moralism and legalism.

Conclusion

Much more can be said on the subject of the church plant and culture. The purpose of this chapter was simply to raise some issues to encourage dialogue and deeper thinking as church plants seek to be missionaries to the people around them.

We might think that a good, conservative church looks and sounds like the rural, white church with a steeple of the 1950s, down to the padded pews, and anything less is bumping up against liberalism. However quaint such a view is, it is certainly a small minority view in the broader culture. Postmodernity is a teacher; it can teach the church plant a few things about ministering to the culture at large. We don't jump into the postmodern culture, yet neither do we strive to go back to modern culture and traditions that went with it.[20] In other words, it is simply wrong to say that the modern period was conservative and the postmodern one is liberal.

Stephen Fowl, in his commentary on Philippians 3:12–21 describes the tension of standing firmly on the gospel while allowing for cultural diversity: "To the extent that Christian communities provide not only a witness to God's redemption of the world but a foretaste of that redemption, they will be capable of manifesting a diversity marked by the peaceable harmony of those who have been made into one body of Christ. To the extent that they fail to display God's redeeming purposes for the world, any diversity they sustain within their common life will tend to look like the violent struggle of disconnected individuals, each struggling with and policing each other."[21] Standing firmly on the gospel while being culturally and traditionally diverse is a great witness to the world and a testimony against the manic individualism of our culture.

In summary, the church plant needs to hold loosely to traditions and more tightly to the confessions. Traditions give identity to people and are, indeed, important. It is not that we want to do away with traditions; instead, we welcome and appreciate many different traditions while we are glued together by the confessions. The confessions—which chiefly speak about the salvation from sin and our grateful living—should set the tone for preaching and unity. The church plant must never stop praying for wisdom to engage the culture while standing firmly on the gospel.

---

20. Stephen Nichols says it well: "Culture too easily takes the upper hand once one is freed from creedal formulas" (*Jesus: Made in America* [Downers Grove, Ill.: InterVarsity, 2008], 79).

21. Stephen Fowl, *Philippians* (Grand Rapids: Eerdmans, 2005), 169.

CHAPTER NINETEEN

The Cultural Factor in Church Planting

Mitchell Persaud

In 1 Corinthians 9:22, when the apostle Paul commented that he had "become all things to all men," he likely had in mind a consideration of the cultural context in presenting the gospel and planting churches. Paul undeniably saw the need to adjust under different circumstances, and while he did not adjust the substance of his message, he did adjust his approach in presenting the message.

Paul not only said that he would be "all things to all men," but he expressed this in the context of his goal—that he might bring men and women to Christ:

> For though I am free from all men, I have made myself a servant to all, that I might win the more; and to the Jews I became as a Jew, that I might win Jews; to those who are under the law, as under the law, that I might win those who are under the law; to those who are without law, as without law (not being without law toward God, but under law toward Christ), that I might win those who are without law (1 Cor. 9:19–21).

But Paul did not have to adjust as much as foreign and cross-cultural missionaries have to adjust today. J. H. Bavinck observes, "Paul preached in a world which for the most part had the same culture as that in which he himself had been raised. He did not have to learn other languages but was understood everywhere, and his clothes and customs created no astonishment. He did not have to deal with Nationalistic tensions, nor was he regarded as a representative of imperialism."[1]

Adjusting to a different cultural milieu is something that Bavinck understood. He cited two examples of "being all things to all men":

---

1. J. H. Bavinck, *An Introduction to the Science of Missions* (Philadelphia: P&R, 1960), 93.

The Dutch medical missionary...Johan T. Van der Kemp, who labored among the Hottentots at the beginning of the last century in South Africa, considered it desirable to marry a freed Hottentot slave girl, and to live in a genuine Hottentot house, in order to come as close as possible to those to whom he would bring the gospel message. And when the great missionary Hudson Taylor, the founder of the China Inland mission, began to work in China in 1854, he chose Chinese dress and followed Chinese customs as far as possible. In both of these cases there lies behind these efforts the desire to minimize the disadvantage that accompanies a stranger who enters among a people with old and established customs from an entirely different world...in order not to detract from the message which the missionary had to bring.[2]

With this said, there are some cultures in which a missionary would not want to marry one of the indigenous people, especially if he were a different race. That could be a huge stumbling block. I realize that church plants are not the same as a foreign mission field, but since the landscape of America is changing so much and so quickly, many of the issues facing foreign missions confront those planting churches in North America as well. Consider how different the Hawaiian Islands are from urban New York City or rural North Dakota, for example. A church planter would certainly use a different approach in the Tennessee mountains than he would with the intellectual elite at Princeton. He would also have to consider religious beliefs and would have to adopt different strategies if he were working in an Islamic or Mormon community or an emergent-church hotspot. The growing number of immigrants in North America also presents cultural challenges. We don't have to go overseas to find vastly different cultures! The truth is that we must be "all things to all men" in our cultures today.

Consider for a moment how other apostles dealt with cultural differences. Bavinck writes, "And when Peter entered into the house of Cornelius he was aware of the fact that by his very deed he had broken with the view of the heathen held by those of his day and had inaugurated a totally new relationship.... And when [Paul] spoke a good word for a runaway slave, he knew very well that his whole conduct and attitude with respect to social relationships were of far-reaching significance."[3]

2. Ibid., 94–95.
3. Ibid., 93.

When there was dissension in Acts 15 over whether the Gentile believers were to keep the ceremonial laws, the church at Antioch sent Paul and Barnabas to Jerusalem. It was a clear action of the local church in Antioch. The church at Jerusalem did not impose Jewish cultural and ceremonial laws on the Gentiles, except to the extent that God ordered them: "Abstain from things polluted by idols, from sexual immorality, from things strangled, and from blood" (Acts 15:20).

The point is this: those who argue for a cookie-cutter method miss the instruction in the book of Acts and 1 Corinthians and will find themselves frustrated. This is one of the reasons for burnouts in the mission field and church plants. What worked in Iowa may have to be tweaked considerably in Los Angeles or Seattle. Again, as the subtitle of this book reminds us, we're planting confessional churches, not cultural churches that look culturally alike in every culture. What role does culture play? I will answer that question by illustrating the need and methodology of adjusting to different cultural situations.

Culture and Methodology
Group Approach
The Scriptures give many examples of group or family evangelism in Scriptures and its significant benefits. In Acts 10, we read of Cornelius calling his household together to hear the message of hope. We read of the example of the Philippian jailer in Acts 16. He gathered his family to hear the gospel, and they were baptized.[4] In fact, it was easier to form house churches if the whole family were converted, or at least if they gathered together to study the Scriptures.

Further, the evidence of household baptism is so overwhelming that it is difficult to argue that the whole family was not evangelized at the same time. Missiologists such as Roger Hedlund argue in favor of family evangelism:

> Boer finds that "Acts is pre-eminently a book describing group approach in missions".... A favored technique was to evangelize households. Cornelius "feared God with all his household" (Acts 10:2). It was to this prepared group that Peter was called to proclaim Christ, and it was the people in this group who received the Holy Spirit and were baptized (Acts 10:44, 48). Paul at Philippi baptized

---

4. See chapter 7, "Church Planting: A Covenant and Organic Approach," by Paul Murphy.

Lydia and her household (Acts 16:15), as well as the jailer with his family (Acts 16:31–33). Other recorded instances of household baptisms include Crispus (Acts 18:8) and Stephanus (1 Corinthians 1:16).... As Judge avers, "When the head of a house was converted, its religious unity was preserved. The members were apparently baptized as a group."[5]

Hedlund gives further arguments for this type of evangelism. Family evangelism has been defined as "a strategy of evangelization which specifically aims at winning whole families to Christ and his Church as they respond to the Gospel through mutually interdependent decisions." The house-church phenomenon of the New Testament (Rom. 16:5–15; Col. 4:15; Philemon 2) was an accompaniment of the family evangelism pattern (Acts 16:15). Hedlund explains, "As the church grew in a particular locality, more than one house church would be formed." The apostle Peter finds that "household evangelism and household salvation are the most basic Biblical and cultural expectations and need revival in our days." This approach "honours in evangelism the social unit that God has created." Household conversions support and strengthen the individual believer and result in a stronger church with a greater impact upon the larger community. A saved family has a much greater influence for good upon the community than a group of individuals. In a society of extended families, such as India, the importance as well as the potential of the family/group approach is enormous, as is demonstrated by studies of conversion movements in this country. At least 80 percent of India's Christian population is estimated to have come to profess Christianity through a group decision process.[6]

Practically, the family or group approach has been used successfully, and missionaries should consider it. I have used this method in the Scarborough area of Toronto, Canada, while working among the immigrant Chinese community, and it has been my most successful method. Other Reformed church planters who have used this method are my fellow missionary, Tony Zekveld, in his work among the South Asians, and Paul Murphy in his church plant in New York City.

Covenantally, there is much to be said for group or family evangelism. While individualism, which has infiltrated the church, is promoted in the

---

5. Roger E. Hedlund, *The Mission of the Church in the World* (Grand Rapids: Baker, 1991), 206–207.
6. Ibid., 207.

West, a more biblical method is to try to get the whole family together, seeking and praying for the Spirit-worked conversion of the entire family. According to Matthew 10:14, missionaries stayed with families.

Another important reason for using the family or group approach has to do with the significant role of men in the family. While in post-Christian Western society the father is decreasingly viewed as the head of the family, in most cultures of the world the father is still viewed as the head. In many instances, if missionaries had evangelized a father with his family, many of the struggles that have occurred between fathers and mothers or fathers and children might have been avoided. Even among liberal Muslims, a missionary cannot expect to meet with girls or women without a man being present. The missionary or church planter must make cultural adjustments.

It is common in many societies for women to be at home during the day, and they then become the targets of evangelism. But it would be better to wait until the entire family is available to evangelize. This method would benefit the church in the long term and create more stable leadership. Further, in the church, the pressure to resort to female leadership when male leadership is lacking will be diminished. This is an overwhelming problem in the large but weak churches of China today.

Culture Affects Approach
A church planter must make cultural considerations when he determines how he will approach an unbeliever to present the gospel. We take different approaches depending on the person with whom we are communicating. We speak differently to children than to senior citizens. A mother speaks differently to a child than to her husband. God spoke differently to Abraham than to Moses. Jesus spoke differently to His disciples than to the scribes and Pharisees. Because Jesus wanted to shock the Pharisees into a sense of their sins, He called them "serpents" and "tombs." But He was far gentler in dealing with a fisherman like Peter, who clearly saw his sins.

The Lord also used cultural illustrations to help make His point. He spoke of "rivers of living water" at the Feast of Tabernacles, when prayer for rain was central (John 7:38). He spoke of the "leaven of the Pharisees and Sadducees" when the disciples were thinking about bread. He knew about important historical events in the life of His people, as demonstrated in Luke 13:1–6, where Jesus alludes to people that Pilate had murdered in the temple and those who died when the tower in Siloam fell.

There are two main approaches to presenting the gospel: a direct approach and an indirect approach.

The Direct Approach. The direct approach is a clear presentation of the gospel, and it demands a response. For example, Jesus was quite confrontational with some people. He called the Pharisees "tombs," "leaven," and "serpents" (Matt. 23:27; Mark 8:15; Matt. 23:33). Jesus confronted and chastised Nicodemus, a ruler of Israel, for not knowing how to be saved. The apostle Paul often presented the gospel at his first encounter, as he did in Athens.

This direct method is excellent for instruction in a class situation. When people are confronted, they must immediately examine what they believe and what they should believe. Some cultures are quite blunt and direct. This would work well in some circumstances.

Are there dangers to this method if it is not properly used with a pagan, for instance? Yes, this blunt direct approach can cause permanent barriers to the hearers, especially for those working with Eastern peoples. The one who is evangelizing must not try too quickly to get to the heart. He must consider that the recipient may still have his or her guard up. People often want to see Christianity in the life of the missionary or church planter as something valid before they show interest in it. So it is not wise to stand in the public square in a foreign country or urban neighborhood attacking a sacrifice to a pagan god—or the stock markets! You may not get another audience.

In one case in Toronto, a church planter was invited to the home of a Muslim. Within half an hour after the missionary completed his presentation, he demanded a response. He was surprised that the man did not want to see him again. He shouldn't have been; it was not the proper way for the church planter to present the gospel.

This direct approach has become popular because premillennial dispensationalists have a sense of urgency about the coming of Christ (the rapture) and think that they need to share the gospel as quickly as possible. Often the gospel gets reduced to a few propositions. This method can also give a false sense of salvation, for a person is rarely able to give a full sense of the gospel in a short presentation. This has been one of the difficulties among those who have used D. James Kennedy's Evangelism

Explosion method. While this method can start up interesting conversations, it is not the whole gospel.

Bear in mind as well that when the Lord Jesus Christ was confronting people, they had heard the gospel before and had either rejected or corrupted it. And when Paul preached in Athens, though he called the people to repent after his first presentation of the gospel, the people actually asked him to speak more on the matter. There are times for this approach.

The Indirect Approach. With the indirect approach a person's defenses are broken down through developed relationships as the one who is evangelizing learns what makes the hearer "tick." This method is particularly useful in dealing with people who come from a culture that strongly distrusts Christianity and Christians in general. It has been used primarily among Muslim and Hindu peoples and in Africa where there are large Islamic populations—and in neighborhoods in America with these people groups. With these people, the gospel is presented later rather than earlier, even weeks and months later in some cases. In fact, it could be argued that the indirect approach is the best for most people with whom a church planter comes into contact.

I would immediately lose the interest of the Chinese with whom I work in Scarborough if I called them sinners in our first meeting. Calling someone a sinner without teaching who God is, what His law says, and how man became guilty makes no sense. And even before dealing with the subject of God and His law, we must often sit around some pork fried rice and talk about Chinese history and the richness of Chinese culture and medicines. So this method has its value even among immigrants in Western countries, not to mention Americans who have lived in the United States their entire lives.

Eastern Europeans are quite willing to begin a conversation if you start to talk about their countries. And that creates a door for the gospel. What do you think about the principle of utopia? Why didn't communism work? Why were the Communists so oppressive and cruel? What do you feel toward them? These are some conversation starters that the church planter/evangelist could steer toward the gospel when the time is right. There are other things a missionary can use to develop relationships—things such as food, style of clothing, and sports. Every culture has something that makes it unique. The indirect approach finds it, considers it, and uses it as an opportunity to present the gospel.

There are dangers in the indirect method, even though it has its mer-
its. Sometimes, because the missionary delays in waiting for the right
time, he is never able to present the gospel, and there is no clear call to
repentance. This is a failure of the person, however. It is not a failure of
the method in itself.

A second danger to the indirect method is that the missionary's delay
in presenting the gospel can cause the hearer to believe that the gospel
is of lesser importance. But the missionary needs to make clear that this
gospel is a matter of life and death, different from the other subjects that
they have recently discussed.

A third danger to the indirect method can be illustrated. In history,
some Christian missionaries conceded that both the Jews and the Muslims believed the Old Testament as they did. This unbiblical concession
was made in order to create a relationship with the hearer. But neither the
Muslims nor the Jews serve the God who wrote the sixty-six books of the
Bible. So the evangelist must be careful not to try to show how similar
Christianity is to other religions as a means of developing a relationship.
Rather he should show how different they are.[7] Paul, for example, began
in a somewhat gentle tone in the Areopagus, but by the end of his "street
sermon" he was calling for repentance. He showed the people of Athens
that they were missing the true God and that their gods were nothing.

Understandable Worship
Many people who are from different cultural backgrounds can make little or no sense of what they see in liturgical Reformed worship. But this
does not apply to people from foreign countries alone. Many in Western
countries have been out of the church so long that they have no idea what
a biblical worship service looks like. Most of what many people believe
about worship is determined by Hollywood movies—from noisy Pentecostal worship to Baptists singing "Bringing in the Sheaves" on *Little
House on the Prairie* to the caricature of the born-again Christian character
on many sitcoms. Few people have seen Reformed worship, and it is foreign to those who might come to our worship service.

How can you make worship more understandable? Ask your elders
to help make the worship service more accessible to the unchurched.

---

7. For more on Christianity compared to other religions from an apologetic standpoint, see Kenneth Samples, *Without a Doubt: Answering the 20 Toughest Faith Questions*
(Grand Rapids: Baker, 2004) and other similar books.

You won't make worship more accessible by compromising doctrine or abandoning the regulative principle of worship, but you do make it more accessible by offering explanations during the service that are simple and not filled with theological jargon. You may need to explain what prayer is and why you close your eyes. You might say, "We close our eyes so we can concentrate our thoughts on God." If you are an elder overseeing a church planter or even a member of the core group, you may ask your pastor to explain from time to time why he greets people at the beginning and why he gives the benediction at the end with raised hands.[8]

In Toronto, we have made a list of common theological words that we have translated into Mandarin so the Chinese have a quick reference to them. Further, we send out a copy of the sermons by email on Saturday. This gives the regular visitor or new Christian an opportunity to grasp the sense of the sermon before going to worship. We also have what is basically a full manuscript of the sermon—with all difficult words translated—printed and ready to distribute each Sunday. What we found is that even English-speaking people take copies of the sermons so they can follow it better. This is a wise cultural adjustment that has had good results for us.

My Reformed brothers and sisters would be quick to say that worship is for Christians. They are right. But the Lord might be working in the hearts of those seekers or unbelievers who are there (and even some covenant people who may not be saved), and they need clear guidance.

Simple—Not Simplistic—Evangelism
Church planters, especially cross-cultural ones, need to watch their language. They need to be careful to not overuse unexplained theological terms in their evangelism and even in the pulpit. "Repentance," "justification," and "sanctification" do not mean much to modern culture. These words need to be defined over and over again. Of course, new Christians need to learn precise theological terms, like they would learn a new language, but only after they have been Christians for a while.

---

8. On introducing the unchurched and non-Reformed to Reformed worship, see Daniel R. Hyde, *What to Expect in Reformed Worship: A Visitor's Guide* (Eugene, Ore.: Wipf & Stock, 2007).

Culture and Sociology

There are cultural considerations in making the initial contacts to present the gospel of our Lord. Not many people will walk into a church and say, "Tell me about Jesus Christ." There is often much apprehension and suspicion of the church and Christians, especially because of the numerous sexual abuse allegations in Roman Catholic churches and the corruption of some evangelical preachers. It is difficult for an outsider to know what a good church is.

At other times visitors to Christian worship services experience downright hostility from relatives and friends, especially if they are from a different religious background. I know of people who have been put out of their families for simply attending Christian worship. Mormons, for example, seem to hate Christian pastors. The church needs to be prepared for these circumstances as well.

How can the church prepare on a social level to develop relationships and provide opportunities for the gospel? The following are a few practical ideas.

Practice Hospitality[9]

When you meet visitors at worship, remember to show them hospitality (Rom. 12:13). I don't know of a culture that doesn't like to have neighbors make them feel welcome. And in showing hospitality, you will demonstrate Christian life and living—something the finest church planter cannot do in his sermons. Food and friendship make people drop their guard and relax. Virtually every culture enjoys chatting around food. Be careful not to criticize different foods. You may have to keep your children away if they can't handle spicy food.

A Flea Market/Fair Approach

Flea markets are popular today. Why not use them for Christ's glory? One man I know simply sells a couple of books but has free material, like Bibles stamped with the church's information, worship times, and an invitation to a Bible study or worship. Culturally, this opens doors to discussion in a non-confrontational way. Flea market visitors usually shop regularly, providing an opportunity to develop relationships.

---

9. See chapter 10, "Being a Welcoming Church Plant," by Kevin Efflandt.

A Forum Approach

We have organized forums with Muslims in which Christians and Muslims each have a speaker. After the speeches, we ask people to write down questions, and the two speakers respond. You can also use materials like those published by Answers in Genesis in a home or in church to spark discussions and develop contacts. Have a meal together when doing this. Word spreads, and word of mouth is powerful. Other people simply have a day each month where different people get to speak about their beliefs. By listening to them you get an opportunity to bring the gospel to them when it is your turn to speak—something they might never have gotten if you had not listened to them. This is a great way to meet the university types who like to show off their knowledge.

Resource Library

Have a lending library at your church plant or home with books, DVDs, and magazines that deal with popular topics like evolution, atheism, examinations of other religions, and the gospel clearly but simply put. Remember, many people today have little understanding of the Bible. If someone borrows something, follow up with him to see what he thought about it. Your neighbors might not go to church, but they might sit with you in your garage and talk about what they read. Be prepared to lose some material, however.

Yard Sales

Have a yard sale (at the church-plant building, perhaps) and get rid of the junk around your house, but also have some Bibles, booklets, sermons, and church invitations you can give away for free. This is a project you can do with others in your church. Immigrants love yard sales, and the casual setting makes people feel more comfortable and open to talk. We have made contacts through this method. It works well on a hot day if you offer a free bottle of water and a Bible in your customers' primary language.

Breakfast

Have a free men's or family breakfast on a Saturday morning. Prepare it yourself or simply purchase and provide muffins and coffee. Get "safe" foods. Don't expect Muslims to come if you are cooking strips of bacon. Don't feel bad if a lot of people don't show up, and be satisfied to start with two or three people. This can be a useful outreach method. Advertise the breakfast on the bulletin board at the supermarket or at the community center. You can put a handwritten sandwich sign in front of the church if you serve breakfast there or announce it on the church website or blog.

Bible Studies

Organize a small-group home Bible study. People who are intimidated and would not enter a church building might attend an informal Bible study. Using prepared Bible-study outlines or video presentations, biblically informed men or elders may facilitate small-group discussions about ultimate issues. The lay leader does not have to pretend to have all the answers, but he may promise to ask or investigate a question that a participant asks.

Awareness of Cultural "Sins"

Church planters must learn the differences between culture, sin, and personal preferences. We know that Christians may drink alcoholic beverages without sinning if they drink moderately. But we must recognize that in many nations drinking alcoholic beverages carries a stigma with it, so many people frown on its use. Even though Scripture permits the use of alcohol, you may find it is not expedient to use it, especially publicly. Many people have seen the suffering the abuse of alcohol brings and perceive it as evil. Even in home missions in North America, if a church planter were working with Muslims or Mormons, for example, it would be foolish to do so over a beer. Nor would you invite a Muslim to your home and offer him wine. That might be your last contact with him.

Especially be mindful of a culture's views of women. What may be expected in North America, like hugging a friend's wife or kissing her on the cheek, is forbidden in most cultures. Also, in today's American landscape, there are an infinite number of sexual lawsuits each day, so the church planter has to take every step necessary to remain above charges concerning sexual immorality.

Sometimes there are traditions that might seem strange to the North American mind, but they are simply cultural aspects that one must accommodate in order to do mission work. For example, a family that wants to have nine nights of wake services when a relative dies is operating within their Christian freedom. In fact, their customs may be good therapy and even superior to the North American way of handling funerals.

Spankings that leave welts on children's legs are often perfectly acceptable in some cultures. Church planters need to realize that they do not determine for the rest of the world what child abuse is. The Scriptures alone determine that. Based on many passages of the Bible such as the Proverbs of Solomon, other cultures may have a biblical way of disciplining their children.

Titles of Respect

In church planting, especially cross-culturally, titles of respect are very important. For example, it is common, especially among South Asians—Indians, Pakistanis, and Sri Lankans—for children to call a missionary "uncle" or for adults to call him "brother." If the missionary is older, he might be called "grandpa." A church planter himself must show similar respect to those of different cultures. For instance, if a person in another culture is a doctor, the church planter should not call him by his first name or a nickname. Some people deeply cherish their titles. The church planter's children must show proper respect as well. It can be highly inappropriate in some cultures to call an older man by his first name. And in some cultures, honor is given by age, not necessarily by title. Among South Asians, a church planter may need to put his education degrees on his business card and even wear a clerical collar to be taken more seriously.

Respect for Cultures

A missionary must have respect for the culture and heritage of the people to whom he is ministering. Of course when the culture espouses sinful traditions, the missionary must preach against them, but he must preach with love and care. When a culture, for instance, determines by its law that a Christian may marry another who is not a believer, the missionary must preach against it. On the other hand, if a person is required to marry someone who is chosen by his parents and that person is a believer, he must not speak against that. The church-planting missionary must not act as if he has the real solution for propagating marriages between those who are truly "in love," in light of historical evidence and biblical teaching. These are but a few examples to illustrate the need to be culturally sensitive. Each culture requires its own adjustments that will come with patience and prayer.

Culture, Complications, and Limitations

The Difficulty of Discerning and Addressing Sin

While most Christians believe that the clothes Brazilian women wear in public are immodest, Brazilians often do not think so. Some women are of the opinion they are not to go to church when they are menstruating. Others think to remarry after their husband dies is shameful, and therefore they should not do it. One Sri Lankan Christian man made his wife swear that she would not remarry if he died before she did. Some think that the earlier they can get rid of their daughters in marriage, the better for everyone. Most cultures are far more lenient with young men than young women.

Those who have been Christians for a while understand that these are errors in thinking. But in a different cultural context the church planter sometimes needs to delay criticism of some lesser issues. He needs to concentrate more on the big picture—the preaching of the gospel and administration of the sacraments. When these main areas are addressed in people's lives, the lesser issues will be dealt with, assuming they are real issues that require change.

I have encountered this particularly in the area of child rearing among new immigrant Chinese families in Toronto. Often the children are quite disobedient and selfish. They yell at their parents and even hit them. The family usually eats what the children want. The family lacks discipline, and the children begin to act like the kings or queens of the family. But I have to remember that these children were raised in a one-child-per-family setting. And there were four grandparents to spoil one child. Yes, we need to address this, but it is often best to wait until the Lord changes hearts. Then the parents will see the need to submit to God's way of raising children. Bavinck speaks to this general principle: "In many instances he must feel his way, and although he must constantly view the tribal customs in the light of the gospel he must not be too hasty in pressing the native to abandon these customs. Of course, such practices which are visibly idolatrous constitute an exception."[10]

The people the church planter is working with have been sheep without shepherds for a long time. The missionary should not think he can fix all their problems in a short time. He has been called to preach for the purpose of winning the lost and discipling them, so he must patiently endure the process of leading people to God. And after he "catches" them, he

10. Bavinck, *An Introduction*, 119.

must begin the careful task of cleaning them. And, of course, the church planter has the elders of the overseeing church to help in this task.

To Offend or Not to Offend: What Do I Do?

Another complicated matter can occur if, for example, you are offered something strange to eat when you visit someone's home. What should you do? In most cases a missionary should eat what is set before him and not ask too many questions (sometimes the less you know the better). But what if he is afraid that the delicious "sheep's eye" might make him gag and throw-up? Learn to ask God for much wisdom and a strong stomach.

Imposition of New Culture

Bavinck cautioned that there was a limit to which the church planter may go in making cultural considerations. Others would rather go much further, often a result of their cultural pride. For example, some churches in the United States have tried to go back to cultural costumes, beating drums, and taking cultural names. They argue that they are better able to worship God that way.

While there may be some legitimacy to worshiping God and allowing for cultural influences (North Americans sit on pews, others sit on the floor; North Americans keep their shoes on, others take off their shoes), many have questioned whether a certain practice is a real conviction or a fad. In some ways, it is an imposition of a new culture on the young since not all Americans have strong ties to other cultures. Their culture is American or some sort of a "mix" between American and another culture (or two).

Limitations Regarding Cultural Adjustments to Preaching

Bavinck helpfully and carefully explains this problem in two cases:

> The conclusion might easily be reached that the content of preaching is given in Scripture but that the manner of preaching, and the question of the missionary approach, is a matter of personal tact and of applying oneself to the given circumstances. It might be held further that theology can contribute nothing with regard to the manner of approach, since it is anthropology, ethnology and psychology that are here the experts. According to such a solution, the Bible provides the content, the "what" of preaching, but the manner, the "how" of

preaching must be discovered otherwise. In fact, each missionary must himself seek to discover a method that is proper.[11]

Missionaries may adopt the way of life of a people, speak their language, associate themselves with their religious concepts, utilize sayings derived from their religious literature, and, from the standpoint of ethnology or psychology, all of this may be excellent. Yet it still may be necessary for theology to issue a warning that such efforts, which seek to draw the missionary close to the people, must proceed with caution lest they sacrifice the purity of the gospel. On the other hand, it is also possible to have the best intentions and ignore the cultural possessions of a people and to preach the gospel pure and simple, without any application to their specific characteristics. History has shown that such a strategy is also questionable, for in this instance the missionary supposes that he is simply preaching the gospel in its purity, whereas, in fact, he is unconsciously propagating his own Western way of thought.[12]

Bavinck contends that the content of preaching is related to the method since we must be Reformed in theology and methodology and that this content supplies the principle that determines the method. It is theology that determines the missionary approach, though other sciences "render a most valuable service. The content of preaching, the Word of God, must tell us what we ought in every instance to do and not to do.... What happens on the mission field is most serious and decisive: Christ himself comes to a group of people, to a nation or tribe. And it is for this reason that the manner of the approach, the 'how,' must at every moment be a recognizable expression of Christ's love and unfathomable mercy."[13] He says further:

> Innumerable little things characterize the preaching of Jesus and give it a particular form within the hard reality of everyday life. The glance with which Jesus could sometimes say more than words about the new element that had in him entered into this world. By his entry into the house of Matthew, by his questioning of the Samaritan woman, by the things he did on the Sabbath, indeed by a thousand small and apparently insignificant actions, he broke down the present social and religious order and laid the foundations of a new society in which all would be different.[14]

11. Ibid., 80.
12. Ibid.
13. Ibid., 81, 82.
14. Ibid., 92–93, 94.

Another consideration is the various places where the church planter can approach people to preach the gospel. There is immense variety here. He could share the gospel in a hospital with someone who is sick, with someone who is mourning, or with someone in their home when the church planter feels comfortable enough with him there. The argument, then, is not whether there should be caution in the approach—there must be—but how far should one go.

One of the wisest ways of learning the culture is through children. A church planter can take advantage of this if he has children. Children learn much faster and are less offended when they are corrected. The wise missionary also attaches himself to one or two nationals who serve as his consultants in matters of cultural dos and don'ts. He can learn from the core group who are already living in that city or community.

Conclusion

It is foolish not to consider the cultural context in church planting at home or abroad. Both Christ and the apostles considered and commanded it. Let the church planter beware, then, that he does not try to revolutionize a culture when preaching the gospel to sinners is his real target.

The confessional Reformed church plant must work at changing the sinful traditions of a culture, but often timing is everything. The church planter is to keep his eyes on the big picture of Word and sacrament and deal with the important issues by preaching to sinners. When hearts have been converted, it is easier to fix types of secondary cultural problems. The gospel is hard enough the way it is: adding secondary cultural problems to the mix hurts instead of helps the church plant. The church planter must keep the gospel of Christ at the forefront of his evangelism and church plant. Nothing else will do.

ᴼᴜ

Growing Contextually Reformed Churches: Oxymoron or Opportunity?

Phil Grotenhuis

Dark storms clouds were gathering in America around the turn of the twentieth century. In the Presbyterian Church confessional conservatives were wringing their hands. The seeds of unbelief had infiltrated the church, the Westminster Confession was in the process of being revised along Arminian lines, and, by 1923, over 1,800 ministers signed the Auburn Affirmation, a document that gutted the supernatural character of the Bible and the disciplinary authority of the church.

Among a small group of confessional conservatives within the Presbyterian Church (U.S.A.) was a quiet, irenic, Dutch-born scholar-prophet named Geerhardus Vos. Already in the late 1800s Vos had the foresight to see where the Presbyterian Church was heading and wrote about his concerns—not only for the Presbyterian Church but for Dutch immigrants heading to America. A letter to Abraham Kuyper on July 12, 1890, relates his concerns:

> The evil is not limited to the Presbyterian Church. It has spread in almost all Reformed churches. It is present also in the Dutch Reformed Church, to which a large part of our Dutch people belong. It is in the air here and before one knows it, one is infected with it. It would be very desirable if all the Dutch people of Reformed principles were one, and could form a separate denomination. It seems to me that isolation is the only thing that can protect us against washing away with the current.[1]

Americanization was a deep concern to immigrants. Many believed that the ecclesiastical (church) and cultural scene undermined a Reformed worldview. Some ministers advocated a spirit of ethnic and ecclesiastical separation. Others championed infiltration. Still others did not tip

---

1. Geerhardus Vos, *The Letters of Geerhardus Vos*, ed. James T. Dennison, Jr. (Phillipsburg, N.J.: P&R, 2005), 142.

their hand either way and advised caution. No one, of course, promoted accommodation.

The Challenge of Integrating: Christ and Culture

Contextualization has always been a challenge for the church. The question is how do we adapt the gospel to a surrounding culture without compromise, on one hand, and irrelevance, on the other? The question is a pressing one indeed as a welcome commitment to church planting is increasingly taking root in confessionally Reformed churches. In his series of articles on growing confessionally Reformed churches, Nelson Kloosterman states, "We would suggest that by the Word of God and the Spirit of Jesus Christ, we as congregations are being awakened to an interest in planting new churches, in communicating the gospel within our own culture and society, and in engaging our life-situations (relationships with co-workers, neighbors and others who render daily services to us) with the truths of Scripture."[2]

The Great Commission and the cultural mandate beckon us to "let [our] light shine before men" (Matt. 5:16). Along with this calling is the tacit assumption that we may not hoard our confessional heritage. Jesus taught, "To whom much is given, from him much will be required" (Luke 12:48). A confessionally Reformed heritage not only bespeaks privilege but responsibility. But the important question is this: How do we carry out our responsibility? Or, to borrow the language of Kloosterman, how do we communicate the gospel in our own culture? How do we engage in life situations (relationships with co-workers, neighbors, and others) with the truths of Scripture? More specifically, how do we effectively grow confessionally Reformed churches in a secular and ecclesiastical culture that has succumbed to the "isms" of our age, namely, individualism, relativism, consumerism, materialism, egalitarianism, feminism, experientialism, anti-intellectualism, and many other of today's idols?

Confessional Calvinism: Fitting Squares into Round Holes

Granted, we Reformed folk are an odd bunch. We talk about absolutes, joyful yet serious worship, confessions, worldviews, unfamiliar theological terms, textual preaching, church membership, baby baptism, and

---

2. Nelson Kloosterman, "Growing Confessionally Reformed Churches: Oxymoron or Opportunity (Part 1)?" *Christian Renewal* 24, no. 14 (April 26, 2006): 16.

fencing the table. The unchurched shake their heads. Evangelicals raise their eyebrows. Confessional Christianity reflects a language and life out of the cultural mainstream. Undoubtedly, we have our work cut out for us. Our history, terminology, and practices fly not only in the face of our secular but our ecclesiastical culture as well.

Again we must ask, "How do we adapt the Reformed faith to our present culture without compromise on one hand and irrelevance on the other?" Such a question is at the heart of what we call "contextualization." Contextualization is simply an umbrella term that points to the relationship between gospel and culture. The Christian faith may find itself in any number of cultural contexts. It may find itself geographically in any continent of the world, regionally in the city or the country, linguistically among English or Russian, racially among black or white, sociologically among blue collar or white collar, or religiously among modern or postmodern.

All churches find themselves in a particular cultural context and reflect it in any number of ways. Think of your typical worship service. The choice of music in your worship, the humor in your fellowship, the terms and illustrations your minister uses in his sermons, the clothes you wear, what you do before and after worship—all betray a certain cultural bent. All of these things move toward the cultural context of some and away from the cultural context of others.

Look at how many contexts are found just in the relatively small URC federation. We have churches in many different contexts: we have rural and metropolitan churches in Southern California, northwest Washington, the Midwest, the East Coast, and dotted throughout the Canadian landscape. The locations of our churches are as far-reaching as Central America and India. Some church members have a long history with the Reformed faith, others are relatively new, and many regularly attending nonmembers have practically no concept of what the word "Reformed" means. And then there are those who have little concept of what "Christianity" means because they were just introduced to your church fellowship through the invitation of a friend. Are we to assume that all confessionally Reformed churches should look alike? Is it even desirable?

Cookie-Cutter Churches? The Pursuit of Unity without Uniformity

Some things never change, and we call them constants. People are people and are in need of the gospel no matter what their background is. They are in need of repentance and faith in Jesus Christ no matter what context in which they find themselves. There are also non-negotiables for office bearers who give their "I dos" to the form of subscription. They are bound by vow to a commitment to the Scriptures, Reformed confessions, and church order as well as synodically adopted and required liturgical forms. But how these come to expression is determined in part by the cultural contexts in which churches find themselves. I will address this subject in more detail later in the chapter.

Contextualization: Watching Out for Land Mines

Contextualizing the gospel is fraught with danger, and confessionally Reformed churches are not immune to it. Some churches contextualize very little—whether they are part of a homogeneous rural community or planted in a larger, multicultural city. Sometimes this stems from sheer thoughtlessness. Other times it stems from historical and ethnic considerations. And still other times it may stem from suspicion and a fear that the gospel may be gutted for the sake of relevance.

For some churches vocabulary and practices remain unanalyzed for years. Terminology in sermons, music selection, order of worship, when to stand and when to sit, pre- and post-worship ways of fellowshipping—all of these are understood and practiced by "the herd" but are unintelligible to the newcomer. The result is what Jurgen Moltmann calls a "fossil theology"—faithfulness without relevance. But there is an opposite danger. It is what Moltmann calls a "chameleon theology"—relevance without faithfulness where the church takes on the color of its surroundings to such an extent that it cannot be distinguished from it.[3]

It's a generalization: confessionally Reformed churches have historically tended to insulation, and modern evangelical churches have tended to accommodation. The answer: confessional orthodoxy clothed in words and deeds that are accessible to the culture. Granted, it's not an easy task. Being "in the world but not of the world" has always been difficult to implement. But the attempt must be made through sanctified common sense informed by the Scripture, confessions, and church order.

---

3. As quoted in Michael Goheen, *"As the Father Has Sent Me, I Am Sending You": J. E. Lesslie Newbigin's Missionary Ecclesiology* (Zoetermeer: Boekencentrum, 2000), 338.

Insulation or Infiltration: A Look at Scripture

Examine the Scriptures and you'll find a number of examples where the gospel penetrates culture without fossil or chameleon residue.

Jesus and the Gospels

In contrast to the prevailing sectors of Judaism, Jesus presented the gospel in many different contexts: in the city and the country, to rich and poor, healthy and sick, Jew and Gentile, sinful tax gatherers and prostitutes and "saintly" Pharisees and scribes. Jesus' willingness to contextualize the gospel contrasted sharply with the Judaism of his day. The prejudicial Pharisees (literally "separated ones") separated themselves from their culture. The Roman-collaborating Sadducees blended with their culture. The sword-bearing zealots ruled over their culture, thinking that the kingdom advanced through revolution. And the pietistic Essenes ignored their culture and withdrew into an isolated community, believing their surrounding culture to be beyond redemption. Jesus, in contrast, penetrated the culture with the life-transforming message of the kingdom and mingled unhesitatingly with the needy. "Those who are well have no need of a physician, but those who are sick," said Jesus. "I did not come to call the righteous, but sinners, to repentance" (Matt. 9:12–13). Jesus' disciples took their cues from Jesus and also infiltrated their culture with the gospel. Matthew targeted Jews, Mark the Romans, Luke the Gentiles, and John the Greeks. The gospel remained the same, but it was presented in the thought forms and language of their audiences.

First Corinthians 9:20–22: Jews, Greeks, and the Weak

First Corinthians 9:20–22 is a contextualist favorite. "To the Jews I became as a Jew…to those who are without law [Greeks/Gentiles], as without law…to the weak I became as weak." While this passage has been used to support all manner of pragmatic approaches to contextualization, it does provide an insight into the gospel's target groups: Jews, Greeks, and the weak.

Fundamentally, Jews, Greeks, and the weak were the same. They were sinners in need of the gospel. The point of contact was the same. All three were inherently religious (*sensus divinitatis*) and image bearers of God (*imago dei*). But all three were different in their worldview orientation and required different approaches and different emphases. Paul identified with all three. To the legalists (Jews), he became a legalist to win them to grace and freedom. To the licentious (Greeks), he became licentiate to sin them to godliness. To the weak, he became weak in order to disciple them further in the gospel. Paul understood and identified with each target group in order to bring them a "tailor-made" gospel— one in essence, varied in approach.

Acts 16–18: Triple Play

Acts 16–18 also provides many insights into the matter of contextualization. Once again we find three target groups (Acts 16): Lydia, a businesswoman; an unidentified slave girl; and a Philippian jailor. Each was vastly different in background, need, status, and worldview. Lydia was Asian, well-off, and religious (God-fearer). The slave girl was likely Greek, poor, enslaved to demonic powers, exploited by businessmen, and without God and hope in the world. The Philippian jailor was Greek, a man of responsibility and power, who was also in need of the gospel.

Tim Keller, senior pastor of Redeemer Presbyterian Church in New York City, notes three different approaches to each person.[4] Lydia was approached with the Word-gospel. Paul spoke to the assembled women, and God opened Lydia's heart to respond to the things he spoke. The slave girl was approached with the Word-deed gospel. Paul commanded the evil spirit to leave her, and she was freed from her slavery and exploitation. The Philippian jailor was approached with the Word-embodiment gospel. He was shocked by the prayers and singing of Paul and Silas as they suffered victoriously for the cause of the gospel. Again, all three were the same. They were Christ-less and in need of the gospel. But each target group was different in background, need, status, and worldview, and Paul tailored his gospel approach accordingly.

The Bible teaches us that the apostle Paul was a busy man. Like his Lord, Paul welcomed sinners of various stripes and pursued a number of different contexts within which to present the gospel. He spoke in the synagogue (Acts 17:1–2, 10–11; 19:9), the marketplace (Acts 17:17), and the university (Acts 17:19). He spoke to religious leaders, government officials, businessmen and businesswomen, slaves, jailors, uneducated, and intellectuals. Each needed Christ and the gospel. However, each required a different starting point, method, and conclusion in the presentation of the gospel.

---

4. Tim Keller, "Study 16: Three Surprising Conversions," in *Evangelism: Studies in the Book of Acts,* leader's guide (New York: Redeemer Presbyterian Church, 2005), 135–49.

John: Subversive Fulfillment

The gospel of John also provides an interesting lesson in contextualization. John goes so far as to adopt the language of his gospel-hostile culture in presenting the Christian faith. He employs the Hellenistic term logos (translated "Word" [1:1]) to describe the revelation of God in Christ and dualistic language to describe the antitheses between light and darkness, above and below, as well as references to truth, light, and life. Lesslie Newbigin notes, "Here the language and thought-forms of the Hellenistic culture are so employed that Gnostics of all ages have thought that the book was written especially for them. And yet nowhere in Scripture is the absolute contradiction between the Word of God and human culture stated with more terrible clarity."[5]

In each biblical case we have examined, we have an example of faithful contextualization. We find what Lesslie Newbigin calls "subversive-fulfillment"—the penetration of the gospel into culture without accommodation on one hand and irrelevance on the other.[6] The gospel of the early church was neither a "fossil theology" nor a "chameleon theology." Many more examples could be given that could shed some light on the matter of contextualization. For now, we are perhaps wondering, "But how does this play out in our church? If growing confessionally Reformed churches is not an oxymoron but an opportunity, how do we go about it? To put it succinctly, how do we "contextualize" our faith in word and deed without falling into either accommodation or irrelevance?

Finding Our Way: Practical Considerations

As already noted, not all churches are the same regarding place, people, history, size, and gifts. So, too, the geographical and cultural contexts in which they minister are equally different. But the differences don't end there. The people to whom they minister are also varied as to ethnicity, sex, temperament, history, education, and worldview. We quickly understand, then, that there is no "one size fits all" approach to contextualization. There are things that we all share as confessionally Reformed churches. We share one Lord, one faith, one baptism. More specifically, we share the Scriptures, the Westminster Standards, the Three Forms of Unity, a church order, and essential commitments to prayer, fellowship,

---

5. As quoted in Goheen, *"As the Father Has Sent Me,"* 338.
6. As quoted in ibid., 337.

and mission. But we all find ourselves in different contexts that require analysis and a faithful application of the gospel.

Theoretically, these are the basics. But what does it look like in practice? Every church has a different story. A church planter in New York City ministers in an urban professional and multicultural immigrant setting. Another may find himself in a large, culturally diverse city ministering among a particular ethnic group such as a Sikh or Chinese community. Still others may find themselves facing unique challenges in places as distinct as Southern California or Hawaii.

My previous experience as a church planter in Springfield, Missouri, was also unique among the churches in our denomination. It was geographically located in the northern tip of the southern Bible Belt (Ozarks). Politically speaking, most people there are conservative Republican. Religions in the area are predominantly Pentecostal, Baptist, Disciples of Christ, and secular. Racially, the area is predominantly white. There is a disparity between educated (Springfield is a college/university town) and poor, uneducated. There were many other factors locally that helped shape our ministry to Springfield, just as there are many unique factors in large cities, Southern California, and Hawaii. As a confessionally and contextually Reformed church in Springfield, our desire was to make our ministry accessible (readily available), intelligible (readily understood), and credible (faithful). How does this come to expression in any church-plant setting?

It comes to expression through trial and error but also through dogged persistence and reliance upon the Lord of the harvest. Our trust is in His Word: "Do not fear, little flock, for it is your Father's good pleasure to give you the kingdom" (Luke 12:32). But again, what does this look like—not just in theory but in practice? Let's peer through the window of one church plant's budding ministry. It's here where we find how one congregation seeks to be both confessionally faithful and contextually relevant.

Mission Committee vs. Mission Identity

Confessional/contextual ministry does not occur only in worship; it occurs throughout the week as well. Regularly, the unconverted are kept before the eyes and ears of the church plant's community of faith—whether they are parents, children, brothers, sisters, fellow employees, fellow students, or others. This is an obvious and rudimentary point, but it is easily sidestepped even in church plants. The pastor and members of the church plant try not to let this happen, and it takes conscious effort.

Church members and regularly attending nonmembers are encouraged to bring unconverted friends, family, and co-workers to Sunday worship. These people are frequently prayed for by name throughout the week and especially at the Wednesday night prayer meeting. The goal is that mission becomes ingrained in the psyche of members to the end that it forms the core of their identity and is not merely an addendum to their ministry. This is an important point. Many churches view mission as something they do rather than who they are. Churches that are intent on contextualizing the gospel need to view mission as part of their identity.

The Nations Shall Worship Before You (Ps. 22:27)

The Bible assumes that non-Christians may be present in the worship of the church. The great desire of a confessionally Reformed church is that non-Christians and yet-to-be-discipled Christians will come into the context of the worshiping community, where they receive the means of grace and see firsthand the loving community of faith. They observe with their eyes the worshiping community. They touch with their hands the extended hands of welcome. They hear with their ears psalms sung, prayers uplifted, and the Word proclaimed. They smell the bread and the wine as it is passed from one repentant believer to another.

What goes on before Sunday worship is extremely important. A designated greeter (in addition to members) keeps an eye out for newcomers. Sometimes the newcomer will come through the invitation of a member, and other times he will come through other avenues such as website, radio ad, word of mouth, or a simple Sunday drive-by. Once he arrives, he is given a personal welcome and is offered an order of worship, his questions are fielded, and brochures are made available to him on how we worship and how to choose a church. Greeters typically hand out visitor cards and return them before worship begins.

A book table is readily accessible with Reformed literature tailored for both Christian and non-Christian. A detailed children's bulletin is handed out that follows each stage of worship as well as highlights the main points of the pastor's sermon. This is designed not only to aid children in their worship but to make worship intelligible and accessible to the unreached, undiscipled, or underdiscipled newcomer.

Before worship begins, members and visitors converse freely with each other. However, approximately five minutes before worship begins, lights flicker on and off and those assembled quiet down to prepare themselves for worship. This reminds everyone, including newcomers, that we have been drawn by His Spirit not primarily to socialize but to worship.

God Is in This Place! (I Cor. 14:25)

Faithful contextualization requires that the worship of the church be accessible, intelligible, and credible. A church's worship may be quite simple, but it should never be dull. How can the gospel (the drama of redemption) be dull? A church plant's desire should be to focus on sin and grace, law and gospel. Christ must always remain preeminent. Terse explanations are intermittently given during worship, especially in connection with songs. Such brief explanations make the various components of worship understood and accessible. They also provide a wonderful opportunity to connect hearers to significant figures and events in church history—an important factor in an age when people are largely ignorant of those saints who have gone on before us.

God's people regularly voice corporate amens following the opening greeting, throughout and at the conclusion of congregational prayer, following the sermon, and benediction. Such amens allow worshipers to voice their confirmations. It also helps keep them conscious of each facet of worship without "tuning out" until the sermon. In addition, visitors cannot help but hear God's people worship. The early church father Jerome noted that when people visited the early church they were commonly frightened at the amen—it had the sound of thunder.

Periodically, psalms are read responsively in worship. They may be psalms of praise or thanksgiving or confession. Congregational singing includes songs that are God-centered and tie us to the church throughout history and the world. New songs are occasionally sung that reflect musical and lyrical integrity.

Preaching is an area that requires great diligence in making the gospel accessible and intelligible. Textual/thematic preaching need not be "dumbed down" to be accessible to worshipers. People who are hungry want meat. But "meaty" sermons do not require that they be unintelligible. Faithful preaching requires that literary and historical contexts as well as theological terms are explained and not simply assumed. I would encourage fellow ministers of the gospel to compose and preach sermons as if non-Christians are present. If we do, non-Christians will come because members will have reason to invite them.

But what about the other means of grace? The sacraments (both baptism and the Lord's Supper) provide wonderful occasions beyond the wording of the liturgical form to declare the gospel. For visitors who merely observe the sacraments, the gospel the sacraments confirm can be explained and a plea for repentance and faith can be given. Visitors may not receive the physical elements of water, bread, and wine, but they may receive the One to whom the sacraments point, namely Jesus Christ.

The ultimate desire at this church plant is to strengthen the saint and convert the sinner. The pastor and congregation have a sincere desire that visitors will have no other recourse but to say, "God is truly among you" (1 Cor. 14:25).

Sunday's Over—Now What?

Once worship concludes, informal fellowship gradually resumes. Sincere (not manufactured) transparency is important. Never leave visitors alone after a worship service. This doesn't require smothering, but it does require sincere attention and a willingness to get to know them. Most visitors readily welcome it, and if they don't, you probably won't see them again. The Lord will retain whom He will.

Hospitality, however, must extend beyond an initial handshake and introductory greeting.[7] It also must include an invitation to home fellowship. Home hospitality allows extended intimacy with members, regularly attending nonmembers, and visitors.

Small-group fellowship during the week also allows the opportunity to minister to newcomers who live in an individualistic and fragmented culture. It allows newcomers to hear church members bring prayer requests, offer thanks for answered prayer, and share their faith. Currently, the only small group at this church plant is the Wednesday night prayer meeting. Here members encourage one another and show to visitors that they are not only committed to orthodoxy (right doctrine) but orthopraxis (right living).

Occasional conferences boost congregational morale and provide excellent opportunities to promote Christ and the Reformed faith. Such conferences allow people to be introduced to confessional Christianity. It

---

7. See *POPC*, 66.

also allows a time for Christian fellowship that often extends beyond the borders of the Reformed faith.

A point worthy of noting is that confessionally Reformed church ministries have historically, in some cases, tended toward reductionism and rationalism in their ministry. There has been a rigorous commitment to instruction in the Word and confessional orthodoxy. But as vitally important as they are, sometimes they have been maintained to the neglect of relational ministry and an embodiment of the gospel (communion of the saints), especially as they are exercised toward visitors. In an experience-based culture, it is vitally important that confessionally Reformed churches express warmth, hospitality, and transparent, genuine love to visitors (Heb. 13:2).

The early church provides us with a good balance. There was a fundamental commitment to a ministry of Word, sacrament, prayer, spiritual fellowship, and transparent and selfless acts of love. The result? Church growth (Acts 2:42–47).

An Encouragement

A credible, intelligible, and accessible ministry is possible, but it doesn't guarantee fruit. A church may have a very appealing website. It may be committed to the fundamentals of Acts 2:42–47. It may also be contextually self-conscious. But these things don't guarantee immediate results. Beware of formulaic methods! The Lord Jesus reminds us who grows confessionally Reformed churches. Jesus says, "I will build My church, and the gates of Hades shall not prevail against it" (Matt. 16:18). It is "God who gave the growth" (1 Cor. 3:6).

On a Parting Note

Our North American culture cries out for a gospel that answers the vanity and fears of our times. There are threats from without and within. Threats increase as militant Islam gains ground. Nerves in some sectors are becoming frayed. Simultaneously, moral threats abound as militant sexual deviants slowly unravel our society. Talk to pastors across the denominational spectrum and they will tell you of increasing cases of family breakdown, divorce, Internet porn and gambling, and other sins that affect both world and church.

Interestingly, younger Christians are not oblivious to this downgrade and deeply desire to see the church respond to the challenges of our age.

Many of them are seeing through the cosmetic responses of the church and desire to see an authentic and robust confessional response. They above all want to see confession put into practice. But in many cases they're not seeing it.

They see through the baby boomers' preoccupation with self. They are tired of the moralistic, therapeutic, self-absorbed psychobabble they hear from many pulpits. They scoff at outdated and contextually impotent seeker-sensitive talk and megachurches whose massive structures bespeak wealth, influence, and success but inwardly are whitewashed tombs. They simply can't understand Spirit-filled folk who embrace old-style fundamentalist theology but whose rate of divorce is on par with and sometimes exceeds that of the surrounding culture. The mainline liberal church isn't even on their radar screens as Sadduccean compromises have made it culturally irrelevant. Younger folk are surveying the ecclesiastical landscape, and they see the church as culturally compromised and contextually impotent.

The time is ripe for confessionally Reformed churches to make their voice heard. Granted, confessionally Reformed churches don't hold the high ground. An increasingly post-Christian society and compromised church make growing confessionally Reformed churches an extremely difficult task. But there is also great opportunity. In the midst of an increasingly self-absorbed, cosmetic culture, people are looking for substantive churches that are confessionally rigorous and readily accessible.

CHAPTER TWENTY-ONE

Does Anybody Really Know
What Time It Is?

Michael S. Horton

Contextualization is hot. Basically, it is the attempt to situate particular beliefs and practices in their concrete situation. Migrating from the rarified confines of secular sociology (especially sociolinguistics), hermeneutics, and missiological theory to practical theology departments and ministry, the imperative to contextualize the gospel has become something of a mantra among pastors, youth ministers, and evangelists. In an age of niche marketing, contextualizing refers not only to the need of aspiring missionaries to understand the culture to which they will be sent but also to the specialized demographics of our own consumer society.

I won't mention names, but many evangelical seminaries offer a panoply of elective courses on contextualized ministry (i.e., urban, youth, sports, suburban, emergent, African American, Latino/a, men's and women's ministry). Obviously, something has to give; the seminary curriculum can handle only so many credit hours. Increasingly, at least from conversations with friends, it seems that it is the core courses in biblical languages, systematic and historical theology, church history, and more traditional courses in pastoral theology that are being pared down to make room.

As a result, many American pastors, missionaries, and evangelists today may know more about their target market than they do about the "one Lord, one faith, and one baptism" that they share with the prophets and the apostles, the church fathers and Reformers, or their brothers and sisters in China, Malawi, and Russia. As recent events in the Anglican Communion have demonstrated, many bishops and pastors in Africa and Asia are more insistent than their British and American colleagues on being defined by this shared ("catholic") faith rather than their own

Originally appeared in *Modern Reformation* 18, 1 (January/February 2009): 14–18, and is reprinted with permission.

cultural context. It's not difficult to determine whose witness right now is more "relevant."

In the 1920s, Princeton New Testament professor (and founder of Westminster Seminary) J. Gresham Machen was already issuing the complaint that the obsession with "applied Christianity" was so pervasive that soon there would be little Christianity left to apply. Are we seeing the effects even in evangelical and Reformed circles of a pragmatic interest in the methods of ministry that downplays interest in the actual message? Do our pastors coming out of three or four years of seminary education really know the Bible as pastor-scholars, ready to proclaim, teach, and lead the sheep into the rich pastures of redemption? Are they becoming technicians, entrepreneurs, and bureaucrats who know the niche demographics of this passing age better than they know the Word by which the Spirit is introducing the age to come?

In some ways, the concern with contextualization has been an understandable response to a naive modern assumption that truth is simply universal, timeless, and changeless. Just as postmodern theory has reacted against the modern "textbook" approach to knowledge and attempted to "situate" thinking in the lived experience of social practices in which we are embedded, contextualization can be a welcome dose of realism. We don't just have ideas; our beliefs are shaped to a great extent by the cultural habits, language, customs, and practices of particular groups. Covenant theology makes a lot more sense in feudal societies than in liberal democracies. Faith in a God who is King of kings and Lord of lords, who saves sinners by His gracious action rather than by putting Himself on the ballot for a general election, may be less plausible to successful capitalists and politically empowered feminists than to prisoners or oppressed workers. "Christendom" was largely a secular construction of a particular empire borrowing Christian language, and we cannot understand the rise of revivalism apart from the Industrial Revolution, or contemporary evangelicalism apart from the massive technological and social revolutions of recent history. It is easier for American Christians to take contextualization seriously when we're preparing for a mission trip to Africa; we are less sensitive to the ways in which our own faith and practice are shaped for good or for ill by our own location.

The most prevalent analogy in Christian calls to contextualization is the incarnation. Just as the Word became flesh, God-with-us, individual believers and the church corporately must "incarnate" Christ's life in the present, we are told. But is this a good analogy? In this article I want to offer some cautions about using it.

A Savior, Not a Symbol

Ironically, a naive kind of contextualization can actually serve the interests of cultural hegemony, power, and pride:

- "This is just the way we are."
- "Young people are like that, you know."
- "You have to understand the social forces that have shaped that group."

There is always some truth in these imperatives. Ethnic churches, urban churches, and suburban churches, for example, can be impervious to the differences of those outside their circles and the ways in which their own cultural assumptions have made them seem alien even to fellow Christians. But is the answer simply to follow enculturation more deeply, to contextualize more broadly, to "incarnate" Jesus more fully by our activity? Or is it to allow the incarnate Savior and Lord Himself to redefine our churches, to re-contextualize our churches around Him and His kingdom as He reigns at His Father's right hand by His Word and Spirit?

Jesus is a Savior, not a symbol. His incarnation is unique and unrepeatable. It cannot be extended, augmented, furthered, or realized by us. It happened; Jesus is God from Bethlehem to eternity. He did not come to show us how to incarnate ourselves but rather to be our incarnate Redeemer. There are a few places that indicate we are to follow the example of Jesus Christ, but not many. In fact, the most obvious one is Philippians 2, where we are told to follow the example of Christ's humility demonstrated in His incarnation. On the other hand, there are many New Testament passages on our union with Christ and the works that result. Christ does not stand at a distance, leading us by His example; the Spirit has united us to Christ so that we actually become one with Him. But nowhere, even in Philippians 2, are we told to imitate, repeat, or extend Christ's incarnation. The redeeming work of Christ is finished; our work is a response of gratitude to that completed work. The qualitative difference between the person and work of Jesus Christ and the person and work of believers makes it impossible to see the incarnation as a paradigm for our ministry. Rather, Christ's incarnation is the reason that a ministry exists at all in the first place.

Contextualizing Contextualization

If we are going to understand our times—and how the gospel addresses us in them—contextualization itself will have to be "contextualized." In other words, we have to realize that this concept too belongs to a particular pattern of thinking and web of assumptions we have inherited as denizens of a certain time and place. The gospel has been around a lot longer than has the doctrine of contextualizing. It has survived martyrdom, Christendom, heresy, and schism—even the myriad symptoms of the "American Religion"—and is no worse for the wear. Kingdoms and empires come and go, but this one endures from generation to generation.

Philosopher Ludwig Wittgenstein observed that we use language to participate in a "form of life" that already existed before we arrived on the scene. From our earliest communication in childhood, we use words to get things done and in so doing eventually become part of the game already in progress.[1] This idea that knowledge is social rather than simply the result of an individual's apprehension of "clear and distinct ideas" has led sociologists like Peter Berger to speak of "plausibility structures."[2] It's not that one cannot escape the paradigm that has shaped his or her language and therefore beliefs and practices. However, conversion from one paradigm to another is not simply an act of the will. If one shares the presuppositions of atheistic naturalism, the claim that Jesus rose from the dead will be implausible, just as a sixth-century European peasant would have found it implausible that a person struggling with epileptic seizures could be treated by medicine rather than by exorcism.

Historians of science have followed this train of thinking in recent decades by showing how scientific paradigms govern the progress of the sciences, resisting anomalies (i.e., observations that seem to count against the theory) until they gang up on the theory and overthrow the whole paradigm. Until then, the community of scientists (not unlike a church or denomination) retains their confidence that the paradigm they now hold makes the most sense of the data. But the paradigm itself plays a large role in their interpretation of the data and the plausibility of that data in challenging their broader system. Reformed apologist Cornelius Van Til underscored the importance and inescapability of presuppositions in a way analogous to this notion of plausibility structures.

---

1. *The Encyclopedia of Philosophy*, s.v. "Wittgenstein, Ludwig Josef Johann."
2. Peter L. Berger and Thomas Luckmann, *The Social Construction of Reality: A Treatise in the Sociology of Knowledge* (1966; repr. New York: Anchor Books, 1967), 157.

Recognizing, however, that a particular culture's worldview, paradigm, plausibility structure, and presuppositions are formative is different from the assumption that they are determinative. As in the natural sciences, an entire system can be overthrown even by a single anomaly—if that phenomenon is significant enough to cause a paradigm–revolution. The resurrection of Jesus Christ is just such an anomaly. It is significant that when Paul addressed the philosophers in Athens (Acts 17), he knew his audience well enough to connect with their reigning paradigms; but instead of showing how the gospel substantiated their worldview, he used the truth in their own confused system to unravel the system itself. His speech culminated in the greatest anomaly of all: the resurrection of Jesus Christ, which demonstrates the inevitability of the last judgment. The only responsible conclusion, he says, is to repent and believe the gospel. To be sure, most of Paul's auditors thought he was crazy; their stubborn commitment to their reigning paradigms screened out the possibility of bodily resurrection and a final judgment. But some believed. That's the way it goes. And it has gone that way ever since, because the Spirit is at work opening blind eyes and deaf ears. That's where our confidence must be placed.

When we make a particular context normative, we essentially concede that there is a captivity from which Jesus Christ cannot liberate. This is the doctrine of historicism, which assumes that a particular belief can be explained adequately simply by defining the context in which it came to be believed. Workers accept their lot in life because they assume the capitalistic paradigm as a given, Marx argued. People hold certain convictions because of their context. Historicism became the dominant way of thinking in the culture that produced Protestant liberalism. So, for example, Rudolf Bultmann accepted as a fate the supposed impossibility of people using electric lights and radios believing in a world filled with angels and demons. Retired Episcopal bishop John Shelby Spong has repeated this refrain in recent years, insisting that it is ridiculous to expect contemporary people in highly developed societies to believe in the supernatural religion that is revealed Christianity.

While this trajectory of historicism has made us more aware of our contextualized existence, it has, ironically, become its own kind of dogmatic, universal, and totalizing claim. If people could only believe things that were determined by their context, there could be no revolutions in science, art, politics, and other fields of cultural endeavor. As a "theory of everything," historicism is manifestly false when applied to Christianity. Christ's resurrection was not an idea whose time had come in the evolution of Second Temple Judaism. Although it grew out of Israel's story, it was a radical anomaly even in the thinking of the disciples themselves. The resurrection—and the gospel to which it is attached—possessed sufficient power to overthrow the reigning paradigm of many, as the Spirit drew them to Christ through its proclamation. Since Jesus Christ has been raised, whatever paradigms have shaped us must be called into question. That is Paul's point in Athens. Our context is not a fate to be accepted. The sociological "is" does not prescribe the theological "ought." When Christian writers such as George Barna and many others assume that we must change our message, methods, or mission because of generation-whatever, we recall the words of the Great Commission: "All authority has been given to Me in heaven and on earth. Go therefore and make disciples of all the nations, baptizing them in the name of the Father and of the Son and of the Holy Spirit, teaching them to observe all things that I have commanded you; and lo, I am with you always, even to the end of the age" (Matt. 28:18–20).

Christ Confronts Culture

As Reformed Christians, we must address more constructively how it is that we can proclaim Christ, witness to Christ, and serve Christ in a culture that may tolerate "Christianity" in some vague sense but is increasingly hostile to the particular claims concerning Christ's person and work. So in a certain sense we are also trying to contextualize our witness. However, our assumption is not that our "post-Christian culture" defines how we present Christ but that Christ's objective person and work define how we engage this culture or any other.

Whether we identify them as late modern or postmodern, our cultural assumptions should be studied and recognized not chiefly so that we can make the gospel more relevant and inviting to our neighbors but so that we can recognize the particular ways in which they—and we— have become resistant to the gospel. In other words, by starting with God's Word to us and the assumption that it can create new worlds rather than with us and our assumptions, we expect the gospel's engagement with culture to produce more clashes than accommodations, more dissonance than resonance, more disorientation, confusion, and objections than stability, affirmation, and recognition. Whatever we discover about our culture, at least one conclusion can be easily anticipated at the beginning: the gospel that has always been strange in every culture, for largely the same reasons, is still strange to us and to our neighbors. Its relevance lies not in its repetition of familiar platitudes of natural religion, sentiment, and morality but in its disturbing and liberating power to convert.

A contextualizing approach that assumes a basically affirmative relationship to a given cultural context will accommodate the message, methods, and mission. Paul recognized in the opening chapters of 1 Corinthians that the Greeks of his day had particular trouble even understanding the gospel because it was a solution to a problem they did not even consider. They were looking for philosophical and ethical wisdom, not for a Savior who could raise their bodies to immortal life. Similarly, his Jewish contemporaries were seeking life in their own righteousness rather than looking outside of themselves to the incarnate Redeemer. In that sense, Paul "contextualized" the gospel. Nevertheless, he was convinced that the gospel itself had the power to do its own work (Rom. 1:16).

What Time Is It?

Basic to our working assumptions is the New Testament's distinction between "this passing age" and "the age to come." There is a legitimate place for dividing Western history according to obvious turning points: ancient, medieval, modern, and postmodern. However, the primary division for Christians is "this age" and "the age to come": the era dominated by sin and death, leading to judgment; and the era dominated by the Spirit, righteousness, and life, leading to salvation in Christ. It is not Alexander the Great and Immanuel Kant or Jacques Derrida but Jesus Christ who defines history as "before" and "after." His work represents the most significant turning point in history as the law of sin and death is confronted with the gospel. That is why the New Testament identifies the whole era since Pentecost as "these last days." Wherever we are in our places and times, this is the most decisive context. We are either "in Adam," sharing in the fading regime of death, or "in Christ," with an unfading inheritance.

Protestant liberalism forgot what time it is, accommodating its message, methods, and mission to this passing age. Evangelicalism is in the process of doing the same thing in its call to contextualization. The most dangerous context of mission may not be Paul's: an era of perpetual threat of martyrdom. It is probably not the church in China today that is under the greatest threat but the churches belonging to a "Christendom" that has turned sour on its upbringing, like a wayward adolescent who reacts viscerally against everything that reminds him or her of home. In this case, however, Christendom never was home; it was always an illusion created by a confusion of Christ and culture.

God's Word tells us what time it is. Paul to Timothy: "In the last days perilous times will come: for men will be lovers of themselves," with all of the characteristics of narcissism, materialism, pride, and reckless disregard for authority. People "will not put up with sound doctrine, but will gather to themselves teachers who will say whatever their itching ears want to hear." Paul's prescription is not to accommodate the gospel to this context, but to confront the context with the gospel: "Timothy, preach the Word, in season [i.e., when it is popular] and out of season [i.e., when it's not], teaching, rebuking, and exhorting" (2 Tim. 4:2).

American evangelicals are increasingly aware that we are living in a post-Christian culture. Our brothers and sisters in Europe have known for some time now that this is their lot, as churches are turned into mosques or civic centers—but now it is our turn. In vain will we spend our energies on last-ditch efforts to "take America back," struggling to hang onto some last vestiges of a Judeo-Christian morality even while biblical doctrine, worship, and practice increasingly vanish from our churches. It is time to accept the fact that our neighbors are not "unchurched" but pagans, even though many were raised in at least nominal Christian backgrounds. In some ways, our post-Christian context makes mission a little clearer. Instead of the bland moralism of a pseudo-Christian culture, which distorted the gospel in myriad ways, a faithful proclamation of the gospel and lives shaped will lead to a more explicit, if smaller, Christian witness. We need to reflect more deeply, wisely, and biblically on how our churches can become theaters of grace, nurseries of faith, and engines of mission again. Taking the gospel more seriously than we take our context, we recognize that it is the age to come—breaking into this fading age through the gospel—that is normative. The covenant of grace is the definitive context—"in Christ" the normative location—of every believer, whether in ancient Thessalonica or contemporary Shanghai, Nairobi, or Omaha.

This is what we mean when we confess "one holy, catholic, and apostolic church." It is catholic because it is in Christ. Those who are united to Jesus Christ through faith in the gospel are knit together more intimately than any generation, consumer niche, ethnic group, gender, or other demographic generated by this present age. The age that endures, after the American empire has come and gone like the rest, sets our coordinates as pilgrims in this fading age. We must recover our confidence in the truth that the gospel creates its own paradigm, its own "sociology of knowledge," its own form of life, language game, and plausibility structure from the Word and the sacraments. We must learn to speak our own language again and take our cues from the practices God has instituted for His own work among us as He creates the kind of community that is as strange as its gospel.

Epilogue

Daniel R. Hyde and Shane Lems

We've covered many topics in the preceding pages. In part 1, we looked at the foundation for planting churches. Brian Vos gave us an exegetical, or biblical, foundation for planting Christ-centered churches. Daniel Hyde considered principles of church planting and the leadership of the Holy Spirit in the book of Acts. Wes Bredenhof gave us the theological and doctrinal motivation for planting churches. Michael Horton reminded us of the necessity of the church and its ministry of Word and sacrament.

Part 2 focused on the methods of planting churches. Daniel Hyde drew principles for beginning a church plant from Acts 16. Paul Murphy described the necessary heart preparation for those beginning and involved in church plants and then laid out strategies for outreach and evangelism. Kim Riddlebarger answered the questions, "What do I do if there are no confessional Reformed churches in this area? How do we even start thinking about a church plant?"

In part 3, we described the work of the church plant. Daniel Hyde answered the question, "What does it mean to be a church planter?" and in another chapter explained that public worship is at the heart of evangelism. Kevin Efflandt suggested hospitable church-plant practices that will make visitors feel welcome. Shane Lems gave some pastoral advice to the church planter on balancing all his tasks, which is helpful for the core group and elders of the plant as well. Comparing the church plant to a restaurant, Michael Brown explored the essential ingredients of preaching and teaching, which are vital for feeding God's sheep. He then took up the topic of biblical church membership— from the early days of the plant to organization or particularization and membership transfer. Spencer Aalsburg explained the role of the session or consistory of the church plant and told us how the plant and the mother church relate. Eric Tuininga concluded this section with a discussion of the relationship between the mother church and church plant.

Finally, we offered some insights on the context of planting churches in part 4. Shane Lems introduced the subject by encouraging all of those involved in church planting to be mindful of cultural context and its challenges as a church plant is established and grows. Mitchell Persaud reminded us of the cultural details that church planters and sessions must be aware of. Phil Grotenhuis and Michael Horton gave us cultural contexts to consider when planting. We also read about preaching and teaching in the plant, motivating the plant, and shepherding the plant. We've covered a lot of bases!

In closing, we want to spend just a few paragraphs tying it all together. First, if you've read through this book, we encourage you to press on in the work of church planting. Whatever your role—a member of the core group, an individual who wants to see a confessional church in his area, a seminary student considering church planting, a group of elders studying the topic, or anyone else—please pray hard about church planting and be willing to expend yourself for this great privilege of planting churches. It will not be easy, but no one ever promised that the Christian life—much less evangelism and church planting—would be easy.

Second, be ready to learn from your mistakes and be flexible in many areas. Be patient in your choices, your teaching, your learning, and your advising. Be humble, love your neighbors and your enemies, and focus on the gospel of forgiveness. Planting a church is a tough task, and many problems and heartaches in a church plant feel many times worse because the family is so small. Church planting is not glamorous; it is like slogging through the mud in the rain most of the time.

Finally, showcase the glory of Christ in everything the church plant does. By keeping the gospel center—the five *solas* trumpeted loud and clear—the church plant will glorify God and edify His people, which is the ultimate goal. Even if you slog it out for ten years with a tiny group, if the gospel is front and center and if God's people are built up in the faith, the plant is successful. Church planters should not measure success with the spectacles of the world, where numbers and vast programs mean success, but with the spectacles of Scripture, knowing that if Christ is preached and His people are strengthened spiritually, then the church plant is a success. You'll fail in planting a church if you have one hundred new members in the first year but they know little about Jesus. As Brian Vos noted in the opening chapter, it takes a little dying in the church plant for the living Christ to be in the spotlight. But what a wonderful dying that is, because it results in life!

APPENDIX A

∾

Church-Plant Timeline:
A Big and Brief Picture of a Plant

Daniel R. Hyde and Shane Lems

1. A group (eventually the so-called core group) of Christians in a certain place begins to talk about the need for a confessional Reformed church in the area. These people could be Christians coming to an appreciation of Reformation truths or already Reformed Christians living in or moving to a place where there is no confessional church. See chapter 8, "Planning the Plant: Some Thoughts on Preparing to Plant a New Church" by Kim Riddlebarger.

Alternatively, a confessional Reformed or Presbyterian church could call and send out a home missionary to start a Bible study in an area that has no confessional church. After prayer and studies, the church starts a fellowship or Bible study with the aim of planting a church.

2. The group becomes significant in number—around six families or more. They pray together and study the confessions of a Reformed/Presbyterian church and contact that church to discuss the possibility of a plant.

Alternatively, the home missionary is eventually working with a group of six or more families, and the consistory/session begins to discuss beginning worship services.

3. The Reformed/Presbyterian church contacted by the group works with this group of Christians, teaching them more about Reformation truths, and takes these people into their spiritual care (they join the mother church). The session/consistory could shepherd these members either with its elders/pastor or by calling a man to lead the work. At this point, a church plant is officially started. These initial stages may take from several months to several years. See chapter 8 by Kim Riddlebarger, chapters 14–15 by Michael Brown, and chapters 16–17 by Spencer Aalsburg.

Alternatively, with the home-missionary situation, the work moves from fellowship/Bible study status to church plant. From this point, the rest of the timeline looks roughly the same for both methods of church planting.

4. The mother-church session/consistory can begin thinking about organizing/particularizing the plant when four things come together:

- When the church plant has been holding worship services and has seen spiritual and numerical (a secondary consideration) growth, indicating that evangelism and outreach has been and is continuing to occur.

- When church education has been in place and functioning for a while.

- When the finances allow the church to be nearly self-sustaining.

- When the church has its own officers. The church does not choose officers so that it can organize. Rather, Christ gives the church officers, and then they organize. This stage of organization/particularization should not be rushed: it could take from two to five years.

5. Officers are trained, installed, and ordained by the mother church. The newly organized consistory/session calls a pastor to the newly organized church and also transfers membership of the core group to the newly organized church. Following appropriate church order, these things happen and the church becomes a local, organized church within the presbytery or classis of the neighboring churches.

The Steering Committee

Spencer Aalsburg

We do well to define carefully this group we call a steering committee. Many problems have arisen where the proper boundaries of such a committee are not abundantly clear to all involved. An example of steering committee guidelines is listed at the end.

Committees—Instruments of the Consistory

The biblical authority and duties of the consistory that undertakes church planting have been explained. But what about the administration of finances at the church plant? Who cares for the church-plant building and grounds? Do these duties belong to the domain of the consistory? Monsma instructively answers:

> Yes, inasmuch as the government of the church is the task of the elders and administrative duties are indeed governmental duties. This, however, does not mean that the consistory may not appoint a finance committee or helpers from among able and worthy members of the church.... However, all such helpers and committees should be appointed directly by the consistory for the term of *one* year only and they should know themselves strictly accountable to the consistories.[1]

Indeed, most churches have several committees (e.g., building and grounds committee, nursery committee, education committee, library committee). And these committees derive their authority properly from the consistory. Consistories authorize. Committees evaluate. Individuals implement. It is the consistory that has the authority, so only it has the right to authorize a committee to meet or act, as the OPC BCO notes

---

1. Martin Monsma, *The New Revised Church Order Commentary* (Grand Rapids: Zondervan, 1967), 97–98 (emphasis in original).

well in XII.3. This authorization is usually given by a written mandate, describing exactly what the consistory authorizes a certain committee to do. Committees serve the consistory by evaluating, making recommendations, and carrying out assigned tasks. Individual members then implement the approved decisions.

Committees are entrusted with a limited authority, described in their guidelines. As instruments of the consistory, they have assigned duties to accomplish for the consistory. This will necessarily involve a certain amount of freedom, exercised within limits, in order to effectively operate.

For instance, a nursery committee most likely would not inform their consistory, "By the way, we're going to tear out a wall in the nursery and add on." That would exceed the scope of their authority and corresponding duties. The nursery committee doesn't have the authority to make those decisions. The committee certainly could recommend that idea, but it would need to be approved by the consistory first (and then perhaps be subjected to the congregation's advisory vote).

On the other hand, it would be just as improper if the nursery committee asked for approval to buy additional baby wipes and rearrange the toys in the nursery. The nursery committee ideally would already have the authority to rearrange the nursery in ways it deems appropriate and to buy whatever regular supplies it needs. This doesn't mean the committee members become deaconesses, for buying these items would ultimately fall under the auspices of the established deaconate. The nursery committee would be accountable to the deaconate concerning what it buys.

A Committee That Steers

When a church decides to undertake church planting, there will be a host of goals to accomplish—not the least of which include finding a worship location, developing literature, implementing advertising, organizing fellowship gatherings, and paying bills.

Consider advertising. Just as it would be inefficient for an elder to discuss rearranging toys in the nursery at a consistory meeting, so it may be inefficient for an elder to spend thirty minutes informing his consistory of all the advertising options available for the church plant.

To aid the consistory in this work, a committee can be formed that would—among other duties—gather, analyze, and recommend the most appropriate advertising options for their church plant. Thus the committee would help steer the consistory in the decision-making process and then return to steer the church plant according to the consistory's decisions.

A Working Relationship with the Consistory

It should be noted that a consistory does not need a steering committee in order to plant a church. A steering committee may or may not be desirable, depending on the composition of the consistory and its distance from the church plant.

If the consistory decides to appoint a steering committee, it will likely include in the committee's guidelines the directive to seek name recognition by advertising. So the steering committee would not need to seek approval for every advertising venture, except when particular input from the consistory would be fitting.

What would be a fitting occasion to seek input from the consistory? The answer would depend on the guidelines governing the steering committee, understanding that there will be gray areas even with fine-tuned guidelines. As with any committee of the consistory, trust must be fostered between the steering committee and the consistory.

The best course of action when encountering a gray area—especially early in the committee's life—is to check with the consistory. Consider the implementation of a church logo. What would the consistory think if the steering committee took it upon itself to design a logo? Assuming that the committee's guidelines allow it to produce literature, this could arguably include a logo. Yet one could reason that the permission to produce literature doesn't include a logo, since that would express an important identity of the church plant and, by inference, of the mother church.

Examples like this abound. The best course of action—especially as a trusting, working relationship is being established—is for the committee to work closely with the consistory. And that course of action is built in when elders are properly assigned to serve on the steering committee.

At this point it is fitting to recall that the "consistory is the only assembly in the church(es) whose decisions possess direct authority within the congregation" (URCNA CO, art. 21). And yet the consistory has appointed the steering committee to provide aid with the details of planting a church. If a consistory will second-guess every steering committee decision, it should save everyone time and do the work itself (which would be perfectly legitimate).

On the other hand, the steering committee must understand that the church plant it is steering does not belong to its members. Even if the members of the steering committee are the ones who originally championed the cause of starting a church plant, the church plant does not belong to them. And they must recognize that submission to the elders—ordained to shepherd in Christ's name—is submission to Christ Himself (1 Thess. 5:12–13; Heb. 13:17).

The church plant does not belong to the steering committee. It does not belong to the core group. It does not belong to the 25 percent of the people who do the work. It does not even belong to the consistory. The church belongs to Jesus Christ, who, from His majestic throne, ordains men to shepherd the flock, whether they gather for worship at the mother church or at the church-plant site.

Membership on the Steering Committee

Since the steering committee is formed to steer the consistory with respect to the church plant and since the consistory is charged with planting the church plant, it is imperative that consistory members serve on the steering committee. Just as an education committee will include a consistory member who oversees the committee (since the consistory is charged with ensuring that the congregation is educated according to the Scriptures) and maintains communication between the committee and consistory, so also consistory members will serve on the consistory's steering committee.

Including ordained elders and deacons on the steering committee will ensure this vital communication and accountability between the steering committee and the consistory and deaconate. Gray areas mentioned above will be reduced when consistory members are intimately involved in the operations of the church plant from the start, while trust is being nurtured.

The number of lay members of the committee and the length of the term of service will be at the discretion of the consistory, which will also appoint the specific members. The number of members will depend on the workload. Members should not be drafted merely to get people involved. Moreover, a consistory may pastorally add or remove members from the committee, as it deems appropriate.

While a steering committee may be charged with much busywork, care should be taken to not overly complicate the committee's labors.

Ideally, the consistory will adopt a version of the guidelines listed in appendix C, adjusting them for their particular situation. Accordingly, there will not need to be a host of subcommittees, which are not only unnecessary but threaten to turn the church plant into a bureaucracy.

Not a Mini-Consistory

It should be clear that a steering committee is not a "mini-consistory." A consistory is composed of the ordained minister(s) of the Word and the elders. Thus the steering committee does not rule the church, for "the consistory is the only assembly in the church(es) whose decisions possess direct authority within the congregation, since the consistory receives its authority directly from Christ, and thereby is directly accountable to Christ."[2]

The consistory cannot and may not give away its obligation to shepherd the flock entrusted to them (1 Peter 5:1–4). Even though the consistory may appoint some of its members—along with some church-plant members—to form a steering committee, this committee is not a mini-consistory. The steering committee may monitor day-to-day functions, but that is different from ruling the church in the capacity to which the consistory alone is ordained.

The steering committee will work closely with the church-planting pastor and hold him accountable in the same way that any church member would, but that is far different from officially ensuring that he faithfully discharges his office—a task reserved for the elders alone. The steering committee may organize fellowship events, implement evangelism and missions efforts, visit families, and encourage attendance at Christian school events, but this will be done under the auspices of the consistory, which is ultimately responsible "to maintain the purity of the Word and Sacraments, assist in catechizing the youth, promote God-centered schooling, visit the members of the congregation according to their needs, engage in family visiting, exercise discipline in the congregation, actively promote the work of evangelism and missions, and insure that everything is done decently and in good order."[3]

---

2. URCNA CO, article 21.
3. Ibid., article 14.

A Word about Finances

Two additional matters deserve brief mention. First, while the church is not a business, it has administrative duties like businesses.[4] Not the least of these is managing finances. Handling money and bookkeeping should be performed with accountability, prudence, and wisdom. Remember, the practices you begin will set precedents for years to come. Fostering trust among committee members does not mean accountability may be lacking. Sound procedures should be established for the finance matters of the steering committee.

Second, just as the steering committee is not a mini-consistory, it is also not a mini-deaconate. Since the church plant truly is part of the mother church, the church plant already has a deaconate. Accordingly, any causes of financial support (such as parachurch ministries and missionaries) should be approved by the deaconate, which always renders an account of its work to the consistory (cf. "Guidelines," C.6.g).

There need to be mutual trust and submission concerning money in the church plant. Perhaps a core group had several thousand dollars before joining the URCNA or even bought a piece of property together. All the answers to potential situations cannot be covered here.

We must allow the already established principles to guide decisions, even about finances. The church plant has a deaconate by virtue of being part of the mother church, and that deaconate is called to care for it, just as the church plant (along with the whole congregation) is called to give cheerfully. Moreover, we must remember the stark reality of the warning that Paul gives Timothy: "For the love of money is a root of all kinds of evil, for which some have strayed from the faith in their greediness, and pierced themselves through with many sorrows." (1 Tim. 6:10).

Whatever money is possessed by the church plant or the whole church or any individual, we must remember that we don't own it. It has been entrusted to us to use in serving and loving our generous God and our neighbor. Whether on the steering committee, the council, or in any area of our lives, we're to flee the love of money and all kinds of evil. And instead, as Paul instructs the people of God, we should "pursue righteousness, godliness, faith, love, patience, gentleness" (1 Tim. 6:11).

---

4. Cf. *POPC*, 67–69. This section contains several good suggestions concerning administrative practices.

Guidelines for the Steering Committee

Spencer Aalsburg

The following guidelines can be adapted for the steering committee of any mother church/church plant. For our purposes here, we're calling the church plant "East Avenue" and the mother church "Faith Reformed Church" (FRC). Since all church plant situations differ, it may be necessary to modify these guidelines as best fits the situation.

A. Steering Committee Membership
The committee includes the following members:

1. The associate pastor of FRC, called to pastor the East Avenue church plant (assuming a pastor-planter has been called).

2. An elder (or elders) from the FRC consistory.

3. A deacon (or deacons) from the FRC deaconate.

4. Three male members of FRC who are regular attendees at East Avenue church plant.

B. Steering Committee Authority

1. The committee serves as a committee for the consistory of FRC.

2. The committee has authority to exercise such duties as are assigned to it by the consistory.

3. The committee has authority to pay expenses related to the East Avenue church plant, to maintain the financial books, and to invest surplus moneys.

4. The committee does not have the authority to oversee the church plant or to create new policies. These matters are properly reserved to the consistory of the church, which is "the only assembly in the church(es) whose decisions possess direct authority within the congregation, since the consis-

tory receives its authority directly from Christ, and thereby is directly accountable to Christ" (URC CO, art. 21).

C. Steering Committee Duties

1. Meetings

   1.1. The committee shall hold regularly scheduled meetings, ordinarily once per month.

   1.2. These meetings must be announced to all members of the committee and to the consistory, ordinarily giving notice of at least a week.

   1.3. Minutes must be kept for each meeting, with copies distributed at the following consistory meeting.

   1.4. An elder will ordinarily serve as chairman.

   1.5. A deacon will serve as treasurer.

2. Worship Matters

   2.1. The committee should recommend dates for celebrating the Lord's Supper and for holding special worship services, subject to ratification by the consistory.

   2.2. The committee may approve changes to the bulletin.

   2.3. Changes to the structure of the liturgy must be approved by the consistory.

3. Education Matters

   3.1. The committee will recommend the establishment of classes, the teachers for appointment, and the use of curricula.

   3.2. These decisions must be ratified by the consistory before implementation.

   3.3. The committee may establish and regulate various Bible studies and book studies in the community.

4. Outreach Matters

   4.1. The committee should develop plans for reaching into the community with the gospel, subject to ratification by the consistory.

4.2. The committee has authority to advertise and promote name recognition.

4.3. The committee has authority to develop and purchase outreach tools (e.g., booklets, pamphlets, etc.).

4.4. Decisions to hold seminars, rallies, etc. must be ratified by the consistory before implementation.

4.5. The committee has authority to publish a newsletter to be distributed.

5. Policy Matters

5.1. Policies of FRC are the de facto policies of the East Avenue church plant, unless separate policies are approved by the consistory for this group alone.

5.2. The committee can recommend such policy changes or the adoption of additional policies not addressed by the FRC congregation, but these must be ratified by the consistory before implementation.

6. Finance Matters

6.1. The committee shall ensure that all financial obligations (rent, bills, etc.) are met for the church plant.

6.2. The committee is to maintain the bank accounts established for the use of East Avenue church plant.

6.3. A report of income and expenses should be included in the Steering Committee report (cf. C.1.c).

6.4. The committee should develop an annual budget each year. This budget must be approved by the council and ratified by a vote of the whole congregation.

6.5. Committee members may collect offerings at services and should process them in the presence of at least two members.

6.6. Significant expenses (in excess of $2,000) or changes to the budget (in excess of $2,000) require approval by the council.

6.7. Any causes of financial support (parachurch ministries, missionaries, etc.) should be approved by the FRC deaconate, which always renders an account of their work to the consistory (cf. URCNA CO, art. 15).

6.8. The member who fills out a check for financial obligations will not be the same person who signs it.

Grounds for Guidelines Concerning Committee Membership

1. By providing representation of both East Avenue church plant attendees and its council, this arrangement promotes communication, accountability, and trust between the committee, the church plant, and the men whom God has called to oversee them.

2. By including ordained men, this arrangement ensures that the actions of the committee are not taken by men who lack the authority to guide and oversee the church.

Grounds for Guidelines Concerning Committee Authority

1. These guidelines ensure that everyone understands the origin and limits of the committee's authority.

2. These guidelines ensure that the principles of Scripture and the provisions of the church order are not violated through the exercise of authority not truly possessed by the body.

Grounds for Guidelines Concerning Committee Duties

1. These guidelines ensure that everyone has the same understanding of what duties the committee has been given.

2. These guidelines also hold the consistory responsible for carrying out its God-given shepherding duties.

3. These guidelines offer appropriate freedoms for the committee, thereby laying the groundwork for eventual organization as a particular congregation. Until such time, however, the guidelines ensure that the work of overseeing and ruling the church plant is performed by proper ordained authority.

Selected Bibliography

Bavinck, J. H. *An Introduction to the Science of Missions*. Philadelphia: Presbyterian and Reformed, 1960.

Beeke, Joel R. *Puritan Evangelism: A Biblical Approach*. Grand Rapids: Reformation Heritage Books, 1999.

Beeke, Mary. *The Law of Kindness: Serving with Heart and Hands*. Grand Rapids: Reformation Heritage Books, 2007.

Belcher, Jim. *Deep Church: A Third Way Beyond Emerging and Traditional*. Downers Grove, Ill.: IVP, 2009.

Biblical Evangelism Today: A Symposium. Philadelphia: The Committee on Christian Education of the Orthodox Presbyterian Church, 1954.

Brown, Mark, ed. *Order in the Offices: Essays Defining the Roles of Church Officers*. Duncansville, Pa.: Classic Presbyterian Government Resources, 1993.

Brown, Michael, ed. *Called to Serve: Essays for Elders and Deacons*. Grandville, Mich.: Reformed Fellowship, 2006.

Chester, Tim, and Steve Timmis. *Total Church*. Wheaton, Ill.: Crossway, 2008.

Clark, R. Scott. *Recovering the Reformed Confession: Our Theology, Piety, and Practice*. Phillipsburg, N.J.: P&R, 2008.

Dawn, Marva J. *Truly the Community: Romans 12 and How to Be the Church*. Grand Rapids: Eerdmans, 1992.

De Jong, Peter Y. *Taking Heed to the Flock: A Study of the Principles and Practice of Family Visitation*. Grand Rapids: Baker, 1948.

Driscoll, Mark, and Gerry Breshears. *Vintage Church: Timeless Truths and Timely Methods*. Wheaton, Ill.: Crossway, 2009.

Grand Rapids Board of Evangelism of the Christian Reformed Church. *Reformed Evangelism: A Manual on Principles and Methods of Evangelization*. Grand Rapids: Baker, 1948.

Greenway, Roger S. *Go and Make Disciples! An Introduction to Christian Missions*. Phillipsburg, N.J.: P&R, 1999.

Greenway, Roger S., and Timothy M. Monsma. *Cities: Missions' New Frontier*. Grand Rapids: Baker, 2000.

Hall, David W. *The Practice of Confessional Subscription*. Oak Ridge, Tenn.: Covenant Foundation, 1997.

Horton, Michael Scott. *Christless Christianity: The Alternative Gospel of the American Church*. Grand Rapids: Baker, 2008.

————. *The Gospel-Driven Life: Being Good News People in a Bad News World*. Grand Rapids: Baker, 2009.

————. *People and Place: A Covenant Ecclesiology*. Louisville, Ky.: Westminster, 2008.

Hyde, Daniel R. *God with Us: Knowing the Mystery of Who Jesus Is*. Grand Rapids: Reformation Heritage Books, 2007.

————. *The Good Confession: An Exploration of the Christian Faith*. Eugene: Wipf & Stock, 2006.

————. *In Defense of the Descent: A Response to Contemporary Critics*. Grand Rapids: Reformation Heritage Books, 2010.

————. *In Living Color: Images of Christ and the Means of Grace*. Grandville, Mich.: Reformed Fellowship, 2009.

————. *Jesus Loves the Little Children: Why We Baptize Children*. Grandville, Mich.: Reformed Fellowship, 2006.

————. *Welcome to a Reformed Church: A Guide for Pilgrims*. Orlando: Reformation Trust, 2010.

————. *What to Expect in Reformed Worship: A Visitor's Guide*. Eugene, Ore.: Wipf & Stock Publishers, 2007.

————. *Why Believe in God?* Phillipsburg, N.J.: P&R, 2011.

————. *With Heart and Mouth: An Exposition of the Belgic Confession*. Grandville, Mich.: Reformed Fellowship, 2008.

Keller, Timothy J. *The Reason for God: Belief in an Age of Skepticism*. New York: Dutton, 2008.

Kuiper, Rieneck Bouke. *God-Centred Evangelism: A Presentation of the Scriptural Theology of Evangelism*. Edinburgh: Banner of Truth, 1978.

Kuyper, Abraham, and Harry Boonstra. *Our Worship*. Grand Rapids: Eerdmans, 2009.

Malphurs, Aubrey. *Planting Growing Churches for the Twenty-First Century: A Comprehensive Guide for New Churches and Those Desiring Renewal*, 2nd ed. Grand Rapids: Baker, 1998.

Metzger, Will. *Tell the Truth: The Whole Gospel to the Whole Person by Whole People: A Training Manual on the Message and Method of God-Centered Witnessing to a Grace-Centered Gospel*, rev. and expanded 3rd ed. Downers Grove, Ill.: InterVarsity, 2002.

Monsma, Martin, and Idzerd Van Dellen. *The New Revised Church Order Commentary: A Brief Explanation of the Church Order of the Christian Reformed Church*. Grand Rapids: Zondervan, 1967.

Murphy, Thomas. *Pastoral Theology: The Pastor in the Various Duties of His Office*. Philadelphia: Presbyterian Board of Publications, 1877.

Nevin, John Williamson, and Sam Hamstra. *The Reformed Pastor: Lectures on Pastoral Theology*. Eugene, Ore.: Pickwick Publications, 2006.

Newbigin, Lesslie. *The Gospel in a Pluralist Society*. Grand Rapids: Eerdmans, 1989.

————. *Truth to Tell: The Gospel as Public Truth*. Grand Rapids: Eerdmans, 1991.

Nichols, Stephen J. *Jesus Made in America: A Cultural History from the Puritans to "The Passion of the Christ."* Downers Grove, Ill.: IVP Academic, 2008.

Packer, J. I. *Evangelism and the Sovereignty of God*. Downers Grove, Ill.: IVP, 2009.

Piper, John. *Brothers, We Are Not Professionals: A Plea to Pastors for Radical Ministry*. Nashville, Tenn.: Broadman, 2002.

————. *Let the Nations Be Glad!* Grand Rapids: Baker, 2003.

Piper, John, and Justin Taylor. *The Supremacy of Christ in a Postmodern World*. Wheaton, Ill.: Crossway, 2007.

Poirer, Alfred. *The Peacemaking Pastor: A Biblical Guide to Resolving Church Conflict*. Grand Rapids: Baker, 2006.

Samples, Kenneth R. *Without a Doubt: Answering the 20 Toughest Faith Questions*. Grand Rapids: Baker, 2004.

————. *A World of Difference: Putting Christian Truth-Claims to the Worldview Test*. Grand Rapids: Baker, 2007.

Sande, Ken. *The Peacemaker: A Biblical Guide to Resolving Personal Conflict*. Grand Rapids: Baker, 1997.

Sittema, John R. *With a Shepherd's Heart: Reclaiming the Pastoral Office of Elder*. Grandville, Mich.: Reformed Fellowship, 1996.

Smyth, Thomas. *An Ecclesiastical Catechism of the Presbyterian Church for the Use of Families, Bible-Classes, and Private Members*. Charleston, S.C.: B. B. Hussey, 1841.

Stetzer, Ed. *Planting Missional Churches*. Nashville: Broadman, 2006.

Stetzer, Ed, and David Putman. *Breaking the Missional Code: Your Church Can Become a Missionary in Your Community*. Nashville, Tenn.: Broadman, 2006.

Willimon, William H. *Pastor: The Theology and Practice of Ordained Ministry*. Nashville: Abingdon, 2002.

Willimon, William H., and Robert Leroy Wilson. *Preaching and Worship in the Small Church*. Nashville: Abingdon, 1980.

Contributors

Spencer Aalsburg is the church planter and pastor of the Sioux Falls United Reformed Church Fellowship in Sioux Falls, South Dakota.

Wes Bredenhof has been a missionary to the native people living in Fort Babine, British Columbia, and co-pastor of the Langley Canadian Reformed Church in Langley, British Columbia. Currently he is the church planter of the Providence Canadian Reformed Church in Hamilton, Ontario.

Michael G. Brown is the church planter and pastor of the Christ United Reformed Church in Santee, California.

Kevin Efflandt is the pastor of the Zion United Reformed Church in Ripon, California. Formerly, he was the church planter and pastor of the Bellingham United Reformed Church in Bellingham, Washington.

Phil Grotenhuis was the church planter of the Springfield United Reformed Church in Springfield, Missouri, and is now the pastor of the Phoenix United Reformed Church in Phoenix, Arizona.

Michael Horton is the J. Gresham Machen Professor of Apologetics and Systematic Theology at Westminster Seminary California, co-host of *The White Horse Inn* national radio broadcast, and editor-in-chief of *Modern Reformation* magazine. He was also the church planter and co-pastor of the Christ Reformed Church in Anaheim, California, and is currently an associate pastor at the Christ United Reformed Church in Santee, California. He is the author of many books and articles.

Daniel R. Hyde is the church planter and pastor of the Oceanside United Reformed Church in Carlsbad/Oceanside, California. He is the author of many books and articles.

Shane Lems is the church planter and pastor of the United Reformed Church of Sunnyside in Sunnyside, Washington.

Paul T. Murphy is the church planter and pastor of Messiah's Reformed Fellowship in New York City. Previously he served as pastor of the Dutton United Reformed Church in Dutton, Michigan.

Mitchell Persaud is the church planter and pastor of New Horizon United Reformed Church in Toronto, Canada, where he works primarily among Chinese immigrants.

Kim Riddlebarger is senior pastor of Christ Reformed Church in Anaheim, California, visiting professor of systematic theology at Westminster Seminary California, and co-host of *The White Horse Inn* national radio broadcast.

Eric Tuininga is the pastor of Immanuel's Reformed Church in Salem, Oregon.

Brian Vos is the pastor of Trinity United Reformed Church in Caledonia, Michigan.

Scripture Index

Confessions Index